# TAKE DOWN

## *Inside the Jan Kemp Affair*

**Hue Henry**

*Take Down: Inside The Jan Kemp Affair*



Design and layout by Hope Hilton
Set in Adobe Garamound Pro with headers in Cooper Hewitt
Distributed, printed, and bound by Ingram Spark

ISBN-13 978-0-692-15261-4
ISBN-10 0-692-15261-X
Library of Congress Call No. 2018908362

*Dedicated to the memory*

*of Jan Kemp (1949-2008)*

*and*

*Pat Nelson (1948-2007)*

## FOREWORD

Challenging a prestigious and revered institution requires dogged determination, enduring energy and an infallible belief that a destructive wrong needs exposure and cleansing.

Not only does it subject challengers to unjustified and unrelenting attacks on their professional integrity and judgments, it also burdens them with personal sacrifices brought on by the long hours of exhuming unorthodox and/or incriminating documents that entrenched and powerful people want to keep locked in their private vaults.

Two Athens attorneys, Hue Henry and Pat Nelson, knew and understood the difficulties and hazards awaiting them when they accepted the Jan Kemp case. Kemp was an English professor in the University of Georgia's Development Studies program. Development Studies was created to allow students who were not quite ready for college-level work to improve their skills in courses such as math and English and then move into college courses.

As Henry describes in this book, the athletic department had taken control of the program and stacked it with unqualified athletes who participated in revenue-producing sports such as basketball and football. This was done with the full knowledge and permission of then-President Fred Davison, Vice President Virginia Trotter and Development Studies head Leroy Ervin.

Kemp flunked three football players at the end of a fall quarter when the Georgia Bulldogs were headed to the Sugar Bowl and the possibility of a national championship loomed. Those three football players were needed in that game. So the Davison, Trotter, Ervin tricuspid triple-teamed Kemp. They overruled her and gave the athletes passing grades, allowed the footballers to play in the Sugar Bowl and fired Kemp.

An old adage says, "When the going gets tough, the tough get going." That's what Kemp did. She went to Nelson's office and explained the situation. Nelson took the case, but he didn't want to handle it by himself. He believed that in order to mount a successful challenge of the University establishment, he needed a legal sidekick with the shrewdness of an Einstein and tenacity of a pit bull. Nelson chose Henry.

He chose Henry because Henry had filed federal lawsuits against the University hierarchy before and prevailed each time. Henry details those cases in this book. He also details his first legal skirmishes with then Georgia Attorney General Mike Bowers and prominent Macon attorney Hale Almand.

Bowers, a graduate of the U.S. Military Academy at West Point, had approved and worked with attorneys who had defended the University in previous lawsuits that Henry filed, including one that Almand defended.

Almand and Bowers knew each other well. A few years earlier, Bowers called on Almand to help the state with the Sam Caldwell case. Caldwell was Georgia's labor commissioner at the time, having held the position for 17 years. Among other things, he was accused of running roughshod over employees, misusing state funds and coercing some employees to contribute to his campaigns. Caldwell's case ended up in federal court where he was convicted and sentenced to 21 months in prison.

Bowers chose Almand to help with the Caldwell case because Almand served as an assistant U.S. Attorney in Macon for several years. During that time, Almand was the lead prosecutor in some high profile cases, including an illegal gambling operation that brought Las Vegas attorney Oscar Goodman to middle Georgia to defend the accused gamblers. Almand won the case. He, along with U.S. Attorney Ron Knight, also won the federal case against five Macon police detectives who were accused of taking bribes to protect prostitutes and illegal gambling operations in the area.

Like Henry, Almand enjoyed the reputation of being a pit bull in the courtroom. Almand bantered and cajoled witnesses so much that presiding judges would sometimes rebuke his behavior and order him to back off.

So the stage was set for a vicious battle between two legal heavyweights in the Atlanta federal courthouse. Almand who'd won his legal skirmishes against crooked cops and small-time bookmakers versus Henry who'd tackled University of Georgia officials and won his battles, including one that Bowers had handpicked Almand to defend.

While Almand and Henry swapped legal punches, Nelson served as a friendly attorney who pried essential testimony from hostile witnesses.

In *Take Down: Inside the Jan Kemp Affair*, Henry details events leading up to the Kemp trial and the crucial testimony that ultimately lead to Kemp winning the trial, her reinstatement with damages and back pay and the departures of Davison, Trotter and Irvin from their positions.

A few weeks after the trial and its aftermath, Bowers was asked why – with all the damning evidence that surfaced during the trial – did the State choose to go to court instead of reaching a quiet settlement behind the scenes. Bowers, the West Point graduate, said, "Sometimes a general sends his troops into a battle that he knows they can't win. But it's a battle that needs to be fought."

Hue Henry fought and won his battle with the temperament and vigor of a caged pit bull; now, he relives it in his book. I highly recommend it to anyone who enjoys a first-hand account of hard-fought justice over embedded tyranny.

—Randall Savage

Special Assignment Editor for 13WMAZ Eyewitness News, and formerly a Reporter for the *Macon Telegraph and News*. Winner of 1985 Pulitzer Prize for an investigation into academics and athletics at the University of Georgia and Georgia Tech.

# PROLOGUE

This story will be shocking to most and unbelievable to many. It would have been both to me as well but for a growing number of legal cases involving the University of Georgia (UGA) that landed on my desk before I met Jan Kemp. Those cases portrayed a pathological hostility of UGA's leadership to the constitutional free speech rights of the faculty, staff and student body. What follows is a saga that reveals the courage of those who fought back and forced the resignation of UGA's President Fred C. Davison in 1986 following the verdict in the Jan Kemp federal civil rights case - a case that disclosed explosive details of academic misconduct involving revenue-producing scholarship athletes by some of the University's highest administrators, including Davison. That misconduct precipitated a rebellion by faculty members over interference by those administrators with the faculty's grading standards and related academic issues. Their outrage fueled a nationwide scandal when they testified in favor of Kemp in her highly-publicized trial which led to Davison's resignation.

The University of Georgia has always been a source of pride for the people of Georgia, particularly the citizens of its hometown, Athens. As the oldest state-chartered university in the United States, UGA's power and influence had grown considerably over the years. A winning SEC football program added to its luster. But beneath it all, the harsh reality of the Jan Kemp trial evidence proved the truth of the Shakespearean proverb and Dan Seals' 1986 number one country song, "Everything that Glitters is not Gold."

Before the Jan Kemp trial shameful events on campus, particularly those involving UGA football, were mostly discounted by the school's alumni and ignored by the rest of Georgia's massive "Bulldog Nation." After the trial, the people of Georgia and their leaders acknowledged the truth and demanded reform. They loved their "Dawgs" but came to deplore those who deceived UGA's athletes and demeaned UGA's growing academic reputation.

The damages that Fred Davison inflicted on UGA were manifested in many ways over his 19-year tenure. It is impossible to fully understand the inevitability of his demise without knowing his long history of conflicts with subordinates throughout his tenure. That history was disclosed by faculty members, other employees and students who sought and won federal civil rights cases against Davison and other top-level administrators. I knew Davison's history because I represented some of the plaintiffs in those cases. The following pages describe those civil rights cases that involved the most unethical, unlawful and shameful behavior by UGA's leaders, including Davison, during the 1972-86 academic years.

The Jan Kemp case was a David and Goliath saga of sorts. The "Jan Kemp Affair" not only recalls her bravery in throwing the fatal stone, but also the fortitude of her supporters and her predecessors - other UGA employees and students who simply refused to take it, fought back, and helped oust UGA's politically powerful president, Fred

C. Davison.

Jan Kemp's story is about those events that occurred over 30 years ago. Some readers may remember the Kemp trial. Others may have read something about it since it has been discussed in a number of books, newspapers, magazine articles and scholarly publications regarding collegiate academic-athletic issues. But it is also a story that keeps repeating itself. The "scholarship" aspect of the "scholarship-athlete" profile continues to be ignored or actively manipulated by too many colleges. Taylor Branch's 2011 *Atlantic* magazine article, "The Shame of College Sports," describes the broad scope of continuing misbehavior in collegiate athletics. Recent events at the University of North Carolina and other colleges reveal the continuing infectious influence of the reigning corporate style revenue-producing football machines on campuses nationwide. The "Jan Kemp Affair" is decades old, but the problems it exposed are timeless, and so is the remedy - the courage to confront them.

*The University of Georgia bell tower; photo by Carole Henry*

# CHAPTER ONE
# THE CHAPEL BELL

I was working in my office across the street from UGA's historic North Campus Quadrangle on March 13, 1986, a rain-soaked day, when I heard the pealing of UGA's iconic chapel bell. I looked out the window toward the campus and saw a few people walking beneath umbrellas, but nothing more. The ringing of the old bell was limited by tradition to celebrating UGA football victories, or more rarely, to signal special events. It wasn't football season, so I assumed the sound of the bell was for something special. Was it ever!

Within minutes, the buzz humming through the campus grapevine reached my office. UGA President Fred Davison had announced his resignation sparking a student celebration initiated by the ringing of the chapel bell. I wonder now if those students knew then that the sound of the old bell on that day would be heard longer, louder and in more places than ever before.

The "Jan Kemp Affair" was a phrase coined by news reporters to describe the Jan Kemp case and its aftermath. The case, Kemp v. Ervin, et al., was tried in January and February of 1986 in the United States District Court in Atlanta. The defendants were Virginia Trotter, UGA's Vice President of Academic Affairs, and Leroy Ervin, the Director of UGA's Developmental Studies Division. I was one of Kemp's attorneys along with Joseph (Pat) Nelson, my co-counsel and good friend.

President Davison wasn't a defendant in that trial, but he made himself one in the court of public opinion. His testimony on behalf of Trotter and Ervin included an admission under oath that some UGA student athletes were being taught to "read and write." He justified the presence of illiterate student athletes at UGA because they "were better off" despite their inability to obtain a college degree. If it wasn't already apparent to the jury and the public that he and his administration were complicit in the high-level malfeasance proved during the trial, Davison's own testimony laid any lingering doubt to rest. The verdict attached legal responsibility to the defendants, Ervin and Trotter, but the public and Georgia's political leaders blamed Davison.

The Regents of Georgia's University System took note of Davison's testimony in the Jan Kemp trial. Shortly after the Kemp verdict, they announced the initiation of an internal audit of UGA's Developmental Studies Division. They also deferred Davison's customary annual contract renewal pending release of the results of the audit. More ominously for Davison, he knew that the results of that audit would reveal even more startling evidence of pervasive academic corruption at UGA under his leadership.

The comprehensive audit, conducted by the Regents' staff, was completed four weeks after the Kemp trial verdict was announced. It was delivered to the full Board of Regents at their meeting on March 12, 1986. The chapel bell announced Davison's resignation the following day.

## CHAPTER TWO
## A MEMORABLE PHONE CALL

I was working at my desk on a Fall day in 1982 when my assistant's voice came over the intercom. "Hue, Pat Nelson on line 1." Pat was a personal friend, fellow attorney, and former office-sharing mate. We were both members of what we dubbed "the renegade bar." We saw ourselves as independent lawyers in small firms or solo practices representing ordinary people whose rights were jeopardized by powerful people. We were dead serious about our professional missions. We both believed that our legal training was best used to protect the rights of the powerless against the powerful. Pat was a very good lawyer - a thoughtful person who usually applied his talents with a gentle touch.

I connected to Pat, "Hi Pat, what's up? How's your behavior been lately?" Pat answered, "Not as outrageous as I'd like it to be - no time left to misbehave." "Too bad," I said, "Can I help you get out of this slump?"[1]

"I hope so." Pat's tone of voice shifted - more somber - almost like an opening statement to a jury; a voice that urges jurors to focus on the gravity of what they're going to hear in a trial. "You're not going to believe what I'm about to tell you, but every word of it is true, and we can prove

1 The 'quotes' of conversations that are not memorialized in the trial transcripts are not verbatim since they occurred over thirty years ago. I reconstructed those conversations based on the subjects being discussed, our personal histories, our close friendship, and the sort of banter that was common in our conversations. While the words that I chose as 'quotes' may not be exact, I'm confident that the substance and tone of the conversations are accurate. Other conversations throughout this book are similarly reconstructed, but are always consistent with the considerations noted in this footnote.

all of it."

Pat's words got my attention - "not going to believe", "true", "prove". I urged him on. "Keep talking, Pat!" He had a client named Jan Kemp who was an assistant professor in the Developmental Studies Division at UGA. Developmental Studies was a non-credit program designed to improve the academic skills of marginal students and therefore their chances of success in the regular curriculum. Pat explained that he had already filed a state law civil case for slander that was still pending in the local Superior Court, but he wanted to dismiss it and, with my help, refile it as a civil rights case in a Federal Court in Atlanta.

Pat gave me an overview of the basic facts that we could prove. "Revenue-producing" scholarship athletes and the children of wealthy or otherwise influential parents were being admitted to Developmental Studies by administrative fiat without the consent of the faculty Admissions Committee. The athletes were also being exempted from academic standards and rules limiting attendance in Developmental Studies to four academic quarters to "exit" into the regular curriculum after achieving a mandatory final grade of "C" in each of the program's courses. Some of those students' marginal skills improved rapidly. A few of the success stories were those of "high value" athletes who exited into the normal curriculum and ultimately graduated. They weren't the problem. The problem was the admission and preferential treatment of academically unqualified student athletes - students the decision makers knew beyond question would never earn college degrees.

Pat became more impassioned as he talked about what was going on at UGA. "Jan's getting screwed because she insists on compliance with common standards of academic integrity . . ."

I interrupted, "Whoa! Pat, what in the hell are you getting into? You know you're about to piss off the Bulldog Nation - and that's a lot of people." Pat laughed. "I know, Hue, that's one of the reasons I called you. They're probably already pissed off at you - remember Williams, Lindsey, Dallmeyer? Speaking of Dallmeyer, the other reason is named Hale Almand - you know him - remember?"

I think I spit my coffee through my nose laughing. Of course, Pat knew the answer. While we were sharing law offices a few years earlier, I was handling a case for an Associate Professor of Geology, David Dallmeyer. Davison didn't like how the case was going, so he blamed the Attorney General's Office and lobbied the Board of Regents to hire Almand to represent the dean and department head that we sued. Pat met Almand when he came to our offices to take depositions, and he had heard my stories of how self-assured and combative he was - much like the federal prosecutor that he had been before Davison discovered him.

Pat's personality and history portrayed quite a composite of interesting contradictions. He was a former UGA golf athlete, a graduate of UGA and its law school, a tournament bridge player, a great storyteller, and a gourmet. He was also a former member of the 1960s-radical left UGA Students for a Democratic Society and an exile in Europe as a Vietnam era draft resister. Of particular interest to me, this complicated and interesting man was also an avid fan of UGA's football team. He owned an ancient Mercedes Benz that he had painted *red and black* - UGA's colors. It was only driven on football home game days. So, I had to ask him, "Pat, are you worried about hurting the football program?"

"No," Pat said, "I love the 'Dawgs', but this is a scandal waiting to happen. We need to be on the right side when it blows up in everyone's face. I'm pretty sure that most of the alumni, including the football fans, will be stunned when they find out what's going on. Davison and his buddies are screwing with the academic integrity of our school! I don't think many UGA graduates who worked hard to earn their degrees will be pleased when they find out what's going on - even if they love the Dawgs as much as I do."

Pat was incensed. "Can you believe this, Hue? These severely unprepared football and basketball players are admitted to UGA by the Athletic Association with no screening by the faculty. Then they're protected from being dismissed on academic grounds and afforded other preferential treatment at the behest of UGA's football coach, Vince Dooley, and his go-to assistant Dick Copas." He described the scene in Developmental Studies - a jaw dropping boatload of stories of unbelievable conduct by UGA officials that was demoralizing the faculty to the point of rebellion. "Some of them have resigned in disgust. Others, particularly Jan, have become more and more outspoken." Pat summed up the consequences for Jan. "Ervin demoted her from her 12-month contract to a 9-month contract last Winter Quarter and gave her a notice of nonrenewal of her annual contract a few weeks ago."

Pat said he wanted my help and was confident that we could prove the case. He said, "A number of Jan's colleagues are willing to support her in court. I've already got some incriminating documents that I discovered in the state court case and a few depositions - and the biggest advantage of all - everything we are going to accuse the bad guys of doing is true."

We talked about our roles if I signed on. Pat wanted me to appear as lead counsel, with him as co-counsel. He knew that I had experience trying some bruising cases against federal prosecutors while working for the Federal Public Defender's Office in Atlanta, so he thought that I would be more comfortable than him dealing with Almand's combative litigation style.

I knew that I'd enjoy working with Pat. We had different talents that could mesh into a good trial team. Pat was adept at keeping focused on the big picture, analyzing opposition and potential rebuttal evidence, acquisition and organization of documents, anticipating opposing arguments and developing counter arguments - a gentleman lawyer. I was more into tactics: getting favorable evidence in and keeping unfavorable evidence out, examining and cross-examining witnesses, and making spur of the moment legal arguments to attack or defend whatever was happening. I particularly enjoyed the spontaneous making of and responding to objections. I realized that I enjoyed the combat so much that I sometimes overlooked the point of the war. Pat didn't. He helped keep me focused. I thought that together we had the right balance, and it was always interesting to hang around with Pat. He closed the conversation: "I thought you might be interested in being on the right side again in another brawl with Hale Almand, and hopefully a nice fee after we kick his ass."

How could I disagree? Who could resist this case? The facts were provable; the client was genuine; the mission was important; the defendants and their bosses were vulnerable; the opposing attorney's style would keep me motivated; and the cause was just - a perfect storm! I decided to sign on to help fight the battle if Jan Kemp and I turned out to be a good match. I looked forward to meeting her.

I said, "I'm on board so far Pat. Have Jan call my office to set up an appointment. Hopefully, the three of us will get together to get me completely briefed and plan a strategy."

"Great," Pat answered, "but let me alert you to something from one relatively short guy to another. She's 6'2" tall."

# CHAPTER THREE
# JAN KEMP

As soon as Jan Kemp walked into my office, I knew that she was a formidable individual. Her height, athletic physique, radiant smile, soft Southern accent, quick intelligent mind, and pleasant demeanor were tailor made to get one's attention. She got mine! Looking up from my 5'9" disadvantage, I said, "You must be Jan Kemp - please have a seat!"

In Jan's case, first impressions counted. What I saw over the next hour and a half defined our unusual strategy as we moved into what we all knew would be a bloody street fight with some of the most powerful people in the state. Jan was determined, with or without my help, to disclose what she knew. Her primary goal was to "let the people and the Regents know what's going on." She believed public outrage would force the reforms needed to "weed out the corruption being forced down the faculty's throats."

I rarely had cases where the client's goals were reform first, damages second. Jan was determined to sit on a witness stand to accuse the leadership of UGA and its Athletic Association of academic, ethical and moral malfeasance that was harming students. She understood that resistance to her efforts would extend beyond the Davison Administration. She was challenging a flawed status quo that many citizens and public officials were willing to tolerate. Her challenge would impact a cultural feature of the State of Georgia - some say a religion - UGA football.

I instinctively liked Jan, and knew that we were a good match. Her passion to oppose the abuse of authority granted by the people equaled or surpassed mine. On that score, we were soul mates. With Pat's continuing involvement, I also knew that we could build a great team.

We switched to first names. "So, Jan, what the hell is Developmental Studies? Never heard of it before Pat told me what it was supposed to be. But what is it - realistically?"

Jan smiled and replied, "It's a great idea - we teach basic skills - English, Math and Reading in non-credit courses to kids who couldn't quite satisfy admissions standards. It's a good program, but it's being abused by the Athletic Association with Fred Davison's collaboration. They're exploiting academically unqualified revenue-producing athletes by sheltering them in Developmental Studies to maintain their athletic eligibility. That practice not only insures their failure to graduate, it also demeans the academic integrity of our University and particularly of our program."

I had to chuckle, "Misconduct at the top? Not exactly a novelty at UGA! Which college? Who's the dean?"

"Great questions," Jan said, "Our leader is the Vice President for Academic Affairs, Virginia Trotter. We don't have a dean. Developmental Studies had no tenured faculty members, and no way to get tenure until several months ago when a faculty committee finally developed tenure track standards for the program. It's still an administrative unit whose director reports directly to Trotter who reports directly to Davison."

I got what she was telling me. Developmental Studies had no effective faculty oversight of administrative decisions that violated academic standards. Tenured faculty have job security; they can't be terminated without a specific statement of a reason to revoke their tenure and a hearing before a faculty committee. Untenured faculty members have no such right. Among other things, tenure protects faculty members from unjust retribution by their superiors for arbitrary reasons, like objecting to academic abuses being forced down their throats. Davison was known for always opting for the path of least resistance. In this case that path went straight through a powerless untenured faculty under the direct supervision of the Vice President for Academic Affairs, Virginia Trotter.

"So," I asked, "how does it work? Who decides what standards should be ignored? How do they keep their fingerprints off the record? Who carries out the orders from above?"

Jan was a perfect client. She answered my questions quickly and concisely - a rare experience when listening to new clients tell their story. "Decisions are made at the top - the President's office. The orders are passed to Ervin verbally, and Ervin executes the orders. Davison demands unquestioned loyalty and strict confidentiality at every level of the chain." Jan explained that Davison allocated 50 "administrative" admissions to scholarship athletes and another 25 to "legacy" candidates - the children of wealthy donors or politically important people. There were no standards, no Admissions Committee review - just administrative decisions that the faculty had to live with.

"So, let's think about this, Jan. How does this work? How does Davison get around being exposed? He must have a way to insulate himself if anything goes wrong - you know, wrong, like the existence of somebody like you?"

"Well," she answered, "I think it's more than coincidental that Jim Kenney, Davison's Executive Assistant, is married to Ervin's Assistant Director, Sue McCaffrey. Davison could easily use the Kenney-McCaffrey-Ervin silent telegraph to avoid leaving fingerprints when he's plotting something he wants to disown if he gets caught."

I interrupted, "Well, I'd say that's pretty good circumstantial evidence. I wish I could say I'm surprised, but I know enough about Davison and Kenney to believe that your suspicions are on the mark."

Jan continued. "Communications from the Athletic Association go the other way through the same network. Its agents just tell Ervin what they want. Trotter and sometimes Davison get the message."

I wanted to follow up on this. I sensed that it could become important during the trial to show the jury an overview of the entire academic scam that preempted the faculty's professional judgments. So, I asked Jan, "Is Ervin more than a communications link? Does Davison use him for anything other than a clandestine messenger?" Jan smiled and said, "He sure does. He uses Ervin to lobby regular faculty members who teach our students after they exit the program. Ervin contacts them under the guise of offering supplemental instructions to struggling students, but his real purpose is to convince them to grade athletes on their economic value to the University - not on their academic performance. I know that from personal experience."

I was listening closely to her comments trying to get a grip on how the flow of questionable orders were hidden. My legal mind was reeling with hints of how we might corroborate what Jan was telling me. The circumstances she described were compelling, but sworn testimony and documentary evidence would nail it down. I didn't know it then, but that evidence did exist!

Before ending our meeting, I wanted to give Jan a reality check on what she was getting into. "Jan, I think we both know how malevolent Davison and his buddies can be. You understand that Hale Almand will engineer an attempt to assassinate your character?" I vividly recall her answer. "I'm not worried about any character attack. I don't drink. I've never used drugs. I've never cheated on my husband. I'm a real Christian, and try my best to live like one."

Then she cautioned me. "I need to alert you to something about me that may come up. I understand that the intensity of my resistance to what we saw going on was sometimes annoying to others. If asked about that, my testimony will be that I was comfortable with the passions that drove me. When it came to protecting our students and my alma mater, I was driven. I couldn't live with any other choice. I understand that the tone of my resistance to the abuse of normal standards sometimes offended people, even those who agreed with me but not necessarily with my confrontational stance. I just couldn't tolerate what was happening in front of our eyes. Sometimes I wondered out loud how anyone with even a smidgen of integrity could stomach it. I shouldn't have become that passionate among my colleagues, but I couldn't help it, and thankfully, they are all standing with me on this."

I was impressed. Witnesses who acknowledge their weaknesses strengthen their credibility. "Jan, if you repeat what you just said on the witnesses stand, you'll see a big smile on my face. I'm on the verge of telling you that I hope they attack your character so the jury can hear your answer."

At the end of the meeting, we gave Pat a call to plan a series of meetings to go over our evidence and formulate our strategy. I wanted to draft a civil rights complaint as soon as possible for filing in the U.S. District Court in Atlanta. Pat and I understood Jan's priorities. We were all ready to launch a two-front war against the abusers of the public trust - the dictatorial President of UGA and his lockstep enforcers. The legal war would be fought in the courtroom. The public relations war would be fought in the courthouse corridors and on its steps in full view of the media that any case involving UGA football would inevitably attract.

Jan and I sealed the deal with a handshake. We set up a schedule of meetings with Pat to go over the evidence accumulated in the state court case and get me educated on the narrative that Pat and Jan had promised we could prove. We needed a good chunk of time. The breadth and scope of the academic corruption that we were going to disclose was explosive. Everyone on our team would have to digest a lot of evidence and deliver it to the court and the people of Georgia in a dramatic and persuasive way.

Before Jan left, we had a brief chat mostly about our backgrounds, families, and careers. Jan was particularly interested in Davison's role in the cases involving UGA that I had handled. She had heard about those cases from Larry Blount, a law professor, some other faculty friends, and Pat. I admitted that I knew more about Fred Davison than I ever wanted to - that we had a 'history' one might say. Over time, while traveling from Athens to Atlanta for hearings and depositions, we discussed the four cases involving Davison and his closest allies that I had handled before we met.

# CHAPTER FOUR
# MY PATH TO THE "JAN KEMP AFFAIR"

Before I started my law practice in Athens, I clerked for a highly regarded United States District Judge, Anthony Alaimo, and then served as a federal public defender in Atlanta. My experience in the Federal Court system provided me with a substantial foundation in federal civil rights laws and helped focus my practice as a civil rights litigator. Four of my civil rights cases over the first ten years of practice in Athens involved misconduct at UGA's highest administrative levels up to and including its president.

## Williams v. Kassinger and Saye

On May 14, 1976, Clarke County Georgia Police Chief Winfred "Tate" Brown rear-ended his police car into another vehicle on UGA's campus causing damage to both vehicles and minor injuries to himself and the occupants of the other car. Brown, who admitted to drinking alcohol shortly before the wreck, was the party at fault. Implausibly, that event put me on the path that led to my introduction to Jan Kemp six years later. It also led to my first meeting with Fred Davison in a federal courtroom where he took the stand to defend his handpicked Director of Public Safety, Edward Kassinger, a former FBI agent. Kassinger was on trial along with his subordinate, UGA Police Chief David Saye. We sued both of those police officials for violation of the First Amendment rights of Larry Williams, a UGA Police lieutenant who blew the whistle on a cover-up of Brown's suspected DUI violation on UGA's campus. Williams was fired. He hired me to represent him. We filed the lawsuit in the Federal District Court headquartered in Macon, Georgia where the case was assigned to Judge Wilbur Owens. The pre-trial hearings and the trial were held in the federal courthouse in Athens. Within days of the filing of the lawsuit, Judge Owens ordered the defendants to reinstate Williams to his job. A jury later awarded Williams almost $50,000 in damages. The court then added an award to Williams to recover his attorney's fees and litigation expenses.

Williams was the shift lieutenant when UGA Officer Gene Brewer was dispatched to investigate the Brown accident. Brewer's report was recorded on a State of Georgia mandated uniform traffic accident reporting form which Williams was required to review, approve and sign. It accurately stated: 1) Brewer smelled alcohol while talking to Brown, 2) Brown was staggering, 3) the accident victims stated that they believed Brown had been drinking, 4) Brewer told Brown that he would be transported to a hospital for an examination of a small cut on his forehead and for blood to be drawn for a blood alcohol test, 5) a Clarke County patrol car then arrived at the accident scene, and Brewer allowed the Clarke County officer to transport Brown to the hospital where Brewer would meet them, and 6) Brown never arrived at the hospital.

The report, signed by Brewer as the investigating officer and Williams as his shift lieutenant, was sent through normal channels for filing and submission of a copy to Georgia's Department of Public Safety. Williams habitually made copies for his personal files of all reports containing his signature – a habit that in this instance preserved a document that became Exhibit 1 in the ensuing lawsuit against Kassinger and Saye.

The following morning, Brown showed up at UGA Police Chief David Saye's office for an hour and a half meeting. During that meeting, he admitted consuming "a couple" of drinks at his home before the accident.

After his meeting with Brown, Saye called Brewer in to review his report. He instructed Brewer to change the report by eliminating all information about alcohol and Brown's failure to obey his order to report to the hospital. Then Saye made some fatal mistakes. Rather than ordering Brewer to prepare a new report, Saye made him alter the original form using "white out" to eliminate checked boxes that referenced alcohol on the form and a notation to "See Supplemental." He ordered Brewer to redraw empty boxes over the white out and discard the lengthy supplement to the report that detailed the removal of Brown from the accident scene by a Clarke County police officer and Brown's failure to report to the hospital. Williams was not notified, and a copy of the altered form, containing his signature, was submitted to the Department of Public Safety.[2] Saye kept the original with the white out clearly visible on it.

---

2 The version of OCGA 16-10-20 applicable in 1980 defines a felony when, "A person who knowingly and willfully falsifies, conceals, or covers up by any trick, scheme, or device a material fact; makes a false, fictitious, or fraudulent statement or representation; or makes use of any false writing or document, knowing the same to contain any false, fictitious, or fraudulent statement or entry, in any matter within the jurisdiction of any department or agency of state government or of the government or any county city, or other political subdivision of this state."

Trusting Brewer, an honest cop, to protect him from disclosure of his misconduct was also a big mistake on Saye's part. Brewer told Williams what had occurred. Williams verified Brewer's information by contacting the accident victims who gave him a copy of the altered report they had obtained from the Department of Public Safety.

Williams then wrote a letter to Kassinger and Saye in which he demanded correction of the report or a written exoneration of himself to keep if needed to defend the fact that his signature remained on the bogus report. Neither Kassinger or Saye responded, so Williams' father, a UGA chemistry professor, gave the damning documents to a news reporter for a local newspaper. The reporter then questioned Saye, showed him a copy of the original accident report and a copy of the altered version, and a copy of the letter that Williams had sent to him and to Kassinger. Enraged by the disclosure of the cover-up to the press, Kassinger demanded that Williams appear that night for a meeting to discuss the release of the Brown accident reports.

When Williams arrived with his father, they were ushered into an office where Kassinger, Saye, and Assistant Police Chief David Morris were waiting. The meeting was not pretty. The panel of the United States Court of Appeals for the Fifth Circuit that reviewed the record on appeal in the Williams case described the meeting in these words: "Williams arrived with his father and after some disagreement whether his father should be permitted to remain, the meeting began. The problem with the reporter was first discussed: appellee (Williams) denied that he had divulged the report. When asked if he knew who had, Lt. Williams replied that he could 'speculate' as to the identity of the person but did not know. At this point, Williams' father admitted that he had given the reporter copies of the report and letter. By way of explanation, Williams stated that in the course of obtaining advice from his father he had given his father copies of the reports and of his protest letter.

Tempers flared. Chief Saye, a larger and younger man who played football at UGA in the late 60s, pounded his desk and threatened to sue the father 'in every court in the land.' He also warned, 'I'll whip your ass.' Then Saye became physically menacing to the extent that another officer intervened to restrain him. Kassinger immediately fired Williams for leaking the accident report."

I met Larry Williams and his father William 'Bill' Williams a few days after their meeting with Kassinger and Saye. Larry was a serious young man intent on making a career in law enforcement. His father, a UGA professor in his 60s, was a slightly built man. David Saye was a large man, but he was a coward who chose to intimidate the oldest and smallest person in the office where the meeting with Larry Williams and his father was held.

When Williams showed me the original and altered reports, I knew that I was looking at hard evidence of a civil rights "whistleblower" violation of the free speech clause of the First Amendment. This was a case that had to be pursued. I cobbled together a complaint with copies of the original and altered reports attached and filed it in the Athens division of the U.S. District Court for the Middle

District of Georgia. Among other things, we asked the court to schedule a hearing on our request for a preliminary injunction reinstating Williams to his position. Judge Wilbur Owens was assigned to handle the case.

Judge Owens reacted quickly. He ordered Kassinger and Saye to appear the following week in his court to explain the two versions of the accident report and provide a constitutional reason, if possible, for firing Williams. Because the judge ordered an immediate hearing as soon as the case was filed, no attorney had filed a notice of appearance as Kassinger and Saye's counsel. Therefore, the judge ordered me to immediately serve copies of the complaint and hearing notice on them.

I brought those documents to the police department in envelopes addressed to each. I intended to leave the complaints with the receptionist, but when I arrived I was escorted into Kassinger's office. I laid the envelopes on his desk and told Kassinger that I was serving notice of the expedited hearing at the direction of Judge Owens. He went into a rage much like Saye's reaction to Williams' father, except he didn't threaten to whip any part of my body. He jumped up from his chair, leaned over towards me and slammed both hands down on his desk. He launched into a loud semi-lucid denunciation of me, my legal education, and "my lawsuit" as evil behavior for selfish purposes by an "obviously incompetent lawyer."

I had some familiarity with FBI intimidation tactics from my time in the Federal Public Defender's office. I handled a number of cases referred by the FBI to the U.S. Attorney's

Office for prosecution. Bullying people in FBI custody was not uncommon, and often got results from people being charged with federal crimes. But I was not in Kassinger's custody, and I was not the one in this picture who committed a crime. He aided and abetted Saye's submission of a false report to the Department of Public Safety which was a felony under O.C.G.A. 16-10-20. I was there as an attorney in a federal case acting by law as an officer of the court carrying out a federal judge's instructions. Kassinger knew that the federal complaint that I filed would expose conduct that he couldn't defend. He couldn't deal with being handed a notice to appear in a Federal court to answer to charges knowing that he was guilty. His behavior showed me that Kassinger was no stranger to the use of thuggery. In fact, he had allowed Saye to threaten and intimidate Williams' elderly father in his presence. I had delivered the hearing notice, so I left. Kassinger may have been disappointed over my matter-of-fact reaction to his outburst, but he was definitely frustrated over his inability to intimidate Gene Brewer and Larry Williams into abandoning their commitment to the rule of law.

Shortly after we arrived at the courthouse a few days later for the hearing, Kassinger learned that he wasn't going to get the reaction he wanted from a federal judge either. The purpose of the hearing was for the judge to consider Williams' request to be reinstated. Kassinger and Saye were represented by Assistant Attorney General Mike Bowers, who later became Georgia's Attorney General. He was assisted by Al Evans, a senior Assistant Attorney General who took charge of the case for the defendants after the initial hearing. Bowers, Evans and the other assistant attorneys general involved were always competent, professional and efficient, but they walked into a firestorm that morning.

I had subpoenaed the original altered accident report, but when I asked Bowers before the hearing to show me that document, he told me that he didn't have it and didn't intend to produce it. It took only seconds for him to change his mind after Judge Owens took the bench and asked the attorneys if there were any preliminary matters that needed to be addressed before the hearing began. I advised him of the non-production of the subpoenaed accident report. Judge Owens' response telegraphed his displeasure over the arrogance exemplified by a litigant who intentionally ignores a federal subpoena. He asked Bowers for the location of the original accident report. Bowers responded. He told the judge that the report was at the UGA police department on UGA's campus several blocks away. Judge Owens then asked how long it would take to have it brought to the courthouse. Bowers told him that it would take about 20 minutes. The judge's response was curt and chilling. "OK, I am going to recess for 20 minutes." Pointing his finger at the surface of the bench, he continued, "When I return, I want that report to be right here." He then abruptly left the bench.

The judge returned promptly in 20 minutes and picked up the report that Bowers had placed on the bench. After a few minutes perusing it, he looked at me and said "Mr. Henry, call David Saye to the witness stand." I immediately responded, "Your Honor, the plaintiff calls David Saye." Those were the last words I spoke until the judge had finished nailing Saye for falsifying an official record. His examination of Saye was brutal. As soon as Saye took the stand, Judge Owens handed him the original falsified accident report and the Uniform Accident Report Instruction Manual that the Department of Public Safety provided to all traffic enforcement agencies. Leaning toward Saye, Judge Owens locked eyes with the witness. "Now, Mr. Saye, who put the 'white outs' on the original report?" Saye admitted that Officer Brewer did at his direction. "Who redrew the sobriety box on the form?" Saye gave the same answer. "Who whited out the reference to supplemental pages in the Conclusion section of the report?" Once again Saye responded that Brewer did that at his direction. "Alright," the judge said, "so show me the provisions in the manual that permits 'white outs,'' retracing parts of the form, and changing the information on the form to a version other than what the investigating officer reported?"

Everyone in the courtroom got the message. Nevertheless, Kassinger and Saye continued to claim that Williams' firing was justifiable because he had compromised the "security and confidentiality" of falsified police records.

At the end of the hearing, Judge Owens ordered Williams' reinstatement to his position with retroactive restoration of all benefits that he would have received had the defendants not violated his constitutional rights. The judge also ordered the defendants to send the original accident report to the Department of Public Safety, along with a transcript of the hearing that had just been concluded. The case moved to the damages phase to be tried by a federal jury.

Davison appeared as a defense witness in the jury trial several months later. My cross-examination of him during the trial was my first opportunity to actually speak with him. Remarkably, he shamelessly endorsed Kassinger's and Saye's illegal actions in that federal courtroom in sworn testimony before a judge and a jury - a decision similar to his taking the stand ten years later to defend the indefensible in the Kemp case. His appearance as a defense witness in the Kemp case was my only other verbal exchange with him. In both instances, he was under oath. His demeanor under oath was consistently arrogant and condescending. In the Williams case, he appeared to believe that he was the only person involved who really understood the important policy and legal reasons that compelled Williams' firing for compromising the confidentiality of police misconduct. In the Kemp trial, he "explained" the problem to the jury and blamed others for his failures. He didn't have to testify in either case, but he chose to do so, and in the process, came to own both scandals.

Davison's lecture on the need for confidentiality of a fraudulent accident report didn't impress the Judge who had a decidedly different view - one that assumed all citizens, including police officials, were subject to the rule of law. He refused to allow the jury to consider any legal theory that would protect wrongdoers from disclosure of their falsification of official records. Kassinger's and Saye's arguments also failed to sway the jury. The court clerk read the jury's verdict: $16,000 in compensatory damages and $20,000 in punitive damages against Kassinger, but the lesser amounts of $4,750 in compensatory and $8,000 in punitive damages against Saye. So, Kassinger, the former FBI agent who condoned the cover-up, stood silent when Saye threatened physical harm to Williams' father, fired Williams for telling the truth, and reacted with fist pounding threats when I notified him that a federal judge was about to examine his ethical and legal lapses, received the justice that he dreaded and deserved. The jury verdict in favor of Larry Williams was affirmed by the Court of Appeals in Williams v. Board of Regents of the University System of Georgia, 629 F.2d 1350 (5th Circuit 1980). The defendants then appealed the decision to the U.S. Supreme Court which denied certiorari at 42 U.S. 926 (1981) (Rehnquist Dissenting).

The trial and verdict played out in the local press. The jury's verdict added shame to Kassinger's and Saye's vaunted police administrator resumes. The following November, the people of Clarke County rebuked Kassinger and Saye again when they rewarded Williams by electing him as their Sheriff.

One thing that I learned with great clarity after the Williams case was that Fred Davison was a powerful person. He had just testified in a Federal Court in defense of UGA's highest police officials who falsified an official accident report to the Department of Public Safety. Judge Owens ordered the transmittal of a record of the hearing and the original "white-out" version of the police report to the Department. The Attorney General's Office, the top law enforcement agency in the state, represented the UGA police officials who had clearly violated their oaths of office. The Attorney General's Office also represented the Department of Public Safety, the agency that was defrauded by the false reports submitted to it that caused the unwitting release of a false report to the injured traffic accident victims. Those circumstances clearly created a conflict of interest between the Williams case defendants and the agency that processes accident reports. What happened to these public officials? Nothing! Two state agencies had the chutzpah to ignore a federal judge's finding of police misconduct. I knew from that point forward that Davison and his circle were being protected by very powerful people. In all honesty, that motivated me. I looked forward to the next opportunity to ask a federal judge to take a look at ethics-challenged officialdom at UGA under Davison's leadership.

The Williams case was the first to expose Davison's propensity to protect his hand-picked aides even when their conduct was reprehensible. Larry Williams was the first person to challenge the legitimacy of Davison's presidency in a public courtroom. By unnecessarily testifying that his top police officials' misconduct was proper, and by taking no personnel action against them for violating the rights of Williams and Brown's accident victims, Davison became a part of the UGA police scandal that Williams disclosed. Assisted by Davison's poor judgment, Larry Williams opened UGA's exit door for Davison - a door Jan Kemp slammed shut in another federal courtroom ten years later.

## Lindsey v. Regents

After the Williams verdict, I began meeting with a number of UGA employees with complaints about mistreatment by Davison and his allies. It was a big group. One of them was Bryan Lindsey, an untenured Assistant Professor in the College of Education. Lindsey had crossed Davison during the Spring of 1975 by creating and circulating a faculty survey that Davison saw as criticism of his leadership. The instructions on the survey directed the participants to mail the completed form to the Regents. That was enough to incite a swift reaction by high level UGA administrators, including once again the misuse of UGA's police powers by Ed Kassinger.

Kassinger's use of UGA's police powers to intimate Lindsey predated the firing of Larry Williams by a year. I didn't know until Lindsey hired me that the mistreatment of Williams and his father by Kassinger and Saye was a repeat performance; they had already used police threats against Lindsey for exercising his constitutional right to speak freely.

The similarity of the retaliations against Lindsey and Williams was chilling. In Lindsey's case, it happened when Assistant Police Chief David Morris, the same command level officer who physically blocked David Saye from assaulting Larry Williams' father, went to Lindsey's office to read him Miranda warnings for unauthorized use of copying equipment and "harassment through the mails."

Lindsey initially believed his to be a lost cause, but Judge

Owens' harsh criticism of the defendants in the Williams case changed his view. He decided that he did have a shot at Davison and his enforcers in a Federal Court. He read the tea leaves accurately.

Bryan Lindsey's case fit the classic Davison model for dealing with targeted employees who strayed from the lock-step loyalty that he demanded from every UGA employee. Those with the temerity to openly oppose him on any matter, no matter how slight, invariably suffered undeserved retaliation. Bryan Lindsey was a prime example, but he fought back and turned the tables in the case of Lindsey v. Board of Regents that I filed for him in Judge Owens' court.

The source of the order to intimidate Lindsey could be easily discerned by the circumstances. Who had the motive? Davison's thin skin was no secret. Lindsey had made him the subject of a faculty survey that directed participants to send their answers to the Board of Regents. Who besides Davison possessed the power to order UGA's top police officials to threaten Lindsey? Put these circumstances together with Davison's track record, and it became clear that retaliation was inevitable. No one on campus, other than Davison and his cadre of enforcers, had any motive to initiate an abuse of UGA's police power to harass a professor who hadn't committed any crime. It was crystal clear to me that Davison was not above the abusive use of UGA's police force, headed by Kassinger, his hand-picked Director of Public Safety. The malice implicit in such tactics was incomprehensible. Having an armed command level police officer barge into a faculty member's office to read Miranda rights cannot be interpreted as anything short of reprehensible. Small wonder that Judge Owens who heard this case declared in his findings that "President Davison was a part of this."

Enraged by the police threats, Lindsey reported the incident to a news reporter. During the reporter's interview, Lindsey said that being subjected to such abuse was intolerable, so he intended to resign at the end of the academic year. The UGA administration seized upon that comment, and notified him that his contract would not be renewed in light of his statement to the reporter. Lindsey then notified his superiors that he had changed his mind. His contract was renewed for the following year, but then non-renewed one year later. No reason was included in the notice of non-renewal. The "give no reason" tactic for non-renewals of non-tenured faculty, mandated by the Attorney General's Office, is based on the assumption that the statement of any reason may be vulnerable to challenge for violation of constitutional rights. While probably prudent from a risk management viewpoint, that practice seemed to implicitly demonstrate a lack of confidence in the ability of UGA's administrators to frame constitutional reasons for discharging employees.

Shortly after we filed a complaint, Judge Owens conducted a non-jury trial. His ruling enjoined the defendants from failing to offer Lindsey another annual contract and from any unfairness in considering him for promotion and tenure. The court's fact findings and legal conclusions included:

The preparation and circulation of the questionnaire was constitutionally protected speech under the First Amendment to the U.S. Constitution.

Lindsey's contract was non-renewed in retaliation for his exercise of those rights.

The reading of Miranda rights was improper since the use of copying equipment for personal reasons by faculty members was commonly tolerated, and "harassment through the mails" wasn't a crime in Georgia.

During the trial, Judge Owens was openly skeptical about the reasons claimed by the defendants that justified a Miranda warning. Although I represented Lindsey, Judge Owens was the person in that courtroom who nailed down the absurdity of the claim that the police had good reasons to send a uniformed armed Assistant Police Chief to Lindsey's office to read Miranda rights to him. He focused on the absence of any evidence of actual restrictions on the common practice of administrator and faculty members' use of copying equipment and supplies for personal reasons. They couldn't identify any other instance of a police investigation of that common practice or of a "Miranda" intrusion into a faculty member's office for using the mail to circulate a faculty survey.

The Attorney General's Office appealed. Judge Owens' decision and opinion were affirmed by the United States Fifth Circuit Court of Appeals at 607 F.2d 672 (5$^{th}$ Cir. 1980).

The newspaper coverage of the Williams and Lindsey cases educated UGA's students and employees. Some came to believe that those legal victories would make UGA's administrators understand that they were vulnerable to the possible disgrace and financial consequences of conduct that deprived their victims of constitutional rights. Future events, particularly the Jan Kemp case, proved that UGA's top two administrators, Davison and Trotter, didn't get the message, and both paid a heavy price.

### Dayan and Shelledy v. Regents

In 1979, Marshall Dayan and David Shelledy were undergraduate honor students at UGA. They had some ideas to improve the University System's core curriculum that they wanted to present to the Board of Regents.

The Regents had two categories for processing requests to speak at their meetings. One category, for the general public, required submission of requests to speak to the Regents' Chancellor who in consultation with the Board's Chairman accepted or rejected them. The citizens making the requests were then notified of their decision with an explanation of reasons if the requests were denied. The other category, for students and University System employees, required them to submit their requests to speak for a pre-screening by the president of the institution where they were employed or enrolled. Dayan and Shelledy complied with the policy by submitting their requests to Davison. The policy specifically required the institution presidents to "carefully consider" those requests and transmit them to the Chancellor with their recommendations. Davison failed to comply with his obligations under the Speaker Policy. Instead, he deposited the students' requests in a black hole. He delegated his obligations to a subordinate with no deadline - a bureaucratic maneuver typically used to avoid his obligations as UGA's president. Dayan and Shelledy had no option other than a lawsuit if they wanted to bring their concerns to the Regent's attention. They were smart, articulate, and likeable. They wanted to address the Regents about academic policies that affected their educations. Their complaint was just. Once again, citizens were sitting in my office seeking legal advice because Davison or his agents violated their constitutional rights.

Shortly after we filed the lawsuit, Al Evans, the Assistant Attorney General handling the case for the Regents, informed Davison that he was obligated to comply with the Speaker Policy, and it was damn good advice. To comply with Evans' directions, Davison forwarded the students' requests to the Regents, but with negative recommendations. His compliance, albeit untimely, mooted our best argument - that the Speaker Policy, even if facially constitutional as written, was "unconstitutionally applied."

Despite Davison's capitulation, we continued prosecuting the lawsuit because we believed the policy itself was unconstitutional. The district court disagreed. Judge Owens ruled that the Speaker Policy did not curtail free speech - that it only imposed rational measures to control the time, place and manner of speech "in order to assure efficient conduct of the Regents' business." The Court of Appeals affirmed the District Court decision.

We disagreed with those decisions because they ignored the fact that the initial decision maker, an institution president, has a substantial role in the process that often concerned his or her own conduct, policies, or decisions. That reality chilled the free speech of students and employees with complaints against institutional actions or policies - particularly at UGA because Davison never hid his tendency to punish his perceived enemies. Other citizens had no state-imposed impediments to the free exercise of their right to criticize public institutions and/or policies. Nevertheless, two Federal Courts disagreed with our constitutional analysis of the Speaker Policy.

The significance of this case was the trial judge's decision to award attorney's fees to Dayan and Shelledy because the filing of their lawsuit caused Davison to comply with the Speaker Policy. For the first time, a Federal Court ruled that Davison personally breached a mandatory legal duty - a breach significant enough to order him to pay the students' legal expenses. Davison couldn't hide behind subordinates this time. He owned the suppression of students' constitutional rights. Consequently, he felt the sting of a court decision punishing him for his senseless inaction.

In June of 1980, the Court of Appeals affirmed the trial judge's decision awarding attorney's fees and litigation expenses. It ruled, "As to the award of attorney's fees to the plaintiffs, the district court found that the plaintiffs obtained substantial voluntary relief as a direct result of their lawsuit. Consequently, the award of attorney's fees was proper."

This case marked yet another instance of Davison's aversion to the First Amendment rights of individuals who happened to be subject to his authority. He simply ignored the rules enacted by the Regents to provide UGA employees and students an opportunity to communicate with the governing body of their university. This case unveiled the remarkable scope of Davison's hostility to the free speech rights of UGA's students and employees. No attempt to speak one's mind openly was too trivial to suppress. Why would Davison force students to file a federal lawsuit to compel him to perform duties imposed by the Regents - duties that were so clear that the Attorney General ordered him to comply as soon as the lawsuit was filed? Why did Davison fear the prospect of two honor students speaking to the Regents about a system-wide curriculum?

Ironically, the Regents granted speaking privileges to Dayan and Shelledy over Davison's belated negative recommendation. There was no doubt. Davison had been caught red-handed. He was ordered to pay his opponents' litigation expenses, and the Regents rejected his attempt to deny the students' effort to exercise their constitutional rights. The Regents repudiation of Davison's recommendations was clearly an ignoble moment for a man characterized by an elevated sense of power and importance. Yet, he apparently learned nothing from the Speaker Policy case. He continued ignoring or intentionally suppressing the constitutional rights of UGA employees.

## Dallmeyer v. Regents

David Dallmeyer was a tenured associate professor of geology when his department head brought false but serious charges against him. He was notified at 3:30 P.M. on a Thursday afternoon in February of 1980 that he was being ordered to report the following day to the office of Jack Payne, Dean of the College of Arts and Sciences. He was given no reason for the Dean's order. When he appeared for the meeting, he was confronted by his department head, Don Eckelman, with what turned out to be totally baseless allegations of plagiarism and sexual harassment - the top two academic sins which, if proved, would destroy any professor's career. Payne ordered Dallmeyer to submit a letter of resignation by the following Monday and instructed him to "keep quiet" about it. Payne told Dallmeyer that a refusal to resign would initiate procedures to revoke his tenure resulting in a public disclosure of the charges that he faced. While Dallmeyer was meeting with Eckelman and Payne, UGA security personnel were sent to his laboratory to evict his technician, shut down the lab's equipment, lock the lab, and change the locks. Then, to add insult to injury, UGA's eviction team also posted a public notice on the laboratory door stating, "Entry Only with Permission of Geology Head" - an unnecessary slur because the lab was locked down.

At the time of this incident, Dallmeyer was ascertaining the age of rock samples that he had brought to UGA from Greenland. The age determination process required the uninterrupted use of delicate equipment over a fixed time period. As a result of the closure of Dallmeyer's lab, the equipment shut down, the analysis was lost, and the equipment was damaged.

Dallmeyer immediately contacted representatives of the American Association of University Professors for advice and assistance. Its representatives suggested that he contact me to discuss possible legal remedies. I met with him on the following day, a Saturday. It was immediately obvious to me that the aggressive actions of UGA's high level administrators required an aggressive response. Dallmeyer agreed, so I drafted a complaint and shipped it to Macon to be filed on Monday in the U.S. District Court for the Middle District of Georgia. Judge Owens was assigned to the case. His office notified me and the State Attorney General's Office that he was scheduling a hearing in Macon on Tuesday of the following week to consider Dallmeyer's request for a temporary restraining order prohibiting UGA officials from banning him from access to his office and lab. We appeared as ordered. After Judge Owens heard arguments from both sides, he ordered the defendants' attorney, Assistant Attorney General Linda Birrell, to have UGA's file on the attempt to remove Dallmeyer's tenure brought immediately to his chambers in Macon. After his review of the records, Judge Owens not only reinstated Dallmeyer to his position, he also restrained the defendants and their agents from interfering with Dallmeyer's research projects, from initiating any tenure removal process for any reason without first procuring permission from the District Court. Once again, the Attorney General filed an appeal from Judge Owens' ruling.

Enraged over Judge Owens' orders in the Dallmeyer case, Davison wrote a memo to the Regents bitterly complaining about the quality of legal representation provided by the Attorney General's Office and seeking authority to retain Hale Almand.[3] That memo was not penned for the eyes of the public, but a copy was accidentally included in a 'discovery dump' that Almand delivered to my office. Discovery dumps are used by some defense attorneys with superior economic leverage to increase the workload of plaintiff's attorneys. As it turned out however, Almand or someone on his staff inadvertently included Davison's memo to the Regents' Chancellor in the discovery dump. The memo, dated February 22, 1980, reiterated the false allegations against Dallmeyer, criticized Judge Owens, and railed against the representation received from the Attorney General's Office. The Regents apparently bought into that narrative and allowed Davison to hire Almand to handle Dallmeyer's case.

The significance of the Dallmeyer case to the "Jan Kemp Affair" was Davison's decision to introduce Hale Almand, a private attorney and former Assistant United States Attorney, as the litigator whom he believed would do a better job than the Attorney General's Office. Almand convinced Judge Owens to allow UGA to proceed with tenure revocation proceedings, but that decision backfired when the faculty committee appointed to hear the case exonerated Dallmeyer. The sexual harassment charges

3 Davison's memo reads in part: "The deans also operate under the assumption that the Attorney General's office is prepared to successfully defend their actions. It would seem that this was not the case in Judge Owens' court this week. It is appalling that, in a matter critical to the proper functioning of Board policies and institutional decision-making, the University was represented by someone who understands neither."

were abandoned before the hearing because there was no evidence to support them. The faculty committee then dismissed the plagiarism charges because they were based on Dallmeyer's use of U.S. Geologic Survey public domain maps with proper attribution.

Dallmeyer's victory was particularly sweet because it was a faculty committee that stood up to Davison, and he couldn't do a thing about it. Normally, he overruled faculty committee decisions that displeased him, but this time a federal judge was looking over his shoulder. At the end of the Dallmeyer case, two developments leading to Davison's ultimate demise had occurred: the empowerment of an angry faculty, and the retention of Hale Almand as Davison's hand-picked trial lawyer.

Dallmeyer returned to his career, and performed his duties admirably until he retired as Professor Emeritus in 2010. He is and was a good person and a great professor. He was also another innocent victim of a Davison style assault - false accusation, ambush, exile, and threats of public ruination in the absence of instant capitulation. Dallmeyer resisted. He used the rule of law to save his career and to help set the stage for the "Jan Kemp Affair."

The Dallmeyer case is the only one discussed here that was not filed for violation of the plaintiff's First Amendment rights. It was filed on the theory that UGA agents violated Dallmeyer's Fourteenth Amendment right to "due process of law" by evicting him from his lab and shutting down his equipment without affording him an opportunity to defend himself in a fair hearing before taking such drastic action. It was also a very significant development because it introduced Hale Almand as Davison's go-to lawyer just in time for him to engineer the legal train wreck that followed.

# CHAPTER FIVE
# FRED DAVISON

Fred Davison was already an insider when he was appointed as UGA's interim President in February of 1967. He was inaugurated as President the following year on July 1, 1968 when he was only 37 years old, but he had already served as the Dean of the University's School of Veterinary Medicine and as a Vice Chancellor of the University System of Georgia. I imagine the University community was pleased that its new leader was a talented young man who could bring new ideas and great energy to a growing UGA baby boomer student body.

I had no idea who Fred Davison was until I began law school at UGA in 1969 and then paid scant attention to him. Those times were turbulent throughout the country. The civil rights movement, the war in Vietnam, and the generational divisiveness flowing from the 1960s cultural revolution took center stage. As UGA's chief executive, Davison drew heat from student protesters who were becoming active on campus, mainly because he was completely insensitive to the legitimate issues involving their lives.

Later, as the twists and turns of my professional life played out, I learned that Davison had alienated a large number of faculty members and other UGA personnel. His tenure as UGA's President was fraught with needless controversies, most of which grew from his extreme sensitivity to any criticism - constructive or otherwise. He was stunningly unpopular with the large Liberal Arts, Journalism, and College of Education faculties.

Davison conducted himself as an elite intellectual with few if any peers. His language exemplified the condescending manner of far too many academics who consistently address others as their underlings. Within two years after his inauguration, Davison had evolved into an isolated, authoritarian executive in constant conflict with faculty members who he treated like military camp recruits. In fact, he admitted as much in a post-Kemp trial interview by Jerrold Footlick, a prominent writer on educational issues, during which he described UGA's deans as his "field generals."[4]

That admission may be the most honest self-assessment by Fred Davison ever publicized. His actions throughout his 19-year tenure as UGA's President painted the picture of a remote but powerful military commander - more like the leader of a military coup d'état than a leader of a major research university. He ruled through a cadre of carefully selected aides whose unconditional loyalties to him were handsomely rewarded with the largesse that he could gift out as UGA's President: excessive salaries, sky-box seats at UGA's football games, guest status at bowl games, and "official trips" to UGA's study-abroad facilities.

---

4 Jerrold K. Footlick, an attorney, *Newsweek Magazine* Education Writer and prolific author on higher education issues wrote *Truth and Consequences*, a book describing a number of university related public relations disasters, including the "Jan Kemp Affair." His interviews focused on the absence of any public relations effort to counter the national press coverage that savaged UGA's reputation during the five and one-half week trial. *Truth and Consequences* contains the only published interviews of Davison and his close advisors.

Davison's closest advisers occupied the highest levels of administrative positions with salaries that dwarfed faculty incomes and benefits. Those aides included the Kemp trial defendants, Virginia Trotter and Leroy Ervin, but they were really in Davison's second tier of loyalists. His closest aides were:

Ralph Beaird, his legal advisor and the Dean of UGA's School of Law who engineered some of the legal fiascos that characterized Davison's presidency.

James Kenney, aka "The Undertaker", his Executive Assistant, whose typecast drill-instructor demeanor fit his role as Davison's bearer of bad tidings. He was married to Sue McCaffrey Kenney, Leroy Ervin's administrative assistant.

Barry Wood, Davison's personal public relations spokesman who protected him from news reporters and issued carefully parsed public statements for him.

Edward Kassinger, Davison's hand-picked Director of Public Safety and former FBI agent who headed UGA's police force that he and his high-level subordinates used to intimidate UGA employees.

The environment at UGA during the Davison era provided the backdrop for the "Jan Kemp Affair." The unrelenting episodes of surprisingly pointless controversies that Davison incited over many years alienated people ranging from UGA's faculty and staff to Georgia's political leaders leaving him with a trail of enemies. His mistreatment of UGA personnel created a fearful environment intended to intimidate, and it did. But when the Kemp trial exposed him, the fear he intentionally created exploded in his face. Nineteen years of abuse had created broad based faculty and political demands for new leadership that suddenly became too powerful for Davison to withstand. He had to face the fact that he had written his own professional obituary.

Davison's needlessly authoritarian leadership style may have benefited him in some ways - perhaps it resolved issues quickly if not fairly. But, it also signaled the inevitability of the humiliating circumstances of his departure. Always acting through his aides, Davison imposed no limits on intimidation tactics available to his enforcers; the most vicious included the thuggish abuse of his perceived enemies by UGA's top level police officials in the Williams and Lindsey cases and the seizure of Dallmeyer's laboratory. The ugly characteristics that appeared in the earlier cases reappeared in the Jan Kemp case. The jury's verdict in her case was a resounding condemnation of UGA's leadership that led directly to Davison's resignation. His vindictive instincts had already been on display in numerous instances, all of which set the scene for his downfall, but none that garnered anywhere near the press coverage that the Kemp case attracted. Davison's circle of loyalists diminished precipitously after the Kemp verdict. Since he had already alienated a significant portion of the faculty and several deans and department heads, it was no surprise that "friends" of Davison on UGA's campus became a rarity after Kemp blew the whistle that signaled the beginning of the end of his presidency.

According to a number of faculty surveys, Davison was already exceptionally unpopular when the "Jan Kemp Affair" emerged in 1981. After the Kemp verdict, *Athens Observer* reporter Phil Sanderlin put the trial in historical context in an article recalling Davison's history of conflict and divisiveness. Sanderlin's recap of Davison's troublesome tenure described his alienation of a wide cross section of the UGA community beginning in the early 1970s, including faculty, deans, department heads, students, and public officials. It also recalled his fatal mistakes: condoning and participating in conduct that alienated people whom he couldn't control – like federal judges and citizens serving as federal jurors.

Sanderlin described 1973 as a contentious year; one that set the tone for the events to come. Davison was actively resisting implementation of the recommendations of a 1970 UGA Steering Committee self-study. The conclusions of the study were critical of Davison's administrative style. The recommendations included major delegations of operating responsibilities to the leaders of UGA's Schools and Colleges. Davison ignored the study.

Meanwhile, the faculty of the School of Journalism passed a vote of "no confidence" in their dean, Warren Agee - a Davison insider. Davison threw a temper tantrum. He released a presidential statement characterizing the Journalism faculty's no confidence vote as, "beyond the bounds of professional conduct." Then he convened the Journalism faculty for a three-hour browbeating concluding with his advice that, "Journalism is a buyer's market, so disgruntled faculty members can leave."

Davison's hostility toward any faculty concern that deviated from unquestioned loyalty to him was so severe that it drew public criticism from powerful state officials. Governor Jimmy Carter weighed in to support the Journalism faculty. He said, "The department heads ought to be given a greater role in the final determination of pay and promotion. I've known for several months of the potential problems at the University of Georgia. It is serious. Those who have resigned are good people." Davison ignored the Governor's criticism and disregarded his instructions to engage the faculty in policy discussions that affected them.

Reacting to Davison's blatant retaliation against dissenting faculty members, Clarke County's legislative representative Chappelle Matthews told the press that the Board of Regents should investigate the UGA campus tension. He warned that if the Regents didn't take responsibility, a legislative committee would. He described mistreatment of the Journalism faculty as "the tip of the iceberg", which caused him to worry about "much deeper morale problems." Davison hardly noticed the disharmony being openly discussed in the press and among Georgia's leaders.

True to form, Davison expressed no reaction to the results of another faculty survey by the Student Government Association in 1974. It found 62.5% of the respondents characterized the Davison Administration as unresponsive to their legitimate concerns and needs. The following year, a 1975 Arts and Sciences faculty "report card" resulted in an overwhelming majority grading Davison in 21 categories with D's and F's. Again and again, Davison closed his eyes to these ominous messages from UGA's faculty - a habit that ultimately drove his failure to make the decisions needed to quell the rebellion by an abused Developmental Studies faculty, a rebellion that ripened into his personal Waterloo: the "Jan Kemp Affair."

Davison's authoritarian management style wasn't limited to his dealings with alienated faculty members. He also antagonized several deans and a department head to such a degree that they resigned. In 1972 Lindsey Cowen, UGA's nationally renowned Dean of UGA's School of Law, resigned after Davison revoked the faculty's traditional autonomy over recruitment, promotion, and retention. Cowen's successor, Neil Alford, Jr., followed his lead and resigned in 1977 for the same reasons.

That same year, John Stephens, Dean of the College of Arts and Sciences resigned after Davison threatened to dismantle that college in retaliation for 80% of its faculty responding to yet another survey that overwhelmingly concluded that Davison did not inspire confidence in the faculty. Davison wrote, "We are a house with 12 windows – light shines through all but one." Bill Shipp, an *Atlanta Constitution* editor, condemned Davison in an editorial that noted, "In an apparent fit of pique, President Davison has announced his intention to dismantle the college. Davison's proposal amounts to an all-out declaration of war on the College of Arts and Sciences which makes up the nucleus of the University and, in the end, provides the courses that make the difference between having a college education and not having one."

Dr. Calvin Brown, a Rhodes Scholar and founder of the *Georgia Review*, a prestigious UGA literary journal, was the Head of UGA's Department of Comparative Literature in 1973. Commenting on the Davison-faculty tensions, Brown told a reporter, "The whole business runs head on into a flat contradiction: in the long run, the sort of faculty that the University of Georgia pretends to want simply will not tolerate the sort of dictatorship it seems determined to have." Brown elaborated when he retired in 1977. Commenting on the lack of any reform since the 1973 controversies, he said, "The concept of a community of scholars just doesn't exist. The concept is that of the factory or of the army, with people who give orders and people who take them."

Many other incidents during Davison's presidency kept him in negative territory with the faculty, including his ouster of Dr. Hardy Edwards as the Dean of the Graduate School for refusing to sign a "loyalty letter" prepared by the President's Office regarding the Arts and Sciences survey. The use of the "dean's loyalty letter," generated in the president's office and circulated among the deans, was a common Davison practice in response to the flood of controversies he unleashed on UGA throughout his presidency. Deans who refused to sign such letters were always punished. A clear example of that reality came on the heels of Dr. Edwards' exile when Davison forced the resignation of Agriculture Dean Henry Garren, the only dean who refused to sign yet another "loyalty letter" that supported Davison's decision to fire Dr. Edwards.

Davison's management style also reflected his inflated self-esteem which he himself touted when he told a group of presidents of the other institutions in the University System of Georgia that he "had no peers in the room; his peers were the presidents of institutions like Cornell University and the University of Wisconsin."

Davison also misused his authority to punish tenure protected senior faculty members who dared to disagree with him over policy issues. A good example was his blacklisting of a distinguished professor from being mentioned in any of UGA's official publications. The case of English professor Marion Montgomery vividly demonstrated Davison's vindictiveness in reaction to even moderate criticism. Montgomery criticized the management styles of Davison and his Provost, S.W. Pelletier, over procedures used to select the new editor of the *Georgia Review*. Davison's reaction was described by Karen Kephart in a letter to Montgomery in May of 1974. Ms. Kephart was the editor of UGA's Public Relations publication, *Columns*, which routinely published news of faculty accomplishments to be distributed throughout the faculty and the UGA community. After the publication in *Columns* of an article on Montgomery's newly published novel, *Fugitive*, Ms. Kephart was told by her superiors that *Columns* was not to print photos of Montgomery or articles written by him. She was subsequently reprimanded when she authorized three sentences about Montgomery to appear in a "Campus Capsule" note. She said her superiors told her that "the official administrative policy regarding Professor Montgomery was absolutely no publicity. Fred Davison does not like to see Professor

Montgomery's name or picture in *Columns*." This incident exposed a level of petty vengeance that corroborated the opinions of many faculty members and others who suffered under Davison's leadership.

# CHAPTER SIX
# REVENUE-PRODUCING ATHLETES AND CHILDREN OF INFLUENTIAL CITIZENS

Pat gave me reams of information he discovered in the State Court case that he had filed for Jan. The document productions enabled me to acquire a broad overview of the narrative that we could use to develop a civil rights case premised on the theory that Jan was unlawfully punished for exercising her First Amendment free speech rights. We dismissed the State Court case in order to litigate the issues in Federal Court.

The narrative that we developed focused on three conflicts between Jan and Ervin that proved his motive for demoting and firing her: her refusal of Ervin's request to seek a grade change for Herschel Walker's sister, her refusal to abandon a disciplinary case against the son of a wealthy alumnus of UGA's law school, and the "exit" of nine revenue-producing athletes from Developmental Studies into the normal curriculum despite their failure to pass mandatory courses.

Jan not only resisted those blatant breaches of academic integrity, she also threatened to publicly expose the details of those events - in other words, to exercise her right to speak freely.

We scheduled three separate meetings to discuss the details each of those events.

## Grade Change for Herschel Walker's Sister

The first meeting, the one regarding a grade change for Herschel Walker's sister, took place at the end of the Winter Quarter of 1982. Ervin asked Jan to contact an associate professor to see if she would change the grades of two female track stars who were former Developmental Studies students, one of whom was Veronica Walker.[5]

Jan explained what happened. "Veronica exited from Developmental Studies after the Fall Quarter of 1980. Some of us let Ervin know that she wasn't ready, but he ignored our advice. Veronica then failed a basic first quarter course in UGA's English department in the Winter Quarter of 1981. That's when the trouble started." Jan continued, "When Ervin learned that Walker and another female track athlete failed the introductory English course, he blew his top. He barged into my office. He was very upset. He said he was embarrassed that these particular 'exits' from the Program had failed a preliminary introductory English course created specifically for students coming out of Developmental Studies. He was really in a snit. He paced back and forth, flailed his arms and told me in no uncertain terms that 'we can't allow this to happen.' His tirade raised my blood pressure to a boiling point. He was asking me to lobby a fellow teacher to change a grade. I said, 'No, no way! It's insulting to think you could involve me in this. My integrity's not for sale.'"

---

5 Unless called as a witness, students were identified by their initials, but Veronica Walker's name was introduced by the defendants' attorneys. Three other football players were identified however because they testified – Kenney Sims and Antonio Render were called by the defense. We called Ronnie Stewart at his insistence to testify for Jan.

Jan's resistance infuriated Ervin. He raised his voice and asked her, "Who do you think is more important to this University, you or Dominique Wilkins?" Jan said she was flabbergasted. Wilkins was UGA's most famous basketball player - a superb player known as a "human highlight film" who went on to become a nine-time NBA All Star with the Atlanta Hawks. Ervin's statement was not only offensive, it was nonsensical. Wilkins had nothing to do with Ervin asking Jan to lobby a fellow teacher to change a grade for Veronica Walker, and he wasn't among the athletes who received preferential treatment.

Jan stood her ground. She let Ervin know in no uncertain terms that she would never interfere in any way with any other professor's academic discretion, particularly the assignment of grades. Ervin's response tipped his hand. "Your opinion doesn't matter anyway - this is bigger than both of us. It's already been taken care of. Others have called me about this, like Fred Davison for one."

Jan laughed, "That's one of the few things Ervin ever said that I believed. And by the way, Hue, almost all my witnesses will tell you that he's a habitual liar." She was right. When we interviewed her colleagues, they verified what Jan told us. We were confident that we could prove Ervin's reputation for dishonesty at the trial, and we did. A number of faculty members testified that Ervin had a bad reputation for truthfulness, and that they would not believe anything that he said whether or not he was under oath.

I followed up on a discussion we had during our first

meeting. "Jan, we both know how careful Davison is to insulate himself from personal blame by always operating through other people. You filled me in on the Davison to Kenney to McCaffrey to Ervin line of communication. What we need to know now is how do we unveil it for the jury at the trial? Where are the chinks in the armor?"

Jan thought about my question for a moment before responding. "That's a tough one. The whole point of avoiding transparent lines of communication is to hide Davison's involvement. It might be helpful if you and Pat could get access to the grade change forms and any transmittal memos regarding the forms. You might find some hint of involvement by Jim Kenney or even by Sue McCaffrey. The fingerprints of either may show up. Wouldn't that be nice?"

I was familiar with Jim Kenney's reputation - no one was closer to Davison. There was no doubt that Jan's instincts were right. After hearing her answer, I told Pat that we needed to pin this connection down. I asked him to make a note to remind us to file discovery demands for everything that might relate to grade changes involving Veronica Walker. Pat nodded his agreement. We both knew that we could find the truth during the discovery phase of the upcoming federal lawsuit. Grade changes can't happen without documentation.

By the end of our Veronica Walker grade change meeting, I was even more convinced that Pat's promise that we had proof of everything Jan was going to tell us. My previous experience in cases involving Davison cemented my confidence in Pat's promise. I had every reason to believe that his agents, including Ervin, would use any tactic they could to protect UGA's high value athletes from the rigors of the normal college curriculum. Capturing the revenue that they produced appeared to be Ervin's highest priority.

Jan made her view of Davison clear before we concluded our meeting. "Davison may not be a defendant," she said, "but he's got to be the target of the public relations war that I hope my case inspires - the war for reform. It's wrong what he's doing. He's got to be held accountable or all of this is for nothing."

We filed the lawsuit against Trotter and Ervin because they had both admitted their roles in firing Jan. There was no evidence that Davison was directly involved in that decision. That was fine with us. Adding Davison as a defendant was unnecessary and would complicate the presentation of our evidence. We all agreed: put Trotter and Ervin on trial in the courtroom; put Davison on trial in the press.

**ML**

A few days after my first meeting with Jan and Pat, we met again to discuss Jan's second collision with Ervin. This time it involved her actions regarding a student admitted as a "legacy" applicant - in this case the son of a Florida attorney and UGA Law School graduate.

"So, Jan," I facetiously asked to kick off the conversation, "any chance we could have gotten one of these legacy admisions?" She laughed and said, "No. For three reasons:

we're not rich, we're not powerful and Fred Davison hates us!"

We laughed and then Pat spoke up. "Let me give you an overview of this one, Hue. Twenty-five slots are reserved for 'students of special value' to UGA. They're admitted just like revenue-producing athletes with no review by the Admissions Committee. 'Special value' is supposed to be a term describing students with outstanding talent in art, music, dance, and so on. What it really means is the children of friends of high level UGA and Regents' officials - particularly friends that have large fortunes or political connections." He turned to Jan, "Fill Hue in on the Parental Involvement Plan."

Jan took over. "We call it PIP for short. This is what separates the legacy students from the athletes. When parents get involved in raising funds for UGA, some of them expect access to Davison or his closest aides to influence academic or disciplinary decisions made by the faculty. The parents of athletes, on the other hand, have no influence with UGA's leadership, but believe me, the Athletic Association does. The PIP is tailor made as a forum for parents to trade money or influence for favoritism on issues involving their children."

"So," I asked her, "what if anything was your involvement in the PIP?" She paused momentarily and then explained that although she had some serious reservations about becoming involved, she went ahead and helped organize it. She felt that if the faculty didn't participate, the field would be open for Ervin to make whatever deals were necessary to get more money. Her thinking was that at least with faculty members present, academic integrity would be on the table when the trading took place.

Unfortunately, Jan found out that faculty involvement in the PIP didn't deter Ervin from subjecting the program's mission to its utility as a money funnel. "We were all concerned that our grading and disciplinary decisions would be compromised by parents with deep pockets. In my case, that's exactly what happened."

She explained that ML, the son of a PIP member and donor, was admitted to Developmental Studies as a legacy student after rejection by the Admissions Committee which she served on. Ervin attended those meetings. When ML showed up in Jan's class, she challenged Ervin during a committee meeting to say whether he met minimum requirements, Ervin responded, "I think you know very well that he does not."

Jan continued, "I told Ervin that I didn't want students whose parents were making donations placed in my class, but he enrolled ML anyway. He didn't do very well in my class. My impression was that he always got his way because of his father's wealth and influence. He thought he could just cruise through my course and Ervin would take care of the rest. I let ML know that he was failing and needed to start working if he planned on staying at UGA."

Jan paused and took a deep breath before continuing. "Not long after that conversation, I got a profanity laced night time phone call from ML. He didn't identify himself, but I knew who he was because I recognized his voice and his manner of speaking. I reported the incident to the UGA police department, but I didn't want him to face criminal charges, so I filed a complaint with UGA's student judiciary. When Ervin found out about the student judiciary charges, he went ballistic. He called me at home several times complaining that the police had threatened to 'throw ML in jail.' He also called UGA's police chief to ask him to drop the charges."

Later, Jan learned that Ervin told an assistant to write a memo stating that ML was removed from Jan's class after consultation with her which was untrue. "So, I called him to ask for an explanation. He angrily replied that he had to fix a bad situation that I caused by overreacting; that I was 'using an elephant gun to kill an ant.'"

Pat had already taken Ervin's deposition in the State Court case during which he revealed Davison's role in ML's case. In that deposition, Ervin admitted that he received a phone call from Albert Jones, an Assistant to the President, questioning the evidence before the student judiciary. Jones said that he was calling "in terms of reviewing the situation with the president." Ervin also attended a meeting with Jones and two of Davison's top lieutenants, his legal counsel, Ralph Beaird, and his Executive Assistant, Jim Kenney. ML was found guilty by the student judiciary and sentenced to 10 hours of community service and the loss of the use of his student I.D. to attend UGA functions. Davison subsequently vacated his punishment. No one ever explained why Davison would be interested in a student judiciary proceeding, but the Developmental Studies faculty understood his motive - to protect the flow of revenue from wealthy donors like ML's father who expected favors in return.

Jan described the effect of the PIP on the faculty. "Hue, Ervin was stunningly transparent about using the PIP as a fundraiser. Albert Smith was a research coordinator in the Developmental Studies Program who worked on the development of the PIP. He quit his job and moved away, but he'll be happy to give us a deposition. He attended a PIP organizing committee marketing workshop where the participants discussed raising money for the program - and catch this - Albert saw ML's father give Ervin a check."

Jan also told me that several faculty members complained about donations being made in their presence. They also felt like they were being lobbied to go along with the influence peddling that seemed to them to be the real purpose of the PIP program. For instance, they were given UGA sports coats supposedly as gifts of appreciation for their work in the program. The subsequent events involving ML proved the validity of their suspicions that "money talked" to the highest levels of UGA's leadership.

Jan wasn't deterred by Ervin's bombastic reaction. She refused to ask for a dismissal of the student judiciary charges and cooperated with the student judges' inquiry into the charges against ML, not just to impose a proper punishment, but because she wanted to teach the young man that his family's influence would not serve to avoid the consequences of his misbehavior. She told Ervin that she intended to continue cooperating in the prosecution of ML's student judiciary case. Ervin's reaction intensified. "For the next two or three weeks, Dr. Ervin harassed me endlessly, trying to get me to drop the charges. He told me how important the student was to the University." Jan stood her ground.

Davison's decision to interfere with this rather mild disciplinary action revealed that his agenda included elevating the status of certain non-athlete students for their potential to produce 'revenue' from their family fortunes. Once again, money preempted academic integrity.

### The Exit of the Nine

The topic of our third meeting was the most sensational of the three main events that we knew we could prove. Pat started the conversation, "Hold on tight, Hue. This one's going to be a mind bender. You know the Dawgs lost the national championship last year to Pittsburgh in the Sugar Bowl. Well, UGA lost more than a football game! Jan, tell Hue what the 'Bulldawg Nation' doesn't know."

Jan took a deep breath, paused briefly, and looked straight at me. I knew right away that this part of the saga was the most painful for her. She began, "At the end of the 1981 Fall quarter, we had ten students who completed four quarters but never made the grades to exit - eight were football players, one was a basketball player, and the other a female non-scholarship student. Under Regents' rules, all ten students were automatically dismissed, and that was a problem for the bigwigs. The football players were scheduled to play in the Sugar Bowl on New Year's Day. The prospect of playing athletes who've been dismissed for academic reasons must have made Davison and UGA's football coach Vince Dooley pretty nervous. The next thing we knew was that Trotter had simply exited the athletes from our program by administrative decree. She snapped her fingers and 'poof'! Our academic judgments, along with Regents' policies, vanished like in a magic show. Excuse my language, but a good part of our faculty was pissed off!"

Jan must have seen the expression on my face. I was stunned with the passion behind her words. If a jury saw what I was seeing, they would see the truth - no doubt about it. After a few silent moments, Jan continued; this time in her softer slower Southern voice.

"Our students were being told they could succeed in normal college courses - that was an intentional lie. This may sound melodramatic, but we loved those kids. We wanted no part of a charade that was all about money no matter the human costs. It was wrong. How can they possibly justify deliberately moving these young men into an academic track with a dead-end sign posted for them because they 'produce revenue'? It's not just wrong. It's evil!"

"And the female?" I asked. After a short sarcastic laugh, she answered by asking me, "What do you think? A female that had no economic value to UGA? Why would the big shots care about her? She just disappeared like others who didn't make it."

Pat interrupted, "I'll tell you this, Jan: what happened to her isn't going to disappear! You can count on that. But go ahead; tell Hue about the warm reception you got from Ervin and Trotter when you objected to what was going on."

Jan continued, "A group of us formed an ad hoc faculty committee to protest. We met on January 18, 1982. The members of the committee were livid over the exit of the nine. I was asked to draft a protest letter to Trotter. We scheduled a meeting for January 27th for the committee to review and revise the letter. Some revisions were approved. I agreed to complete those revisions for the committee to review at a meeting that we scheduled for January 29th. Additional revisions were requested at that meeting. I made those revisions and got the final version delivered to the committee members on February 1st." I asked her, "What did the committee do with the letter after those revisions were added?"

Jan chuckled and replied, "Nothing. Trotter scheduled a meeting with the committee for February 2nd. I didn't have time to make a few additional edits of the letter requested, and I couldn't attend the meeting - I had a doctor's appointment. But I don't think the meeting did a bit of good. Nothing changed. In fact, it got worse, particularly for me. Ervin demoted me the following day – February 3rd."

Jan paused. She seemed to be struggling with the reality of what she had just said. "I took my job seriously. We were the last hope for those kids who couldn't quite meet admissions standards, but who had the potential to succeed with our help - intellectually and personally. Ervin never got it. We were invested in those kids' future; we had a stake in the success of every one of them. I knew getting demoted was only the first step. Ervin was going to destroy my career." She paused and looked down for a moment. I saw that her eyes were moist when she looked up again.

I thought she'd appreciate some help controlling the feelings that her story was evoking, so I asked, "Did he give you a reason for the demotion?"

She regained her composure quickly, and answered my question, "No. He never did, but the handwriting was on the wall. I was pregnant. Starting a family wasn't cheap. I needed my job and the extra income from serving as a coordinator. I was desperate. I knew Larry Blount. He taught in the Law School, so I contacted him and he agreed to handle a grievance to challenge my demotion. I appreciated his concern and his help, but there was really nothing he could do. The appeal had to be filed with - guess who - Virginia Trotter."

Pat spoke up. "Wait until you hear about the 'fair' hearing Jan got. Run that by Hue, Jan."

# CHAPTER SEVEN
# A FAUX GRIEVANCE HEARING

Jan seemed to perk up a bit. She smiled, not a joyful smile, but one that silently repeated Pat's sentiments. "Wait until you hear this! Larry filed the papers to start a grievance. We got a notice of a hearing to be held in Trotter's office. She and two other vice presidents would also be on the panel. The other two were Davison's Vice Presidents, Eugene Younts and Robert Anderson. And, guess who else was present - Ralph Beaird, the Law School dean. I wasn't sure whether he was there to make Larry uncomfortable or to be Davison's guy in the room or both. But I did find out that his presence didn't intimidate Larry who fought tooth and nail to protect me."

I was pretty sure that I knew why Davison sent Beaird, so I offered Jan my opinion. "Pat and I know the answer to that one, Jan. Beaird was there to cover Davison's ass if the conversation drifted toward his knowledge of any 'inconvenient' information. You said it best - he was Davison's guy in the room. Believe me, Beaird is the first of many layers of a built-in 'deniability' protocol to protect the chief. And, knowing Larry, I doubt that Beaird thought he could intimidate him."

Jan agreed. "No surprise to me, Hue. Larry filled me in on Beaird. Larry thought he was there to pull the trigger if necessary; I mean to make sure we didn't really get a hearing about the real reasons I got demoted. And that's what happened, but not before they let Ervin go off the rails about what a bitch I was . . . excuse me!" We cracked up! Pat managed to spit out, "Well said, Jan!" "Well, anyway," she continued, "I did get to tell the vice presidents the things that were going on that nobody wanted me to talk about: overriding Admissions Committee decisions, grade changing, and administrative exits. They heard me out, asked no questions, and then announced their decision: 'We are not here to review the merits of the decision to demote you, but only to determine if the proper procedures were followed in reaching that decision.' That was it for me with those people. I hired Pat to file a lawsuit because they left me no other choice. He filed it in the Superior Court. Then Ervin fired me."

Jan paused. I understood that the days and months after that parody of a "hearing" were the darkest of her life. I asked her if she wanted to take a break. She smiled and said, "No, Hue - task completion! Remember, I'm a career teacher."

So, after laughing about being scolded by a teacher, not an uncommon event in my youth, I asked her, "Did you hear what happened at the committee meeting that you missed?"

"Sure," Jan answered, "Nothing of substance. The committee members objected to administrative exits: first as a breach of ethics - no one should be put on a road to failure, and second as an inexcusable affront to the faculty's professional judgments. They also wanted Trotter to address other academic issues like admitting illiterate athletes and granting them more than four quarters to exit. Trotter just listened and made notes and did nothing. Oh, and she did talk about me like the whole mess was my fault. What a clown! 'If it weren't for that bitch Jan Kemp, we wouldn't be having this meeting - this is not a problem except in her mind!' Ha! We'll see about that, won't we?"

Pat answered, "I sure hope so, Jan. If we can't rattle their cage with this case, we may as well go home and let them go ahead and run an elementary school with a great football team - and call it a college."

Pat turned to me, "Let me bring you up to date on how we got to where we are now. Larry gave me a call after the 'pretend hearing' by Fred's vice presidents. He told me what was going on. He said he called Trotter. He told her that limiting the scope of the hearing to the merits of the process used to reach an unjustifiable decision means Jan hasn't had a hearing, and she wasn't going to throw in the towel. He said he was obligated to refer her to an attorney to file a lawsuit if she couldn't arrange a meaningful hearing by an impartial faculty committee."

Jan interrupted. "Larry told me that he would recommend one of two lawyers, you or Pat." She laughed before continuing, "I picked Pat because Larry said you'd just file a lawsuit, and Pat would at least contact the Attorney General's Office to see if we could settle our dispute. He did. They referred him to Hale Almand. When that happened, Pat knew that UGA's defense was under Davison's control. Then Ervin notified me at the end of August that I'd be fired in nine months."

Pat continued. "I knew as soon as I got involved that Jan's job was on the line, but since she was entitled to at least nine months' notice of a non-renewal of her contract, we had some time to get ready for the inevitable. I didn't want to wait for the axe to fall before starting to investigate Jan's story. I put together a complaint for defamation against Ervin to file in the Superior Court here in Clarke County. To be honest, I did it to start a discovery process so we'd have a head start on a civil rights suit. The plan was to dismiss the State Court case as soon as Jan got the notice of nonrenewal, and then get you involved and file a civil rights suit. Then, as expected, the axe fell: Jan got the non-renewal notice at the end of August. And that's how we got here."

# CHAPTER EIGHT
# JAN'S ATTEMPTED SUICIDES

Pat had already filled me in on Jan's personal problems resulting from her resistance to the breaches of academic integrity by UGA's administrative leaders at the behest of Vince Dooley, Director of UGA's Athletic Association, and his staff. We needed to discuss those issues for a couple of reasons: to prove damages at the trial for the emotional suffering caused by the deprivation of Jan's civil rights, and to respond to questions about Jan's mental health that the defendants might try to exploit at the trial. So, I had to ask her, "Jan, you know we are going to have to deal with the psychological issues that Pat briefed me on. Are you comfortable talking about that?"

Jan sat up and looked straight at me. I could almost see the story that she began painting with her words - her face revealed her pain as she recalled the events that led to her attempts to take her own life. "Yes, I'm fine with talking about it - honesty is my best therapy. I tried to kill myself twice. I regret what happened, but I'm not ashamed of it. I was sick. Of course, I was under a lot of stress at the prospect of losing my job - or possibly my career. I didn't know if I would ever teach again. But then, the unthinkable happened - worse than just losing a job. I found out that Ervin was approaching some of my students to solicit letters from them criticizing me with outright lies - accusing me of wasting classroom time to make sexual remarks and other offensive statements. I wondered if taking a stand on the stuff going on over there had been worth it. My students - the most important people in my life outside of family, were being used - made to lie about me in exchange for being allowed to remain in the program beyond the four quarters allowed to exit. It was sickening. They were harming me and my students."

"I had always thought I would be too shy to teach - My father is shy, and when I was growing up I was a daddy's girl. But I did grow up and became a teacher, and I loved it. And now I was losing it. Then my beautiful baby, Will, was born, and I believed I was harming his future. The pressure mounted. I lost belief in myself and tried to kill myself."

Jan stopped talking. After a brief but uncomfortable pause, she continued, "Hue, I am psychologically vulnerable - I understand that. I was treated for depression a few years before coming to work at UGA. That worked out, and I felt like I was strong enough to deal with just about anything. Then this unbelievably vicious campaign to destroy my profession plunged me into a living hell. People were suffering on my behalf. Life wasn't worth living."

I was speechless - her suffering and the strength that she mustered to overcome it was a compelling story. After taking a pause to absorb what I was hearing, I spoke up, "Jan, you seem so together - how in hell did you survive?"

"That's an easy question, Hue. My parents love me unconditionally - I knew that - I knew that they would die for me, but I also realized - a little too late unfortunately

- that my urge to end my life would devastate them if I succeeded. And when I looked into my baby's eyes, I saw the most important reason to live. I believe God saved me for those reasons."

As we progressed through trial preparation, it became obvious to me that Jan's counter attack was her best therapy. She remained strong, focused and persistent until she accomplished her goals. Her strength was driven by her firm belief that she, along with other courageous colleagues, would unveil the wrong-doing by UGA's top administrators.

I was convinced. Jan was going to fight to the bitter end. She knew that the brickbats to come would be thrown by powerful people, but she was steadfast in her willingness to accept the pain that she might suffer in an effort to rescue UGA from the clear and present danger being created by its leaders. She knew that her cause was just, her story was provable, and her colleagues supported her. Her mission to expose the high-level abuses of fundamental ethical and academic principles at UGA motivated her, her colleagues and her attorneys. Nothing was going to stop her - Davison and his cohorts targeted the wrong person this time.

## CHAPTER NINE
## THE LAW - 42 USC SECTION 1983

After getting a grip on the facts of Jan's complicated story, I drafted a civil rights Complaint against the Regents, Virginia Trotter and Leroy Ervin. The complaint alleged a violation by the defendants of Jan's First Amendment free speech rights. We chose to file the complaint in the United States District Court for the Northern District of Georgia. We assumed that potential jurors in the Atlanta area would be more sympathetic to Jan's case and less susceptible to potential influences of jurors by UGA sympathizers than if the trial was conducted in Athens.

The federal statute that we intended to enforce was 42 USC Section 1983. That section of the United States code provides a legal remedy to "any citizen of the United States or other person within the jurisdiction thereof" for the deprivation of constitutional "rights, privileges, or immunities" by anyone acting "under color of law." We were convinced that we could prove the three key elements of this statute: 1) that the defendants' actions subjected or caused Jan to be deprived of her employment, 2) which violated her First Amendment rights of free speech, and 3) while acting "under color of law."

Trotter and Ervin couldn't deny that they "subjected or caused" Jan to be deprived of her employment while acting under color of law as State of Georgia agents in their positions as a UGA Vice President and as a UGA Assistant Vice President and Developmental Studies Director. Their defense was that Jan was demoted and fired for her alleged failure to progress toward tenure and her disruptive behavior—not for exercising her First Amendment rights to criticize the preferential treatment of revenue-producing athletes. The only issue that had to be resolved by the jury was the true reason for Jan's demotion and the subsequent non-renewal of her contract. Whether Jan's activities and statements regarding academic corruption at UGA were constitutionally protected by the First Amendment was a "question of law" to be decided by the court rather than the jury.

We were confident that Judge Ward would find Jan's speech to be constitutionally protected because he had denied pretrial defense motions challenging that protection. It was highly unlikely that he would find that Jan's speech was not constitutionally protected on the eve of the trial. The record also included a document with a handwritten notation by Trotter relating to Jan's grievance that read, "She is threatening to go public." Speaking publicly about matters of public interest, such as academic abuses at a university, is a protected First Amendment right. Trotter's notation was an admission that she knew of Jan's intent to exercise her free speech rights. Based on the controlling case law, we were confident that any federal judge would find that Jan's communications about academic corruption were protected speech.

The judge's finding would be critically important not

only because it satisfied our duty to prove the third element of the statute, but also because the court's decision would be announced to the jury during the court's final instructions before they began their deliberation. So, while the judge would instruct the jury that liability under 42 USC 1983 required the plaintiff to prove all three elements of the statute, he would then immediately advise them that that they did not have to consider whether Jan's communications were constitutionally protected because the court had determined as a matter of law that they were. That instruction coupled with the defendants' admissions that they acted "under color of law" would then reduce the jury's duty on the question of liability to a single issue: was Jan demoted and fired for exercising her constitutional rights or was she demoted and fired for the alternative reasons claimed by Ervin and Trotter - lack of research and inability to work cooperatively with supervisors and colleagues?

The pre-trial work was done. The witnesses were ready. And we were ready!

## CHAPTER TEN
## HALE ALMAND FOR THE DEFENSE

The biggest impediment to achieving our goals was Hale Almand, Fred Davison's choice to handle UGA's litigation instead of Georgia's Attorney General. Davison knew that Almand's tenacity would preclude any serious effort to settle the Kemp case before the trial. He seemed to want the fight as much as we did. We were also inflexible because Jan wanted a public trial to insure disclosures of the misconduct that caused the faculty rebellion.

Having dealt with Almand in the Dallmeyer case, I knew we were in a tough contest, but that was fine. We had the facts on our side.

Given our combatant personalities, Almand and I never became chums. but I know that there was respect for the opposition by both legal teams. Both of us benefited from our early training in the Federal Court system: his as Assistant U.S. Attorney prosecuting defendants in a broad range of federal criminal cases - mine as a law clerk for United States District Judge Anthony Alaimo writing orders in civil and criminal cases, and then as an Assistant Federal Public Defender in Atlanta representing individuals in a broad range of federal criminal cases.

Our personal backgrounds were different. His was tailor made to fit comfortably into Davison's military style command structure. Almand was a large man, a graduate of the Citadel and a Vietnam Vet. My background was the opposite. I was a 5'9" community college graduate with limited military experience during one misspent year as a freshman in a Catholic military high school. Almand used his legal education to prosecute people. I used mine to feed my innate suspicion of authority.

I believe Hale Almand was an honorable man determined to represent his clients to the best of his ability. He was a good trial lawyer - a very good prosecutor. He gained notoriety early in his career as a federal prosecutor in the Middle District of Georgia, headquartered in Macon. He also served as a State of Georgia special prosecutor after leaving the U.S. Attorney's Office. He obtained a good reputation in a highly publicized criminal case in which he convicted Georgia's long time Commissioner of Labor Sam Caldwell of theft by deception, extortion, false statements, and false swearing. He was a formidable opponent, but we also had a boatload of legal experience and, more importantly, the facts and the law were on our side.

One pre-trial "non-event" caused considerable consternation among Georgia's political elites after the trial - the absence of any effort to try to settle the Kemp case before it became a public relations disaster. The Monday morning quarterbacks were incredulous that UGA's leadership failed to resolve Jan's complaints to avoid the drubbing they took in the trial. In fact, there were never any settlement negotiations. Settlement was never under consideration - never even mentioned. The lawyers for both sides knew that the Kemp case would be tried. Davison had never authorized settlement discussions in any case that I was involved in, and I had no reason to believe this case was different, particularly since our demands were not negotiable. Jan didn't want to settle because her goals were not economic. She consistently insisted on reform that would completely eliminate the academic abuses in Developmental Studies - a condition we knew was unacceptable to Davison and his Athletic Association collaborators.

All of the post-trial finger pointing at Almand for not settling the case before the trial was misdirected. The corrosive "Davison culture" that had caused so much controversy at UGA precluded concessions by either side. Almand's hands were tied. There was never any doubt; the outcome of the Jan Kemp case would be in the hands of a federal jury.

# CHAPTER ELEVEN
# JUDGE WARD

Horace T. Ward, an African American, was assigned as the District Court judge to try the case. That random selection surely caused some consternation in the halls of UGA's administration since Judge Ward's 1950 application to UGA's School of Law was denied for the blatantly transparent reason that he was "not qualified." That conclusion was preposterous given his outstanding academic history. It didn't take much imagination to realize that Judge Ward's race was the only reason he was denied admission.

Judge Ward persisted in trying to discover the official reasons for the denial of his application to no avail. After months of evasion by UGA officials and the adoption of racially motivated changes in the application process by the Regents, Ward filed a lawsuit seeking a court order requiring UGA to admit him to the law school. He was represented by legendary civil rights attorneys Thurgood Marshall, Donald Hollowell, Constance Baker Motley and A.T. Walden. Then Ward received a 1953 draft notice of induction. His lawsuit was dismissed by a federal judge in Atlanta in 1956 after Ward completed his military service. UGA remained segregated. Ironically, Judge Ward played a role in ending segregation there several years later.

Judge Ward decided to attend law school at Northwestern University. He earned his law degree in 1959, and returned to Georgia to join Hollowell and Baker Motley in their successful legal effort to integrate UGA. Their lawsuit was resolved by U.S. District Judge William Bootle who issued a January 6, 1961 order requiring UGA to admit two black applicants, Hamilton Holmes and Charlayne Hunter.

UGA's leadership ultimately repented and awarded Judge Ward an honorary doctorate of law degree at its 2014 graduation ceremony - sixty years after he would have earned a UGA law degree had he not been African American. UGA now proudly claims him as one of their own.

Given Judge Ward's history with UGA, we thought Almand would move to disqualify him, but that never happened. On second thought, I realized that UGA had no choice. How would they explain a second snub of an iconic federal judge - particularly one who battled the injustices of segregation until he prevailed? Judge Ward gained the love and respect of Georgians of all ethnicities who came to know him, including those who had earlier opposed his right to obtain a legal education at their flagship university. We couldn't have found a better judge - he was totally fair to both sides of the Kemp case, but it was a great comfort to us that we had a judge who had fought battles on the same terrain where Jan was fighting her battle.

# CHAPTER TWELVE
# OUR PRETRIAL MOTION FOR A PRELIMINARY INJUNCTION

The first hearing in the case may have alleviated the defendants of any residual anxiety about Judge Ward. He granted our request for a hearing on a motion for a preliminary injunction that we filed seeking an order restoring Jan to her faculty position pending the outcome of the case. After the hearing, he denied our motion. We weren't surprised. Preliminary injunctions reinstating public employee plaintiffs are rarely granted, particularly in complex cases. Nevertheless, even if the odds of success are slim, early hearings provide good tactical opportunities. The presence of a federal judge is an excellent opportunity to discover a significant volume of the opposing parties' evidence in advance of the cumbersome formal "discovery" process. This affords aggressive defense attorneys an opportunity to hinder the process through "objections" to questions being asked by plaintiff's attorneys. Since there is no judge present to rule on those objections, additional time and expense is needed to resolve the discovery issues through additional motions and hearings.

Although Judge Ward denied our application for a preliminary injunction, he did allow us to conduct a five-hour hearing which included comprehensive cross-examinations of Trotter and Ervin. Among other evidence, we got admissions from Trotter that she was the administrator who approved the demotion and firing of Kemp, and that she did it based on Ervin's recommendations. That testimony eliminated any issues regarding the identity of the state officials who actually violated Jan's First Amendment rights.

The preliminary hearing also provided an opportunity to force the defendants to state their "reasons" for firing Jan. They testified that there were two reasons: lack of research and a disruptive personality. This was very important testimony because we were confident that we could disprove those defenses at trial through Jan's colleagues whom we knew would refute both of those reasons. Our witnesses were prepared to testify that:

- Developmental Studies faculty members were not on a tenure track until a few months before Ervin fired Jan;
- No Developmental Studies faculty member had ever been required to conduct research - a major component of the promotion and tenure process;
- The faculty's Promotion and Tenure Committee charged with developing guidelines for the proposed Developmental Studies tenure track recommended deemphasizing the "research" component because it was a "teaching" program.

In addition, the "disruptive personality" reason presented us with an intriguing opportunity - one that cut to the heart of the case because it raised the question: "How should a devoted professional educator behave when faced with the shameful practices of a corrupt administration?" That issue set up a problem for the defendants to deal with that they didn't need, and one that we couldn't wait to exploit after a jury was empaneled. We knew that Jan's colleagues would support our response to that claim. They would testify that "Yes, she was disruptive - stubborn too - when she learned of shameful behavior by her superiors, and rightfully so!" We were happy to let a jury decide if Jan's firing was justified because she dug in her heels over the massive academic abuses being imposed on UGA's faculty and students by the defendants Trotter and Ervin.

We believed the evidence that we put before Judge Ward at the preliminary injunction hearing clearly established that Jan's speech was protected. We were right, again. Just before the trial began, Judge Ward ruled that Jan's speech was protected by the First Amendment as a matter of law, and the jury would be informed of that decision when he gave them their final instructions before they retired to deliberate at the end of the trial.

We still had to do a considerable amount of discovery after the initial hearing to obtain the thousands of documents that we needed to prepare for the large number of witnesses that we intended to call at the trial. Fortunately, Almand was not overly obstructive during the discovery process. He had enough federal litigation experience to know that federal judges don't appreciate having to resolve discovery disputes. Consequently, they sometime penalize the obstructing party in the absence of a damn good reason for causing them to use their time and judicial resources for that purpose. During the discovery process, we were able to obtain student academic records, internal memos, correspondence, and other documentary evidence relating to the multiple instances of academic malfeasance that we intended to prove.

Obtaining the student records was time consuming because we had to comply with the Brady Amendment, a federal law that protects the privacy rights of college students to maintain the confidentiality of their academic records. The Brady Amendment entitled any student whose academic records were being subpoenaed to a notice by the party seeking the records, and a description of the process required to procure those records. Satisfaction of those rules was labor intensive and expensive.

We also had to take trial depositions from several former Developmental Studies faculty members who had left the state of Georgia. We needed those depositions to corroborate the testimony of the former faculty members we intended to call as trial witnesses.

By the end of the discovery phase of the litigation, we were ready to go. We were confident and anxious to expose the fraud being perpetrated upon innocent young men who expected to leave UGA with a college degree. More importantly, we also intended to show the faces of those in power who were responsible for this shameful charade. We were anxious to make those who trampled Jan Kemp's right to speak freely about their malfeasance pay damages and suffer public humiliation for what they did to her, and to UGA.

# CHAPTER THIRTEEN
# PRE-TRIAL SURPRISES

Judge Ward scheduled the trial to begin on August 12, 1985. We could hardly wait to show the court and the jury the mountain of evidence we had assembled to prove that the defendants violated Jan's civil rights. But, as that date approached, two startling developments occurred.

## The Timmons Tape

The first surprise came in a phone call I received from Theresa Timmons, one of Jan's fellow English teachers. Like most of her colleagues, Theresa was scheduled to corroborate some of Jan's allegations. She was a highly-regarded member of the Developmental Studies professional staff. She was well prepared for her upcoming appearance in court. However, Theresa wasn't calling me about that. She was calling to tell me about a meeting that Jan could not attend due to a doctor's appointment. That meeting with Trotter and Ervin occurred in 1982 after the exit of the nine. Theresa told me that Trotter and Ervin made some very candid admissions about the dire chances of the revenue-producing athletes in question to ever earn an undergraduate degree. Then she dropped the bomb.

My best recollection of what she said was something like, "I made a tape recording of most of that meeting. I put it in my purse, so Trotter and Ervin didn't know they were being recorded." Before I could get off the cloud that appeared beneath me when I heard those words, Theresa told me that she wanted to give me the tape, but she had one problem with disclosing it. She was seeking a position at other colleges and didn't want potential employers to learn that she had taped her superiors without their knowledge or consent.

I told Theresa that we wouldn't introduce the tape when we called her to testify, but circumstances might occur that would compel us to put it in evidence. First, we were required under the discovery rules to provide Hale Almand with a copy of it, and we had no control over whether he would ask her about it. Another circumstance might arise if Trotter and/or Ervin denied making any of the statements on the tape. If so, I would feel obligated to introduce the tape to impeach that sworn false testimony. I also told her that any mention of the tape before the jury would compel me to introduce it because not doing so would raise doubts in the jurors' minds about her testimony. Theresa said she understood and would accept the need to introduce the tape under any of those circumstances. She brought the original tape to me. I had a copy made and sent it to Almand. Pat had the tape recording transcribed and made enough copies to provide to the court, Almand, and the jury should we have to introduce the tape.

After Almand received the tape recording, he notified the court and Davison that he had a conflict of interest that would require him to withdraw from representing the

Board of Regents. Almand wasn't required to state the basis of his claim to a conflict of interest because he had an attorney client relationship with all three defendants. It was pretty transparent, though, since he filed the tape recording with the court shortly after we provided him with a copy. The Regents were in no position to condone the behavior revealed by the tape. The Regents' legal staff and the Attorney General recognized that they had no choice: if their agents were required to testify, they would have no alternative to disowning and condemning their co-defendants' misconduct. That dilemma was resolved however when the court entered an order a few days later dismissing the Regents as a party defendant. That ruling caused us some concern because we initially named the Board of Regents as a defendant because it "resided" in Atlanta, which enabled us to try the case there instead of Athens where the two individual defendants resided. We assumed that Almand would soon file a motion to transfer the case back to Athens, but Judge Ward immediately entered an order retaining jurisdiction in his court to minimize costs to the courts that a transfer would entail.

### A Trip to Italy

The second startling development came in a phone call to me from a news reporter on August 9, 1985, three days before the trial was scheduled to begin. The reporter asked me for my reaction to the revelation that Virginia Trotter would not be attending the trial because she had left for an extended visit to UGA's Studies Abroad Program in Cortona, Italy and was not scheduled to return until August 26th at the earliest - two weeks after the trial was scheduled to begin.

We assumed that Judge Ward would be as surprised as we were to learn of Trotter's absence from the trial under circumstances that were inherently suspicious. We notified him of the information provided to us by the reporter. Judge Ward responded as we knew he would. He ordered the attorneys to attend a conference in his chambers the following day. Almand verified the accuracy of the reporter's information, but assured the judge that he could defend the case for Trotter without her presence, and was ready to go forward as scheduled.

Judge Ward didn't buy it. He told us that he couldn't envision a case of this nature being fairly tried when the chief decision maker was an ocean away from the jury that would be charged with reviewing her conduct. Judge Ward tentatively rescheduled the trial to commence no earlier than September 3, 1985, and ordered Almand to have Trotter attend. However, due to the substantial number of trials already docketed in the Federal Courts in Atlanta, the earliest date for the trial to actually get underway was January 6, 1986.

The decision to send Trotter to Italy was obviously made by Davison and his legal advisors, Almand and Ralph Beaird. What were they thinking? Whose idea was it to create a ruse that Trotter's presence was needed in a small Italian mountain town instead of a high profile federal case in which she was a defendant—with nary a mention to

Judge Ward? Did they think the press would ignore that move? Did they think Judge Ward would approve? Even if they got away with it, did they consider how a jury sitting day after day in a jury box looking at Trotter's empty chair might react?

Subsequent events suggested their motive: fear that Trotter would point her finger at Davison. They were right to fear that possibility because that is exactly what she did - not at the trial, but after the trial.

# CHAPTER FOURTEEN
# JAN KEMP'S PRESS AND PUBLIC RELATIONS STRATEGY

It was apparent from the beginning that Jan's case involved broad public interest implications in addition to the issues being tried. She always focused on the broader issues - the ones that affected her profession and the welfare of her students. She never emphasized or even mentioned any prospect of personal economic gain until Almand asked her questions about it during his cross-examination of her later in the trial. Her sole motive was to spotlight the misconduct of her superiors and to force UGA to reform the practices that she deeply believed were contrary to the best interests of the University and its students.

One of Almand's opening pre-trial maneuvers had already boosted our ability to launch Jan's public relations offensive. He filed a motion for a "gag order" restraining Jan and her attorneys from making any public statement about the case until the verdict was announced. What a gift! The motion itself guaranteed media attention - the State of Georgia was asking a Federal Court to gag participants in a First Amendment free speech case alleging serious misconduct by public officials.

Judge Ward heard the motion for the gag order in his chambers. Our response to the motion reminded the court that this was a case about the violation of a citizen's First

Amendment right of free speech. A gag order under those circumstances would mock the First Amendment. Almand was asking the court to limit public access to information and comment by those most knowledgeable about the public corruption being disclosed in a public forum. We assured Judge Ward that we were fully aware of our ethical and professional responsibility to refrain from making statements that might compromise the integrity of the court proceedings, but we were adamantly opposed to waiving our constitutional rights to respond truthfully to questions by news media representatives. Judge Ward agreed with our position. U.S. courtrooms are public forums. Judge Ward's denial of the defendants' motion for a gag order was publicized by the press leaving the impression that the defendants must have something to hide.

We understood that Judge Ward would be monitoring the press and expected him to react harshly if we violated any professional or ethical rules. We also assumed that our public comments would be closely monitored by the defense and expected Almand to repeatedly renew his motion for a gag order on the slimmest of grounds.

We anticipated a counter offensive by the formidable public relations machines of UGA and its Athletic Association, but that never happened with two exceptions. UGA's football coach, Vince Dooley, used a public relations propaganda release as witness notes that he referred to while testifying toward the end of the trial. He then distributed that release to the press at the beginning of a courthouse press conference he convened as soon as he left the witness stand. We had forced him to admit that the press release overstated the percentage of UGA minority athletes who graduated, but he ignored that admission during his press conference. Fred Davison also held a press conference immediately after his testimony the day after Dooley's courtroom and press appearances. As it turned out, their testimonies and press conferences failed to temper the pervasive press condemnations of both. Neither's propaganda moved the jury or the press.

That was it for a counter offensive to our domination of the public airways. The attempts of Dooley and Davison to stanch the flow of daily revelations of serious breaches of UGA's obligations to its students and the citizens of Georgia bombed. The sophisticated public relations pros in charge of defending UGA and the Athletic Association remained silent throughout the entire trial. We answered numerous questions from media representatives, agreed to television interviews, and developed rapport with the reporters covering the trial in the corridors and downstairs cafeteria. Because the defense stayed cloistered, we owned the media's attention.

I learned later from reading Jerrold Footlick's treatment of the public relations aspect of the Kemp trial that Hale Almand had vetoed the use of UGA's public relations assets during the trial resulting in the lopsided win by our team on that front. The trial publicity, more than any other factor, led to the drastic post-trial consequences for Davison and virtually every administrator who testified. Their problem was that the truth led to their downfalls because they had to admit institutionalizing academic fraud to retain functionally illiterate "revenue-producing" athletes. The citizens of Georgia, even the most loyal football fans, could not swallow such a damning self-indictment by those who presented themselves as the academic leaders of the state.

The Kemp case chapter of Jerrold Footlick's book, *Truth and Consequences*, described an intramural conflict in the upper echelons of UGA's administration over Almand's decision to stick to "trying the case in the courtroom." Tom Landrum, then UGA's Director of Public Relations, urged Davison to allow his office to reply to the negative press coverage during the trial. Davison sent him to Macon to lobby Almand to authorize a public relations offensive, but Almand refused. While that decision may have created the illusion that UGA's defense team was operating on an elevated professional level in some people's minds, it was a strategic blunder of major dimensions. Five and a half weeks of unanswered negative daily headlines fueled outrage by UGA's faculty, student body, alumni and benefactors. Jan not only walloped the defendants in the courtroom, she demolished them on the fatal battlefield - the court of public opinion.

# CHAPTER FIFTEEN
# JURY SELECTION

The trial date finally arrived on January 6, 1986. Of course, we were anxious as we entered the Richard B. Russell United States Courthouse in Atlanta, cleared security, and stepped into the elevator to rise to the 23rd floor courtroom of the Honorable Horace Ward. We were also elated. The trial date had arrived, and we were ready to present the volumes of evidence accumulated over three years of preparation.

Our first task was jury selection. Federal civil cases are tried by six-person juries. Judge Ward ordered the selection of four alternate jurors in case we lost any of the primary jurors over the course of what everyone knew would be a lengthy trial.

It should be no surprise that race has been a factor in many cases tried in the deep South, and the Kemp case was no exception. In fact, it posed one of the most intriguing aspects of our case which focused on minority student athletes, many of whom had attended public schools in poor rural communities that didn't provide adequate preparation for the academic challenges they encountered at UGA. The judge and Leroy Ervin, one of the defendants, were also African Americans.

The primary racial issue for us was jury selection. Since the trial would be held in a majority black city, we assumed that a mixed-race jury would be seated. So, we had to decide which racial and educational juror profiles were the most or least desirable.

The race of the judge was not really a factor because jurors inherently trust the judge who is the only disinterested player in the process. The fact that Leroy Ervin was also African-American made us a little nervous for fear that black jurors might resent two white lawyers calling a series of mostly white witnesses to assail the integrity of a high-level minority UGA administrator. Counterbalancing that concern was our assumption that African-American jurors would be enraged when hearing of the crass exploitation by UGA and the Athletic Association of the black athletes being deprived of the college educations they were promised. We believed that factor dominated the assessment. Empathy is a powerful emotion for most humans who feel the pain of persons being exploited by anyone, particularly powerful and wealthy oppressors. We knew beyond a shadow of a doubt that we would be presenting evidence that would outrage any empathetic person. Our conclusion was that African-American jurors would be good jurors for our side of this case because they would identify with the athletes and their families.

So, we decided on juror profile "strike" criteria that did factor in race. We had no problem with any intelligent disinterested juror, regardless of their race, but, of course, preferred those jurors most likely to identify with the athletes and the faculty who protested their mistreatment. All we wanted in terms of white potential jurors were intelligent impartial people unburdened by racial prejudice.

We concluded that Ervin's race would not influence black jurors, but we did decide as a tactical matter to begin our presentation of evidence that was uniformly critical of Ervin's motives and integrity with the testimony of Fred Johnson, a brilliant African-American English teacher. Fred had recently left UGA to teach in a public high school because he couldn't conscientiously remain as part of a program that lacked academic integrity and exploited young men. His negative "character" opinion of Ervin's credibility would set the tone early. Ervin's race was irrelevant, but his conduct wasn't.

After the questioning of the potential jurors, we began the selection process. Jurors are seated through a process of alternate strikes of potential jurors by the parties' attorneys. The reasons for exercising strikes are gleaned from the potential jurors' answers to the attorneys' questions. The purpose of the strikes, particularly when the evidence weighs heavily in favor of the client's claims, is to eliminate any prospective juror with a likely bias against the client or for the defendants.

We were pleased with the composition of the jury after each side exercised their respective strikes. Of the six jurors empaneled to try the case, four were African American and two were white. All were well educated productive citizens, and none had any connection to UGA. Four alternates were selected, but were never seated because the original jury remained intact throughout the trial.

# CHAPTER SIXTEEN
# THE PARTIES' OPENING STATEMENTS

## The Plaintiff's Opening Statement

Pat began our opening statement with the traditional introduction of the attorneys and expression of confidence in our case. Then he defined the ultimate questions that the jury would be called upon to answer after hearing all of the witnesses and reviewing the thousands of documents to be introduced by each side. "What this case is about is your decision based on the evidence that you hear that is properly before you - whether we have carried our burden of proof and whether Dr. Ervin demoted Dr. Kemp because she spoke out on matters of great public concern, and whether the defendants in fact fired Dr. Kemp because she spoke out on those issues."

Then he pivoted to the "preponderance of evidence" standard of proof that we had to carry to prove our case and compared it to the more burdensome "beyond a reasonable doubt" standard of proof in criminal cases. He boldly predicted that the jury, after hearing our evidence, would be convinced "beyond a reasonable doubt" - that Jan's civil rights had been violated when she was demoted and then fired because she dared to challenge the fraudulent treatment of students by the Administration/Athletic Association cabal which was more focused on football than the education of future generations.

Pat praised the jury's power to correct mistakes and/or misdeeds by public officials regardless of how powerful the wrongdoers might be. He explained that the jurors had the authority to render a judgment, to attach the consequences they believed necessary to remedy the wrongs done to Jan, and to punish the responsible individuals.

He followed by giving the jury a comprehensive overview of the nature of the Developmental Studies Program. He told the jurors how Developmental Studies was created to assist marginal applicants learn the basic reading, writing, and math skills they needed to successfully complete the normal academic curriculum and graduate with a Bachelor's degree.

Pat then gave the jury a brief history of Jan's life as a UGA student who obtained her Bachelor's, Master's, and Doctoral degrees from UGA, and joined its faculty where she rapidly gained a reputation as an excellent teacher and a conscientious supporter of UGA's mission - as well as its football team. He emphasized that her criticism was in no way directed toward the University that she loved, but solely toward those whose misdeeds were potentially catastrophic to its health and well-being.

Then Pat outlined a series of three events that led to Jan's demotion, dismissal, and the lawsuit the jury had been empaneled to resolve.

The first event occurred in 1981 when Leroy Ervin approached Jan to ask her to lobby another faculty member to change the grades of two former Developmental Studies student athletes. Jan's refusal threw Ervin into a fit of rage during which he told her that one of the athletes involved was "more important to the University than you are." He also told her that if she didn't do what he was asking, someone else would. That conflict shifted Ervin's attitude towards Jan from admiration to vengeance.

Pat explained that the abuse of UGA's admission standards was not limited to favoring athletes. He outlined the second event that the jury would hear about. There was an unwritten policy of admitting the children of wealthy donors and politically connected citizens to UGA via Developmental Studies. One of those students, ML, had felt so empowered by his family's influence and wealth that he protested a failing grade by making an obscene phone call to Jan who had somehow overlooked his elevated status as a "rich kid." Pat described Ervin's intense opposition to any disciplinary action against ML, and then told the jury how Jan filed charges against ML anyway, and how the student judiciary convicted him. His conviction, as it turned out, was probably the turning point of his college career because he immediately developed into a conscientious student who ultimately exited from Developmental Studies and completed the courses he needed to obtain a college degree.

Pat then summarized the third critical event that led to all of us gathering together in a federal courtroom in Atlanta. That event, the "exit of the nine," put the exclamation mark on the unrestrained academic corruption being tolerated at UGA. He told the jury how nine student athletes were allowed by Trotter to exit into the normal curriculum despite failing grades after their fourth and final quarter in Developmental Studies. He explained that other students were expelled from UGA for failing to achieve passing grades within four quarters. All nine of the students involved were scholarship athletes, and at least eight of them were scheduled to play for the 1981 NCAA National Championship several weeks after they would have been dismissed in the absence of Trotter's intervention.

To conclude his opening statement, Pat explained that the exit of the nine students by executive fiat incited a broad-based faculty protest resulting in the formation of an ad hoc faculty committee to resist that breach of UGA's academic integrity. He told the jury how Jan was asked by her colleagues to draft a protest letter to Trotter on behalf of the committee. Then Ervin demoted her and subsequently terminated her employment with Trotter's approval.

The stage was set. The jury had a comprehensive preview of what we knew we could prove.

## The Defense's Opening Statement

"We may not make a University student out of him, but if we can teach him to read and write, maybe he can work at the post office rather than as a garbage man when he gets through with his athletic career."

Sitting a few feet behind Hale Almand as he stood before the jury, I thought that there was no way I could have heard what I had in fact just heard. I turned to look at Pat sitting at our table to my right. His jaw was dropped, his eyes were wide open, his shoulders were raised, and his palms were up. His demeanor confirmed it. I wasn't hallucinating. The attorney defending high level academic officials of a major state university had just told the jury in a highly publicized jury trial in an Atlanta federal courtroom that the academic bar for student athletes was not to "make a University student out of him" but to teach the skills needed to "read and write" so they could work "at the post office rather than as a garbage man."

Furiously scratching my head - mentally, that is - I began to worry. My inner monologue was reading something like this: What is the strategy here? This lawyer is an experienced trial attorney. This is his opening statement. It had to be thought out. What in the hell is going on? This doesn't compute. How do we react? What trap is he trying to set?

Pat, Jan and I huddled at the next break before our first witness testified. We were all nonplussed. We couldn't forecast the defense strategy. On the one hand, we were thrilled that Almand had admitted a major component of our case: the indefensible abuse of young, mostly minority, athletes by making knowingly false promises of a college education in exchange for the money that their athletic talents would generate. We had assumed that the decision makers on the other side were sophisticated, highly educated, and politically savvy people. There must be some strategy underpinning the notion that there was nothing wrong with setting college level academic standards at elementary benchmarks, but we couldn't figure out what it was. So, we decided to just follow our planned strategy. This enigmatic defense would either morph into a brilliant maneuver, or flame out in spectacular fashion.

It didn't take long before we started getting the answer. The flame out began almost immediately - at least in the media. A furious public, many of whom were UGA alumni, reacted within a day or two. Hale Almand's startling opening statement was widely publicized by the press. Furman Bisher, the *Atlanta Journal* sports editor, published an editorial titled "A Damning Indictment" three days later characterizing it as "a line out of a comedian's mouth in a dingy night club." It was ridiculed by journalists, syndicated columnists, letters to the editorial writers, lawyers, academics, postal employees, sanitation workers, and virtually everyone else who heard of it. To this day, it is referenced in many academic journals, dissertations, and articles on academics and athletics. It has achieved favorite "war story" status in Georgia's legal world. I can't count the number of lawyers who have asked me if Hale Almand really said what the news media was reporting.

At the time, brainstorming with Pat and Jan, I thought maybe the statement was not planned, but rather an off-the-cuff reaction to a pretrial ruling allowing us to introduce evidence of academic favoritism for revenue-producing athletes. The UGA defendants had admitted through Almand's opening statement that student athletes were not subject to the rules governing the academic assessment of other Developmental Studies students because of their unique economic value to the Athletic Association. Given those admissions, Almand filed a motion shortly before the trial began seeking an order barring evidence of such favoritism from being presented to the jury since it was not a disputed fact. Our response was that, while we welcomed the defendants' admissions, evidence of specific instances of academic abuse and the reasons for those practices were still relevant to show the jury the context of the controversy and explain the motives of the faculty, including Jan Kemp, for raising such a ruckus. More importantly, Almand's admissions unveiled the crass motives of the UGA administrators against whom we were seeking punitive damages.

My assumption was that Almand was surprised when the court denied his motion. He faced the reality of the impending barrage of negative evidence by numerous credible witnesses about UGA's exploitation of some of its students for economic reasons. He found himself in a fix. Despite his extensive trial experience, he got a little rattled when the judge called him to begin his opening statement soon after this pre-trial maneuver bombed.

But I was wrong. I discovered many years later when I found a letter from Almand in UGA's Hargrett Library. It was addressed to Fred Davison dated August 8, 1987 - four days before the trial was originally scheduled to begin. The letter laid out the strategy that Almand planned on pursuing in the upcoming trial. It stated that it was being addressed to Fred Davison at the request of Ralph Beaird – neither of whom were his clients. The introductory paragraph read, "At the request of Dean Beaird, I have prepared for you the following brief outline of the defense strategy that we will employ." The letter continues with a litany of admissions of violations of "stated policies of the Division" [Developmental Studies] involving athletes. In light of these provable policy violations, Almand described the trial strategy that he intended to pursue. He wrote: "Therefore, I think at the trial we have to take the position that we admit that these things occurred, offer no apologies and present the University's position in this regard. Accordingly, it is my intention in my opening statement to the jury to advise them that these things occurred, that student athletes were given extra quarters, or administratively exited or admitted pursuant to NCAA guidelines as opposed to Division guidelines and explain the reasons why this was done."

Obviously, Davison concurred since Almand made those admissions in his now notorious opening statement. The wording of his admissions however stunned the UGA decision makers who were complicit in the confessed wrongdoing.

Frankly, I don't remember much more about Almand's opening statement, and I don't think anyone else does either. The press reports of his bizarre assessment of the futures of the student athletes were brutal, to put it mildly. He was roundly criticized for his crass characterization of the student athletes, postal workers, and sanitation workers - and for demeaning the hundreds of thousands of UGA diplomas hanging in the offices and homes of Georgia alumni everywhere. Even Vince Dooley weighed in. According to news reports, he criticized Almand to his face. Dooley made his opinion public in one of his books in which he characterized the Kemp case as being "superbly prosecuted and poorly defended" - a combination of words no losing trial lawyer ever wants to hear.

Almand's choice of words in his opening statement followed him throughout the remainder of his career. While I felt like his opening statement was a gift to Jan and was very glad it happened at the time, I now feel more sympathetic toward Hale as a person. Every honest trial attorney will admit to making mistakes from time to time, and every public speaker "misspeaks" occasionally, but few suffer the consequences of having their words enshrined in Georgia's legal culture and UGA's history.

In any event, when Almand walked away from the jury box, we were ready to roll, and that is exactly what happened for the next five and a half weeks ending with the jury's February 12, 1986 headline grabbing verdict for Jan.

# CHAPTER SEVENTEEN
# TARGETING ERVIN'S REASONS FOR FIRING JAN

During the pre-trial discovery phase of the Kemp litigation, we found a written memorandum by Ervin to Jan's departmental file stating his reasons for firing her. It listed seven reasons: 1) no scholarly publications, 2) no participation in professional associations, 3) no presentation of scholarly papers at professional association conferences, 4) demonstrated inability to work cooperatively with supervisors and colleagues, 5) continually demeaned the need for research in Developmental Studies, 6) failed to encourage subordinates to engage in research, and 7) none of her subordinates produced research.

The problem with Ervin's memo was that Developmental Studies wasn't a "promotional unit" until 1982, the same year Jan's contract was non-renewed. Its faculty members didn't have tenure track jobs which were "up or out" positions, meaning that they had to acquire tenure within seven years from their hiring date to retain their jobs. The tenure process did obligate faculty members in promotional units to engage in research activities, but there was no such requirement for non-tenure track faculty. Since Jan's contract was non-renewed in 1982, she was never in a promotional unit long enough to become tenured.

The dominant issue for the jury to decide was whether Jan was demoted and then fired for exercising her constitutional right to speak freely on matters of public concern, so we had to rebut the reasons stated in the memo which we believed would be an excellent tactic to start our case. To that end, we decided to tender the memo as our first exhibit by putting Ervin on the witness stand for a brief cross-examination to introduce it. Then we could use it as a target for several faculty witnesses whom we knew would swear that they were never notified of any "research" obligations since Developmental Studies was a "teaching" program.

After the opening statements, the judge looked at me and said, "Call your first witness, Mr. Henry." That was the moment we had all been waiting for. I was happy to comply with Judge Ward's directions: "The plaintiff calls Leroy Ervin for cross-examination." Almand rose and asked the judge to instruct the jury on the procedure for the cross-examination of an adverse party. Judge Ward turned to the jury and explained that Almand was not entitled to question his client at this stage of the proceedings, so this witness would be questioned only by the plaintiff's attorney. Ervin took the stand and the race was off!

Ervin had no wiggle room, but he tried his best to find some, and in doing so he gave conflicting testimony about the memo. Initially, he admitted making "notes" of the reasons for his recommendations that Jan be demoted and then fired, but he denied providing a copy of the notes to his lawyers to produce in discovery. That testimony was false. He had obviously provided a copy of those notes to his attorneys to produce in response to our discovery requests, since he alone had possession of them.

When I asked him for the location of the original notes, Ervin said they were in his briefcase that was across the hall. The judge allowed him to go retrieve the notes, but when he returned he said he couldn't find them. His attorneys must have been pretty nervous watching their client because a copy of his memo stating his reasons had been produced during discovery, and I was holding it in my hand while I questioned him.

After watching Ervin's discomfort at the prospect of being questioned about the existence and location of any document that stated the reasons for Jan's non-renewal, I asked him point blank, "Did you ever reduce your reasons for causing the non-renewal of Dr. Kemp to writing?" Remarkably he answered, "I don't think so." I followed up, "Is it your testimony that you have no recollection of doing that?" He responded, "I don't." That answer contradicted his earlier admission that he did make notes but failed to provide copies to his attorneys. His contradictory testimony must have diminished his credibility with the jury - particularly after I handed him our copy of his "reasons" memo. He admitted that our exhibit was a true copy, so it was admitted into evidence without objection. We placed it on the courtroom overhead projector for the jury to see and asked Ervin to read the reasons out loud.

Ervin had badly damaged his own credibility by waffling on the existence and availability of any written statement of the reasons he fired Jan. He was literally forced by the production of our copy of his notes to admit his reasons for doing so, all of which we could disprove.

We wrapped up Ervin's cross-examination, and asked the courtroom Marshal to call our next witness, Fred Johnson.

# CHAPTER EIGHTEEN
# FACULTY WITNESSES

We called Fred Johnson, a former Developmental Studies faculty member, as our first witness. He was an articulate advocate for the restoration of academic integrity in UGA's Developmental Studies Program and a fierce critic of the administrators that encouraged the abuses that led to the faculty rebellion. The fact that he had left his position with UGA in protest of the academic injustices he witnessed made him a strong witness to begin our case.

He described the "exit of the nine" which most of the faculty saw as a grave injustice to the athletes involved, to the non-athlete Developmental Studies students who received no special consideration, and to the faculty who lost their inherent academic authority to grade students based upon their performance. He distrusted Ervin and supported Kemp.

We wanted the jury to understand that the faculty uprising had nothing to do with Ervin's race, so having Johnson, an African American, begin our case could help underscore that reality. We also knew that he could convincingly articulate the faculty's points of view, express his distrust of Ervin, condemn the mistreatment of faculty and students, and rebut the false assertion that the Developmental Studies faculty were required to satisfy tenure track research expectations.

Johnson delivered. He not only painted a complete picture of the prevalent abuses in the program, his testimony also encapsulated the testimony of other faculty witnesses scheduled to appear to support the major themes of our case. He testified that Jan was a dedicated instructor who worked well with her colleagues. He also swore that Ervin had a bad reputation for truthfulness, and that he would not believe him even if he were testifying under oath. With that testimony, Johnson signaled the beginning of one of our trial tactics: to demolish Ervin's credibility by having a number of witnesses confirm that he had an extensively poor reputation for honesty and truthfulness.

Johnson also confirmed that shortly before the team played in the 1982 Sugar Bowl, Trotter "exited" nine revenue-producing athletes who failed to satisfy the standard exit criteria after four quarters. By way of contrast, Trotter simultaneously allowed the expulsion of a non-scholarship female whose potential was at least equal to that of the nine athletes. He also described the faculty's vote to prepare a protest letter and their request that Jan draft it. He told the jury that Jan's firing had a chilling effect on his and the other faculty members' right to voice their complaints about administrative interference with their academic judgments. He also testified that the exit of the nine athletes had a negative impact on other student athletes who assumed they would be treated similarly, and on non-athlete students who resented the leniency afforded the athletes.

Then, without objection, Johnson told the jury that

three other Developmental Studies faculty members had filed and won grievances against Ervin after Jan's contract was non-renewed. A succession of former and then current faculty members' testimonies corroborated Johnson.

Carol Selick, a former faculty member who also resigned over the same issues, told the jury that faculty morale declined after Jan was fired. She also testified that Ervin had a poor reputation for truthfulness and that she too would not believe his sworn testimony. She rebutted Ervin's allegations that Jan failed to support her colleagues and subordinates. She also undermined Ervin's alleged "no research" reason for firing Jan by testifying that she had been told by Ruth Sabol, Jan's replacement as the Coordinator of the English component of Developmental Studies, that its faculty members were not expected to engage in research activities because they were not tenure track professors.

Our next witness, Hyta Mederer, joined the English component of Developmental Studies in 1982. At the time of the trial, she served as the Coordinator of English. Ervin was her immediate superior. We called Mederer to testify about a scholarship football player, Kenny Sims. His name was exempt from the parties' agreement to refer to students by initials only because it was on the defendants' witness list. Sims' story portrayed a critical episode of our trial narrative. He entered Developmental Studies in the Fall Quarter, 1981. Jan was his first English teacher. His grade for that Quarter was an "F." He took English again the following Winter Quarter of 1982 taught by another English teacher, Art Stanley. His grade was another "F."

Developmental Studies students were allowed four quarters to attain a grade of "C" or better to exit into the normal college curriculum, but they had to attain a "D" by the end of their second quarter to remain in the program. Since Sims scored consecutives "Fs," in English, he received a letter of dismissal after the Winter Quarter of 1982.

Sims appealed his dismissal to Ervin who granted him an additional quarter to satisfy the minimum criteria. Sims failed English again in the Spring of 1982 in a class taught by Theresa Timmons, but Ervin, with Trotter's approval, granted Sims a fourth quarter also taught by Timmons in which he finally received a grade of "D." Since he had still not achieved a "C" in English in four quarters, he should have been dismissed under the Regents' four quarters limit for Developmental Studies students. Instead of enforcing that rule, Ervin granted Sims a fifth quarter, and assigned him to a single student class taught by Dr. Mederer.

Mederer told the jury that in her professional opinion, Sims was not qualified to satisfy the demands of the regular college introductory English course, and that he should have been dismissed so he could pursue a realistic career goal. Mederer testified that she didn't learn that Sims had not been dismissed until his name appeared on the football team roster the following season.

It turned out that Ervin and Trotter had approved a sixth quarter for Sims during which he failed once again to earn the grade needed to exit from the program. When that happened, Ervin signed a letter changing that class to an audit rather than a program course. Trotter then approved an administrative exit for Sims who moved into the normal curriculum despite two full academic years of failing efforts to earn a "C" in Developmental Studies' English basic skills classes.

Mederer also told the jury about the lengths the defendants were willing to go to protect revenue-producing athletes. She revealed an example of one track and football scholarship athlete who spent 11 quarters in Developmental Studies - 7 more than allowed under the Regents' rules.

After Dr. Mederer testified, we called Denise Ritter as our next witness. She was a former faculty member and Coordinator of the Developmental Studies Reading component. She corroborated Mederer's testimony regarding the creation of single student classes for athletes. She also described the special studies admission process. A faculty committee made admission decisions for non-athletes. Scholarship athletes were administratively admitted. She knew of only one non-athlete admitted administratively and that student was the daughter of Virginia Trotter's housekeeper.

May Smith, the former Developmental Studies Reading Coordinator from 1975 to 1978, testified the following day. She told the jury about the negative effect on faculty morale that occurred when their judgments regarding academics were overruled by administrators. Those administrative fiats included grade changes, the granting of extra quarters above the Regents' four quarter limitation of students remaining in Developmental Studies, and the provision of one student classes for athletes who consistently failed despite being afforded extra quarters in violation of the Regents' rules.

Smith testified that when she talked to Steve Ender, a staff member responsible for counseling and tutorial services, he admitted contacting a professor about a student athlete identified as GW whose Sociology grade was changed from an F to a C with Ervin's approval. When Smith complained about that grade change to Ervin, he told her to "drop it."

Smith also testified about the troubling climate created among the faculty whose academic judgments were ignored. She related how during a faculty meeting to review requests by failing athletes for an additional quarter, a faculty member stated that AA, a scholarship athlete, was afforded an extra quarter to exit Developmental Studies because he scored the winning touchdown in a game against Georgia Tech, UGA's in-state annual opponent. Almand objected to this testimony because it was hearsay which the judge then ruled was inadmissible and directed the jury to ignore it.

All of Ervin's "reasons" for firing Jan Kemp had been disproved. Almand was unable to mount any credible challenge to the testimony of these faculty members. The jury could either believe the uncontradicted testimony of Jan's colleagues or the word of Ervin whose credibility had taken hit after hit - with more to come!

It was time to reveal Ervin's own words confessing to the actual reasons for his decision to fire Jan Kemp. "Your Honor, we call Velma Scott as our next witness."

# CHAPTER NINETEEN
# VELMA SCOTT

Velma Scott, a Developmental Studies student, was Ervin's "close personal friend." She was older than most Developmental Studies students, but much younger than Ervin. She eagerly volunteered to testify about her relationship with him to explain how she was privy to certain admissions made by Ervin about his reasons for firing Jan. With her help, we had obtained copies of her parents' phone records showing numerous hours of lengthy late evening and post-midnight phone conversations between the two of them to corroborate her testimony regarding their close relationship.

Almand objected to the admission of the phone records and to any testimony by Scott describing her relationship with Ervin as sexual or romantic. He argued that such evidence would be so prejudicial that it would unlawfully influence the jury. We argued that proof of a romantic relationship was necessary to bolster the student's credibility by showing that she had access to Ervin's most intimate thoughts - that he was more likely to make admissions about his feelings toward Jan to his lover than to others.

Judge Ward agreed with Almand that phone records of a sexual or romantic relationship between Scott and Ervin would be unfairly prejudicial to Ervin. But he gave us a way to prove that Scott did have unusual access to Ervin.

He instructed the lawyers and Scott to reference Ervin's relationship with her as a "close personal friend."

Frankly, I believe Judge Ward's decision was correct. Ervin's relationship with Scott was interracial, a type of match that was still somewhat controversial in Georgia in 1986. It was also a romantic relationship between a UGA administrator and a student which many people would judge harshly. Had Judge Ward admitted that evidence, an appeals court might have considered admission of the exact nature of the relationship to be erroneous on the recognized grounds that certain evidence, while tending to prove some relevant fact in the case, may be so prejudicial that proof of it would inject an unfair degree of bias against Ervin for behavior unrelated to the non-renewal of Jan's contract. Therefore, Judge Ward wisely concluded that such evidence should be excluded.

In private, Jan, Pat and I did get a kick out of the notion that the jury might miss the meaning of a "close personal" friendship between a high-level administrator and a student, so denying admission of the phone records and limiting Scott's testimony didn't water down our narrative about Ervin's bad character as described by our faculty witnesses – a narrative that the defense failed to contradict throughout five weeks of trial testimony.

Scott also testified that shortly after the exit of the nine, Jan and Ervin's wife were both pregnant. Ervin told her that "she [Jan Kemp] was another pregnant woman that he was going to get out of his life." Scott also testified that Ervin told her that Jan Kemp was a good teacher but was "crazy as hell, and so are you if you think I'm going to let her run my program. I'll get rid of her before I let her do that."

Those statements, if believed, proved that Ervin knew that the reasons he claimed for firing Jan were false. In truth, she was fired for protesting academic abuses by Ervin and his superiors. Ervin wasn't going to allow Jan Kemp to "run his program" - in effect, he would continue abusing his authority to please the revenue recipients by exploiting the revenue producers and their professors.

# CHAPTER TWENTY
# LARRY BLOUNT

Larry Blount was the African American UGA Law School professor who represented Jan when she filed a grievance challenging her demotion from her position as the English Coordinator in Developmental Studies. He testified that while preparing for Jan's hearing, he asked Ervin to provide him with any evidence that supported his decision to demote Jan. Ervin's answer was devastating - to Ervin that is.

Q. Describe your conversation with Ervin.

A. I asked him whether there was anything in Dr. Kemp's personnel file to support the adverse action against her.

Q. What was his response?

A. "No. Not yet."

Blount testified that he was as appalled as everyone else who knew the inside story of Developmental Studies' role as a substitute for the college educations fraudulently promised to the athletes. Ervin's admission that he intended to pack Jan's personnel records disgusted him. He believed in Jan and did what he could to serve her and UGA by seeking an internal remedy - all to no avail. Blount recognized that the grievance process was a farce created by Ralph Beaird, UGA's Law School dean and Davison's legal counsel. It was controlled by Trotter and two additional vice presidents, Eugene Younts (Vice President for Public Service and Outreach) and Robert C. Anderson (Vice President for Research and President of the University of Georgia Research Foundation, Inc.), all of whom were acting under Ralph Beaird's directions. Judge Ward took note of the absurdity of that process in his post-trial order disposing of the defendants' motion for a new trial. He described the nature of the "process" as follows:

"Thereafter, the plaintiff pursued an administrative grievance within the University of Georgia seeking redress for her removal from the position of Coordinator of the English component. At the hearing, she was represented by Mr. Larry Blount, a faculty member of the University of Georgia School of Law. Defendant Trotter appointed a hearing tribunal, consisting of herself and two other vice presidents, to hear the plaintiff's complaint. There is conflict in the evidence as to what the authority of the tribunal was, and as to the nature of plaintiff's appeal. It is clear that the plaintiff's perception of her endeavor was that she was seeking a review of the merits of her grievance in an effort to have the action of defendant Ervin changed. The tribunal simply reviewed the procedure which defendant Ervin applied to effect plaintiff's removal and found that the procedure was appropriate. Following the hearing, Dr. Trotter prepared a written memorandum in which she underlined the statement that Dr. Kemp 'is threatening to go public.' The evidence further reveals that defendant Ervin attended the hearing before the tribunal, at which time he demonstrated his disagreement and hostility toward plaintiff's presentation."

Blount's testimony was important for several reasons. First, it revealed the nature of the internal "grievance" process as an empty remedy. The panel of vice presidents was convened to simply review the "process" used to deprive Jan of her civil rights with no consideration of the facts. Second, Ervin's "No. Not yet," comment in response to Blount's request for anything in Jan's file supporting her demotion, corroborated Scott's testimony that Ervin's motive for non-renewing Jan's contract was not what he stated in the memo that he prepared, but then "forgot" about. Two witnesses, Scott and Blount, had sworn that Ervin intended to fire Jan for protesting the abuse of UGA's academic standards. Blount had added that Ervin admitted his willingness to create a file after the fact to justify his actions.

Our next witness, a former UGA student athlete, was ready and anxious to tell the jury what kind of teacher Jan really was. I was more than happy to announce, "Your Honor, we call Ronnie Stewart."

# CHAPTER TWENTY-ONE
# RONNIE STEWART

Ronnie Stewart, known as Herschel Walker's escort on the football field, was the fullback who punched holes in the defensive lines of UGA opponents for the Heisman Trophy winner. His was one of the pitifully low number of success stories of minority revenue-producing student athletes at UGA. He was also one of Jan Kemp's students. Ronnie was only the $15^{th}$ minority revenue-producing student athlete in UGA's history to earn an undergraduate degree. He willingly appeared for Jan at the trial where he testified that "if there was any preferential treatment that I got as an athlete, it was from her, because there was no time she wouldn't come to the dormitory to help me. I remember one Sunday when she came to the library and we sat for ten hours while I wrote a paper." Ronnie's "preferential treatment" wasn't like the administrative interference that led to the faculty rebellion. It was a reference to the superlative training that he received in the Developmental Studies program, particularly the education he acquired at the insistence and disciplinary demands of Jan Kemp.

Ronnie's story was an excellent model to describe what benefits were available at UGA for student athletes with the ability to make up for substandard high school educations if they had the motive to do so. After a brief stint in professional football was short-circuited by injuries, Ronnie returned to UGA to complete his education. He satisfied

Developmental Studies criteria, exited into the normal curriculum, performed well there, and graduated with a degree. By the time he testified for Jan, Ronnie had acquired a ServePro franchise which he was then building into a successful business.

I got to know Ronnie during the trial preparation and several post-trial conversations with him. Ronnie even visited my family at our home to express his appreciation to me for defending Jan. I found him to be an outstanding young man - a perfect role model for student athletes. His path to academic success was the same as his path to athletic success: a "can do" mentality, discipline, motivation, and hard work under the guidance of talented teachers and coaches.

Ronnie was a superlative witness. He was articulate, sincere, and believable. He described how Jan spent endless hours tutoring him. He summarized the positive impact that she had on his life. "There is not a finer person. Everything I know I learned from her."

Ronnie's testimony also portrayed Jan as a teacher who was exceptionally dedicated to her students. She even volunteered to tutor some of them after they exited Developmental Studies. Ronnie wasn't the only student athlete who relied upon Jan for help when facing the challenges of the normal academic curriculum. Ronnie's testimony painted a true picture of Jan as a stern but dedicated teacher whose passion to improve the lives of her students became evident to everyone in the courtroom, particularly the jurors. His testimony was the perfect introduction to our next witness: Jan Kemp.

## CHAPTER TWENTY-TWO
## JAN KEMP

Jan strode to the witness stand with an air of confidence, stood facing the courtroom, raised her right hand, smiled and swore to tell the truth. Her testimony was probably my favorite part of the trial because Pat did her direct examination which consumed a Friday and part of the following Monday. I enjoyed the break, but not as much as I enjoyed the show.

The direct examination was comprehensive and illuminating. It came across as an informal conversation between friends about some traumatic events in Jan's life. The cross-examination by Almand was entertaining—Jan dominated one of the best trial lawyers in the state under the glare of the national press.

Jan's demeanor was superb. Trial lawyers usually advise witnesses to just be themselves on the stand. Jan played Jan Kemp exquisitely. It was more than apparent that she was a damn good teacher. Her dialogue with Pat was comfortable; her competency was apparent; and her testimony was honest and well crafted. Jan's presence as a witness was beyond professional. She maintained her composure, gave reasoned responses to questions, looked at the jury when answering substantive questions, and expressed emotions appropriately. She also used her sense of humor effectively. The few tears that she shed were honest and revealed a clear picture of the pain that she had experienced. I felt like standing to applaud when she finished, and the jury members' post-trial embraces of Jan revealed that they felt the same way.

Under Pat's carefully prepared questions, Jan told her story. She told the jury how 75 student slots in Developmental Studies were reserved for "special admissions" and granted without approval of the faculty Admissions Committee - 50 for student athletes and 25 for "political" applicants composed of children of wealthy donors and politically connected citizens. She detailed how some of the donors were also involved in Developmental Studies affairs as members of Ervin's Parents Participation Program (PIP) which Jan and others saw as creating an improper opportunity for parents to influence academic and disciplinary issues involving their children. She illustrated that concern with testimony about the ML profane phone call to her home, her successful prosecution of him through the student judiciary, and ML's father's lobbying of Fred Davison to overrule the judiciary's decision. She told the jury about the relaxation of Developmental Studies grading standards and Ervin's involvement in pressuring Barbara Carson, a regular curriculum English professor, to change grades of former Developmental Studies student athletes. She described the repetitive violations of Regents' imposed time limits on students to exit Developmental Studies, and the creation of "administrative exits" of student athletes when all else failed. She then detailed the 1981 exit of the nine student athletes and the faculty rebellion that followed.

Jan described the escalation of retaliation against her, including aggressive behavior by Ervin, demotion from her coordinator position, and a meaningless appeal to a Virginia Trotter led faux review panel, all of which were followed by the non-renewal of her contract.

Jan continued by describing the most offensive action taken against her by Ervin - the solicitation of her more vulnerable students to write false letters accusing her of making lewd comments in her classes. She told the jury that she believed that any faculty member who supported her would be subjected to similar retaliation.

Jan candidly described her emotional meltdown when her superiors retaliated against her for protesting their misconduct. Jan was a new mother then who was losing her career and her income. She was being slandered by her former students at the behest of an unethical superior. Her friends and colleagues were being threatened for their support. She broke. Her testimony on direct examination regarding the circumstances that led to her suicide attempts was the only time during the trial that that tears ran down her cheeks.

During the darkest time of her depression, Jan fled to the comfort of her parents' home which she described in one of most poignant moments of the trial. Her quiet understated description of driving from Athens to their home in Brunswick, Georgia, and her parents' loving reaction, brought tears to the eyes of some of the jurors. Jan's mother and father embraced and comforted her through a tough night just as they had when she was a small child. Their unconditional love of their daughter played a huge role in both defining and mitigating the emotional costs of Jan's adherence to principle in the face of gross irresponsibility and brutal resistance by some very powerful people.

After slightly more than a day under direct examination by Pat, Hale Almand began his five-hour cross-examination. He should have remained at his table. His biggest deficiency was his prosecutorial experience - he didn't understand that respected academics were not people who had been indicted by federal grand juries. They were witnesses who would be best handled with a gentler touch, but Almand was intent on conducting a criminal case style cross-examination of Jan. He falsely insinuated that she had claimed to be a "linguistics expert" to explain how she had identified ML's voice during the profanity laced phone call he made to her home. Jan never made such claim. She simply stated that she recognized his voice because he had an unusual manner of speaking.

Almand also aggressively challenged Jan's testimony regarding the retaliatory actions against her by Ervin. That tactic was questionable in the face of numerous faculty members' corroborations of Jan's version of Ervin's pattern of retaliatory behavior towards faculty who opposed his manipulation of their program.

Almand also elicited more details regarding her psychological history than Jan had disclosed during her direct examination. His intent in that regard was obvious: to suggest that Jan was not lucid due to mental illness. The problem with that line of attack was that Jan's testimony was clear, concise, and corroborated by a number of faculty members who had no history of psychological illness themselves.

On the other hand, some of Almand's questions seemed like questions that Pat could have asked. For instance, Almand asked Kemp for her opinion of the role of Fred Davison. Her response artfully belittled Davison while insuring that the focus remained on the defendants since they were the ones on trial. "I am pretty sure it was about 16 times that I called him for an appointment and I finally got it. And that was it because there were no reforms. Zilch, zero." Jan described her single audience with Davison who told her as soon as she entered his office that he would be happy to discuss anything with her except issues that were being raised in her litigation against Ervin and Trotter. Jan looked at the jury and asked a rhetorical question: "What was I supposed to say – How 'bout them Dawgs?"

During her cross-examination Almand asked her for her opinion of Leroy Ervin, to which she responded that he was not her favorite person. Almand characterized her response as "sort of a classic understatement" to which Kemp replied, "Not entirely, Mr. Almand. Through nightly prayer, I have conquered my anger and gained personal strength." She also told Almand that she prayed for Ervin every day, and as facially unbelievable as such a statement may appear, her calm demeanor, intelligence, and credibility won the day. There was no doubt in any juror's mind that Jan was capable of forgiveness - her agenda was not the destruction of anyone - it was the resurrection of the academic integrity of an institution that she was totally dedicated to defend and reform in the best interest of it and the students it served.

Perhaps Almand's greatest tactical error in his cross examination of Jan was a line of questions regarding her motive for bringing the lawsuit during which he heavily insinuated was money rather than principle. Her response must have made him wish he had not asked the questions.

Almand: Now, Dr. Kemp, of course, you are asking this jury to award you damages?

Kemp: Yes, sir.

Almand: Monetary damages?

Kemp: Yes, sir.

Almand: And you will want to convince them that your cause is just so you will get money?

Kemp: Yes, sir.

Almand: And to that end you will say whatever is necessary to accomplish that purpose, won't you?

Kemp: No, sir. Money has never been my primary motivating force. Had it been, I wouldn't have become a teacher.

Almand: All right.

Kemp: The principles involved are far more important to me than money.

Almand: So, you would be just as happy if all you got was a dollar?

Kemp: As long as the University was cleaned up, yes, sir.

Jan left the witness stand with her head held high. She had told her story cogently and credibly. She left no lingering problems on that witness stand, except for those that remained for the defendants to deal with. The jury had watched her closely. They were obviously convinced of her honesty and the sincerity of her stated purpose - integrity, not money! The only remaining mistake Almand could do to erode the defendants' case even more was to continue his overly aggressive attack against Jan. He didn't disappoint.

# CHAPTER TWENTY-THREE
# THE PRESS

Since Judge Ward rejected Hale Almand's request for a "gag order," we were free to speak to the press during the trial. Jan had made her motives clear to us - reform was more important than personal victory. We had to let the public, the Regents, and the leadership of the state know that the cat was out of the bag. Georgia's leaders had turned a blind eye to Davison's maladministration for years - particularly the dominant influence of the Athletic Association. The time had arrived to spotlight the serious academic abuses at UGA - to force Georgia's leaders to act.

We had no public relations expertise or experience, and no idea what to expect. So, we decided that we would all simply answer the press reporters' questions. Much to my surprise, Pat and Jan told me that they had voted - I would be the television 'face' of our team - I had no say so. That assignment was more nerve-racking than the courtroom work, but the reporters and their crews were very professional, courteous and easy to work with - and the television coverage of the trial made it almost impossible for anyone to ignore the damning testimony of the witnesses.

Initially, the trial news coverage was limited to the Atlanta and Athens media markets, but that changed drastically as the first week's trial coverage went out over the wires. Of course, Almand's "postal worker trumps garbage man" opening statement also drew broad national coverage.

The editors of *The New York Times* published a January 14, 1986 editorial reacting to the first week's testimony. It concluded with a quotation of Clifford Sjoerd, the Chairman of the NCAA's academic testing and requirements committee and Director of Admissions at the University of Michigan: "To suggest that bending the rules and keeping an athlete enrolled merely because it will make a better postman of him is irresponsible. No university ought to ever contemplate the admission of a student that cannot read nor write."

By the end of the following week, the temperature was rising in the media. On January 17, *The Atlanta Constitution* published an article by sports columnist Dave Kindred containing an assessment of what was really on trial in the minds of his readers. His article, "Black Eye for Georgia is the Price of Expediency", observed that the "halftime" of the trial was nearing, and "Georgia's boys are getting their legal clocks cleaned." His perceptive column framed the bigger issue from Jan's viewpoint by asking, "Can academics and athletics co-exist? Or maybe it's even more than that? Do they have to co-exist? Is education necessarily a part of college athletics? Or is the pretense of education a sop for old time moralists in love with a romantic ideal that never existed."

Bill Shipp, a senior *Atlanta Constitution* editor, weighed in. His January 21, 1986 editorial was headlined, "Kemp Trial Sends Dogs Scurrying with Their Tails Between Their Legs." He began by noting that the state's political leaders and its Board of Regents had not reacted appropriately - no cries of anguish, no calls for reform. He then outlined the three preceding weeks of testimony "for the benefit of those of you who may have been visiting a distant planet." He noted that UGA maintained a "school for gladiators" who are "trained and preened and spoiled and kept mostly separate from the rest of the student body." Shipp noted that they are not "students," but "performers" used to entertain alumni who give large amounts of money. After being used up, they are "left to fend for themselves. It is, to say the least, a barbaric system." Shipp then compared the Kemp Affair to the 1940s Walter Cocking Affair when Governor Eugene Talmadge caused UGA to lose its national accreditation by meddling in University personnel matters. The difference Shipp noted, was the then newly elected governor, Ellis Arnall, "came galloping to the rescue and restored UGA's accreditation." Shipp pointed out that no such white knight had arrived this time, and concluded that, "It's time somebody called for a broom."

Shipp got Jan's message - it's time somebody called for a broom was newspeak for Jan's basic goal: reform or else! Georgia's political leadership was trapped.

Of course, we were encouraged with the evolving public relations battle. Almand's decision to gag UGA's public relations machine insured our domination of press and media coverage of the trial. The publicity was being fashioned by the events occurring in the courtroom. Jan was happy; her story was being told to everyone who needed to hear it - the Board of Regents, Georgia's office holders, the masses of UGA graduates, its faculty, and its students.

## CHAPTER TWENTY-FOUR THERESA TIMMONS

On January 14, 1986, the same day that *The New York Times* editorial was being read nationwide, the events on the $23^{rd}$ floor of the Richard Russell Federal Courthouse sealed the public relations disaster enveloping the defendants and their superiors.

We called Theresa Timmons, the professor who had slipped a tape recorder into her purse and secretly taped a faculty meeting with Trotter, Ervin, and representatives of the Athletic Association. The meeting occurred during the Fall quarter of 1983. Jan was still on the faculty but was in her terminal year since Ervin had notified her that her 1983-84 contact would not be renewed. She didn't attend that meeting, which was a good decision because her presence would have chilled the remarkable candor of Trotter and Ervin captured on Timmons' tape.

Timmons took the stand with the understanding that we agreed to when she gave me the tape. I wouldn't introduce it unless she felt like she had to disclose it in her direct testimony, or if Almand asked her about it during her cross-examination.

Timmons' direct examination was typical of the other faculty members who preceded her, except she was the first witness to testify about the meeting with Trotter, Ervin and the representatives from the Athletic Association. Her courtroom demeanor was perfect. She was an articulate and persuasive witness whose dignified manner boosted her credibility. She testified that she shared her colleagues' concerns about the ethical and moral implications of enticing student athletes to attend UGA with empty promises of college educations in return.

When I asked Theresa why the status quo was unacceptable, she didn't mince words. "To be brought here and be told that if you mind your manners and go to class that eventually you'll graduate is a lie. I felt they should get out of the University and get on with their lives and not get strung out."

"Your witness, Mr. Almand." Almand rose, walked confidently to the podium, and began his cross-examination. His first question exploded in his face. "Dr. Timmons, you tape recorded that meeting, didn't you?"

Eureka! I flew out of my chair. "Your Honor, the best evidence of a tape recording is the tape recording itself. I have the original and transcripts of its content for the Court, the defense attorneys, and the jury. I would like to tender that evidence to help Mr. Almand's cross-examination of Dr. Timmons."

Almand could hardly object since he had raised the existence of the tape with his question, so the judge admitted the tape and the transcripts. The jury listened to the tape and heard the defendants' voices making admissions of reprehensible conduct that not only nailed their coffins shut in the jury room, but also brought more nationwide criticism of the University they purported to lead.

I watched the jury as they listened and followed the transcripts. Some glanced toward the defense table when some of the more disturbing comments were heard.

The tape portrayed Ervin assuming the role of the victim during the meeting - a functionary tasked with the responsibility of carrying out policies that he personally abhorred. Confirming his own duplicity, Ervin admitted his readiness to conceal the ugly truth that everyone in the room knew about. “Let me say what I have to say in this room. I think I have a somewhat responsible position in the University, so I can say what I want to say here, and I guess I might act differently once I leave.” He assumed the role of the disgruntled faculty's leader. “I think what people are saying here is that they are being forced to participate in a kind of chicanery that has somehow placed their credibility in question with their counterparts and colleagues on this campus.”

Ervin had made a huge mistake however by his “identity” with the faculty tactics claim. He made the headline-grabbing admission that “I know for a fact that these kids would not be here if it were not for their utility to the institution. There is no real sound academic reason for their being here other than being utilized to produce revenue. They are used as a kind of raw material in the production of some goods to be sold as whatever product, and they get nothing in return.”

Trotter also acknowledged UGA's student athlete facade,

but rationalized the inherent immorality of that reality by convincing herself that the defrauded young people would be better off having been there. She bluntly admitted that "I think we are really talking through our hats if we think these kids are going to graduate. I do think these students are better off for having been here. I guess you'd have to convince me that they're not better off for having learned to read if they don't know how to read by the time they come here."

The jury had just heard the true story from the horses' mouths. High level UGA officials admitted that the "student" part of "student athlete" was a sham. The athletes were "raw material" used to produce revenue to further enrich the host of wealthy people who ran the Athletic Association, but they were better off because they learned to read - small wonder that the word "Plantation" often fell from the lips of the Developmental Studies faculty.

# CHAPTER TWENTY-FIVE
# RUTH SABOL

Ruth Sabol was the professor who took over as English Coordinator of Developmental Studies after Jan was demoted. She was still serving in that position during the trial, and Ervin was still her supervisor. Nevertheless, she took the stand willingly, swore to tell the truth, and calmly added more weight to Jan's side of the scales. She listened carefully to the questions and gave precise answers.

Sabol was called to show the jury that not much had changed at UGA - the deplorable conditions being described by Jan and other faculty witnesses still prevailed. She also added significant corroboration of previous faculty testimony. Most importantly however, she repudiated the secretly recorded cynical assertion by Virginia Trotter that UGA satisfied their obligations to the athletes by insuring that they would be "better off" when they left the University without a degree.

My next question to her was simple: "Do you believe athletes who do not have the potential to obtain a degree are still better off for having been at UGA?" She paused as if to compose herself to answer - then she spoke, "I firmly believe they are not better off. They're damaged, being used in a system and told that they are going to get a college degree, and hoping, hoping so much from the bottom of their hearts that they will get a degree. It's a tragedy. They do not understand that the University doesn't expect them to graduate. It's a tragedy."

Sabol painted a picture of the continuing problems in Developmental Studies. She described a litany of ongoing Regents policy violations by "administrative pen" that included exits to the regular curriculum, allowing athletes to remain in the program for up to eight quarters, and concealing participation in the program by assigning athletes to single student "tutorials" which were not reported as extra academic quarters.

Sabol also related her personal knowledge of Ervin's pattern of lobbying student athletes in academic trouble to accuse faculty members, including herself, of misconduct during her supervision of them.

Finally, she explained that Jan, by virtue of having written a textbook, had already satisfied any research criteria expected of Developmental Studies faculty initially adopted in June of 1982.

Sabol's testimony vividly described the crippling impact on the young athletes as they navigated their way through cascading academic disappointments. "You're like a coach almost. Those students who are unable to pass from remedial to regular courses after their freshman year begin to wonder during their second year why they are not successful. The third year they become bitter. They feel they will never make it no matter what they do. By the fourth year, they give up."

That testimony must have profoundly affected the jury

- what normal person would abide these administrators' misconduct? A revenue-producing game became more important than the psychological well-being of the young men making it happen. Disappointment and failure were their rewards, and the wrongdoers knew it. The disgust in the courtroom was palpable.

## CHAPTER TWENTY-SIX
## VIRGINIA TROTTER

Virginia Trotter was our final witness. I called her for cross-examination on Friday, January 17, the 10th day of the trial. Cross-examination of witnesses normally follows the direct examination by their attorney, but the plaintiff's attorneys can call the defendants for cross-examination before they deliver their stories through questions by their attorney. We had already called Ervin for cross-examination as our first witness. Trotter was our final witness. We decided to cap the beginning and end of our presentation with the defendants as witnesses because we were confident that their testimonies would harm their case if we were asking the questions.

Our plan was for Trotter's cross-examination to begin after lunch to ensure that I had the entire afternoon to "cover the map" while delaying the completion of her testimony until court resumed on the following Tuesday. The federal courthouse was closed in observance of the first Martin Luther King Jr. national holiday on Monday, January 20, 1986. That recess would give us a few days to hone our final questions.

Trotter seemed surprised that she was being called as one of our witnesses. She wasn't prepared. Her testimony was incoherent. Almand must have also been surprised. He reacted by doing everything possible to keep Trotter from answering most of my questions. He peppered our cross-examination with objections resulting in more time used discussing evidentiary rules with the judge than eliciting testimony.

Almand's basic tactic was to explain his objections through lengthy statements of his view of the facts. That tactic is known in legal circles as "speaking objections." Proper objections simply state the legal basis for the objection such as "irrelevant," "hearsay," "privilege," etc. The judge typically asks the attorney doing the examination to respond to an objection: "What's the relevancy, counsel?" "Are you offering testimony that fits any hearsay exception?" Sometimes, the court asks the attorney making the objection for a clarification such as, "What is the nature of the privilege - attorney-client or marital?" Each attorney gives concise responses, and the judge rules. Speaking objections may or may not state the legal basis of the objection but always offer expansive explanations that misstate or skew the facts for two reasons: to improperly argue their case to the jury and clue the witness to the themes that the lawyer wants voiced. Some judges disallow speaking objections, but to our disappointment Judge Ward permitted them. Our objections to Almand's speech-making instead of stating the legal grounds of the objections apparently won the day with the jurors as reported by one of them who told newspaper reporters after the trial that sometimes Almand seemed to simply be making speeches.

After an hour or so of Almand's objections barrage, the judge ordered a short recess to give the jury a break. A few minutes into the break, Pat and I were summoned to Judge Ward's chambers. When we arrived, we saw Randy Aderhold, Almand's co-counsel, waiting. We were all asked to join the judge in his chambers. Aderhold told the judge that Almand was in the men's room because he was very sick. He said Almand was requesting a continuance of the trial until the following Tuesday. Judge Ward asked us for a response. We were skeptical given Almand's energetic obstruction of Trotter's testimony immediately before he "got sick," so I candidly responded to Judge Ward's instruction. "Your Honor, I take Mr. Aderhold at his word that Almand has sent that message to you, but we want it verified. We want the court to have someone examine him. Frankly, we want to eliminate any possibility that this development is more gamesmanship than medical, and if it is medical, a medical professional should assess him."

I honestly believe most federal trial judges would have wanted more information before adjourning to ensure that Almand was ill but not in any medical danger. That suggestion seemed particularly appropriate in this case because two years earlier Almand had suffered a significant medical event while prosecuting a criminal case against the legendary Georgia politician, Labor Commissioner Sam Caldwell. In that case, emergency medical assistance was necessary, and the event was publicized in the press and on television.

Judge Ward reacted as the gentleman that he always was. "No, I'm not going to do that, Mr. Henry. I'm going to take Mr. Almand at his word, and Mr. Aderhold will be sure that he'll be cared for." Once again, Judge Ward revealed the humanity that caused him to be so revered throughout his life. I wouldn't be surprised if he did find out whether medical intervention was necessary. I have a good reason for these suspicions. The following week, we conferenced again in chambers to discuss some legal matters related to the case. After the conference, Judge Ward asked Almand how he was doing and got a positive response. Then Judge Ward looked straight at him and asked him if he felt like his job was having an impact on his health. He mentioned the medical event during the Caldwell trial. He was genuinely concerned. He sincerely wanted Almand to prioritize his health over his career. Judge Ward was not only an excellent judge, he was a true humanitarian. Pat and I thought he let Almand get away with another questionable attempt to shield Trotter from what he saw happening that Friday afternoon. But nobody blamed Judge Ward. We had to laugh it off - we joked about how Trotter would probably be taking another trip to Italy on UGA business before court reconvened on Tuesday morning. As we left the courthouse, Pat was asked by a reporter to comment on Almand's sudden illness. He couldn't resist replying, "He heard the same testimony you did. It must have made him sick."

Trotter's abbreviated Friday appearance did, however, set the tone of her approach to testifying - evasion! Trotter didn't appear to be any better prepared for her testimony when she returned to the stand on Tuesday. A good example of her inability to provide cogent answers to questions was her response to one of my first questions that morning: "Was there a University policy that specified the standards for granting preferential treatment to revenue-producing student athletes?" She answered that the "policy" was open-ended; exceptions could be made at her discretion. In fact, those exceptions, coupled with the absence of written policies or guidelines, allowed the Athletic Association to engineer the preferential treatment of revenue-producing athletes without regard to their inevitable failure to satisfy normal collegiate curricula. That had already been indisputably proved through her admissions on the Timmons tape.

Additonal testimony from Trotter painted the picture of preferential treatment of other students which was based on whether or not an appeal was made to Trotter as the chief academic officer at UGA. Very few students ever pursued such appeals, however, because there were no notices, publications or other means of knowing of the right to appeal. Moreover, there were no standards to apply when assessing appeals. Neither the faculty committees who rejected unqualified students, nor those who taught failing student athletes were consulted. Invariably, the non-athletic student appeals that Trotter mentioned were from influential and/or wealthy citizens with non-qualifying sons and daughters. Those aspiring students which everyone involved, including Ervin and Trotter, designated as "political" admissions, were favored because their parents would contact their politically connected friends to wire them into the channels needed to override Admissions Committee and other faculty decisions. The parents of other applicants who were denied admission or expelled for failing grades had no such contacts, and no way to learn that there was an appeals process.

Trotter's answer to the questions about those inequities was that she could only act on appeals which once again evaded the obvious question: if that was so, why wasn't the appeal process formalized and publicized in UGA's literature on the policies regarding admissions to UGA and expulsion for failure to satisfy normal academic grading standards? I believe the jury wondered about that too and reached the same conclusions the faculty had: the absence of notice and standards must have been intentional. The appeal process appeared to be nothing more than a ruse to immunize athletes and non-qualified sons and daughters of "favored" citizens from both academic admission screening and dismissal for failing grades. UGA leaders' motives were obvious: to protect revenue-producing athletes and politically influential citizens' children.

Trotter claimed that her only concern in considering application denial appeals was the well-being of the applicants - not their influence - but she couldn't cite a single example of an admissions denial of anyone from an influential family. The sole exception to the privileged class category of irregular admissions was the admission of Trotter's housekeeper's daughter after her initial application was denied. Trotter attempted to justify that decision as an effort to bolster UGA affirmative action obligations, but no other UGA officials tasked with those duties were involved, and the same opportunity was not offered to other unsuccessful minority applicants. Her most cynical rationalization, however, was that her housekeeper's daughter's grades were "similar to the athletes who received preferential treatment."

I asked Trotter if an appropriate factor for her consideration would be whether or not an unqualified applicant's parent was a member of the Board of Regents, and she unequivocally answered, "Yes." That answer confirmed the grim reality for most of the unsuccessful applicants - their opportunity to attend UGA depended upon the size of their parents' bank accounts and/or their ability to benefit UGA in the nether regions of Georgia politics.

I was puzzled by the failure of Trotter's attorneys to fix her standards-less discretion that ignored Regents and UGA's rules before the trial. The lawsuit was three years old when the trial began. Surely that was sufficient time to have a sit down with Trotter to urge her to create a rational appeal protocol available to all unsuccessful Developmental Studies applicants. That would have ameliorated the effect of Trotter's use of arbitrary unwritten policies that implicitly favored the sons and daughters of wealthy and influential parents. Apparently, the decision makers planning the defense for Trotter discounted the power of an apology and change of policy.

Regarding the exit of the nine in 1981, Trotter admitted, "It's my decision. I accept responsibility for it." I asked her if that decision was influenced by the fact that the nine were all athletes in the revenue-producing sport of football or basketball. She first responded, "not particularly," but then modified her answer and swore, "I'm sure that came into it." I asked if she would make the same decision again.

She answered that she would. I later learned that she fine-tuned that statement after the trial when asked by Regents' investigators if Davison had any part in the decision to exit the nine. She told the investigators that she spoke with him in depth and described his reactions as guarded but clear - protect the eligibility of the revenue-producing athletes.

The pressure on Trotter must have been intense because she had an alternative to actually exiting the nine. Although equally improper, a precedent had already been established by Ervin to afford failing athletes more than four quarters with his "permission." Ervin used that process in 1980 and 1981, each time at the end of Fall Quarter - the fourth and final quarter for athletes who failed to exit the program.

The improper underlying motives of UGA's leadership in December of 1981 were recognized in the Regents' office as a ploy to keep some athletes eligible for the upcoming Sugar Bowl in New Orleans. We introduced a Regents official's letter to Ervin signed by a Vice Chancellor approving extra quarters for five other football players which contained a handwritten notation, "Good luck in New Orleans." I asked Trotter why she didn't use the same process instead of ordering the exit of the nine at the end of the Fall Quarter of 1981 - get Regents' permission to grant certain athletes a fifth quarter. That process would have at least afforded the students a reasonable opportunity to exit properly with enhanced chances of survival in the regular curriculum. Trotter answered, "To tell the truth, in 1981 I never even thought about going to the Regents."

Next, we introduced a memorandum that Trotter wrote

after conducting Jan's grievance appeal when she was demoted from her position as English Coordinator. The handwritten memo underlined a part of a statement reading, "She is going public, and Blount [Larry Blount, the law professor representing Jan in her grievance] has advised her to get an outside lawyer." That note was direct evidence that the prospect of Jan exercising her First Amendment rights was problematic for Trotter.

I shifted the focus to two students: Kenny Sims and LS. I directed Trotter's attention to her statements about them that were recorded on the Timmons tape.

Sims was a student athlete who was a superb football player, but also a young man whose prospect of obtaining a college degree was nil. The faculty, Ervin, and Trotter all knew that. The exploitation of Sims was not just shocking, it was very wrong. The UGA decision makers used him to slander Jan. Their attorneys called him as a trial witness which they knew would result in his name being revealed despite the court's and the parties' efforts to limit references to students by initials only.

Sims signed a March 29, 1982 letter addressed to "Whomever It May Concern" accusing Jan of making inappropriate sexual remarks in her class. We understood that Sims was a likely witness because he was listed on the defendants' witness list in the pretrial order. Sims' letter was provided to us during the discovery phase of the litigation, and it was apparent from the beginning of the trial that character assassination was a core component of the defense strategy. So, it was no surprise that the defendants put their own interests over their duty to protect Sims' academic privacy. Jan and others were outraged at the exploitation of Sims, particularly under the circumstances that shed a sinister light on Ervin's conduct - exempting Sims from academic standards applicable to others while grooming him as a witness to be used against Jan Kemp.

I pressed Trotter to explain why Sims was granted a fifth quarter in 1983 over faculty objections, and subsequently an "administrative exit" from Developmental Studies despite the unanimous opinion of the faculty that he would never graduate. Trotter couldn't explain those undisputed facts. Her failure to articulate any reason for her actions in that regard left the obvious inference that there was no sound explanation. The truth was that Sims paid for the academic leniency afforded him by accommodating Ervin in his crusade against Jan. There was more evidence to come when Sims was called as a witness by the defense in the presentation of their case later in the trial.

LS, a female non-athlete, was also granted a fifth quarter simultaneously with Sims, but she was subsequently dismissed for the stated reason that she lacked the ability to graduate. Trotter agreed with the faculty's dismal assessment of LS's inability to succeed in the normal curriculum. When I asked Trotter to explain the distinction between LS and Sims, since the faculty also believed that he lacked the ability to graduate, she responded, "I didn't know that." But she did know. I handed her the transcript of the Timmons tape where she was recorded saying, "We would be talking through our hats if we think these kids are ever going to graduate . . ." She looked at the transcript and replied, "That's just a statement. That's not anything I swore to." Trotter had just told the jury that truthfulness was optional when she wasn't under oath.

Trotter was also recorded on the Timmons tape complaining about the Athletic Association. She said, "I mean, you know, every time we talk about it, we talk about recruiting better students and we talk about, you know, that we talk about the fact that we're really going to go after the athlete that's a scholar as well. All of these things I'm told, and then I'm told by this group right now that they're worse than they've ever been."

Actually, Trotter already knew that the student athletes were worse than ever long before hearing from the faculty on the Timmons tape. I handed Trotter a document that memorialized a 1982 decision by her overruling Ervin's recommendation that a prospective student athlete not be admitted to illustrate that she did in fact know that athletes who were "worse than they've ever been" were still being admitted. She examined the letter before responding, looked up and delivered one of her more preposterous answers. "We were talking about students generally across the country, sir, not University of Georgia students." That response was inconsistent with what she had actually said. The Timmons tape clearly revealed the purpose of the meeting, and it had nothing to do with "students across the country" and everything to do with UGA student athletes who were seemingly unqualified to acquire a college education in any institution of higher learning, including UGA.

I saved our last line of questions to leave a troubling picture in the jurors' minds of the misuse of administrative admissions.

Q. It is true, is it not, ma'am, that there are different standards for admissions with respect to athletes who produce revenue for the Georgia Athletic Association as opposed to scholarship athletes in non-revenue-producing sports?

A. I don't know. I do know that revenue-producing students are admitted that way. I assume that all athletes are, but I don't know. I better – I can't say I know, because I don't. You will have to ask someone else."

But she did know. She knew that UGA policies allowed the Athletic Association to designate a fixed number of revenue-producing athletes for administrative admissions, even those who scored under 650 (of a possible 1600) on the College Board Scholastic Aptitude Test (SAT). Non-revenue-producing scholarship athletes were required to meet the standard admission criteria, including SAT scores over 650, but there was a convenient way around that requirement when the non-revenue-producing scholarship was also a good football player.

I asked Trotter to identify a March 10, 1982 letter written to her by UGA's football coach Vince Dooley recommending an exception for a track athlete, a sprinter who ended up playing wide receiver on UGA's football team for two seasons. She identified it, and we introduced it without objection. Then I asked Trotter to read Dooley's letter to the jury:

"I am recommending an exception to our agreed policy of not accepting for admittance athletes of non-revenue sports, whose score is less than 650 on the College Board. As you can see from the attached, a sprinter from Northside High School in Atlanta is a blue-chip track and field prospect who has received fine letters of recommendation from the principal's office and guidance office. Your consideration of this request will be most appreciated."

That letter and Trotter's subsequent approval of Dooley's recommendation contradicted her sworn testimony claiming that she thought that the revenue-producing athletes' admissions policy was applicable to "all athletes." If that was her belief, why would Dooley be requesting a waiver of "our agreed policy of not accepting for admittance athletes of non-revenue sports, whose score is less than 650 on the College Board"? When Dooley testified later in the trial, he undermined Trotter's credibility further by confirming that waivers like the one involving the non-revenue-producing track athlete were common.

During the trial, I assumed Trotter was simply trying to minimize her own culpability by not answering the questions being asked - claiming she had no memory of an event or that she would have to review records. She also gave confusing, sometimes nonsensical testimony such as her response to a question asking for the terms of a particular policy of hers. "There was no policy - no non-policy on that . . .  I don't remember, one, two, three." She also answered another question asking if all students were special. Her curious response was, "Absolutely. It depends on the context." During her testimony in the earlier hearing on our application for a preliminary injunction, Trotter had famously responded to a question about the volume of preferential treatment of athletes by claiming, "I would rather err on the side of making a mistake." That quote was picked up by *The New Yorker* magazine and published under the heading, "On a Clear Day in Academia."

I later found out from the Regents' post-trial audit of Developmental Studies that Trotter had other motives for her evasiveness - to protect Davison without committing perjury. She feared that she or Davison or both might be asked about his knowledge of the preferential treatment of the student athletes. Little did she know that she was being set up as a scapegoat by Davison and his inner circle. Had Davison been asked, he intended to falsely deny that he had any knowledge of her approvals of the many violations of the letter and spirit of the Regents' rules.

The irony of Trotter's dilemma was that we had no intention whatsoever to point the finger at Davison. Ervin and Trotter both admitted that they were the ones who demoted and then fired Jan. When high level officials admit that they caused the harm, the best legal tactic is to accept those admissions and go no further, particularly if accusing others might erode the jury's certainty about who in fact did fire her. There was no evidence that Davison had any role in the actual firing, so it would have been ill-advised to introduce a questionable argument which tended to exonerate the defendants on trial by providing them with the Nuremberg defense - "I was just following orders." Even worse, the jury may have decided that the decision to fire Jan was in fact Davison's - and guess what - he wasn't a defendant. So, we avoided any suggestion that Davison participated in the challenged personnel decisions. But there was no doubt that he was on trial in the court of public opinion. We did fight that battle, but only outside the courtroom.

We ended the presentation of our case leaving the impression shared by the faculty that Vince Dooley dictated Developmental Studies' admissions policies regarding athletes without interference from UGA's president or any of its high level academic leaders. Trotter did her utmost to protect all of them during her testimony - a decision that she must have regretted when she heard the jury's verdict.

Our case in chief was complete. I was privileged to make the announcement that all plaintiffs' lawyers love, "Your Honor, the plaintiff rests." It was time to hear and challenge the defense.

## CHAPTER TWENTY-SEVEN
## KEMP TRIAL PUBLICITY AND PROTEST

By the end of the second week, the Kemp trial was attracting the national media. In addition to the reporters for the Atlanta, Athens and Macon newspapers, reporters from *The New York Times*, the *Los Angeles Times*, the *Miami Herald*, and the *Orlando Sentinel* attended portions of the trial. Georgia news media represented by reporters included all three Atlanta television stations, the *Atlanta Journal Constitution*, *Morris Communications* (Athens, Savannah, Augusta, and Jacksonville newspapers). *Sports Illustrated* published a January 1986 article on the Kemp case as the third week of the trial was about to begin.

UGA's campus reaction and outrage was also attracting media attention from the *Athens Banner Herald* and UGA's student newspaper, *The Red and Black*. Students were watching. On January 28, two hundred students demonstrated in freezing weather in front of Davison's office. They carried a variety of signs such as "Trotter Gate," "Bulldog Blues," and "Give Truth a Chance." They called upon Davison to appear and address their concerns. He ignored their request. The angry mood of the crowd was summarized by a senior student who told a *Red and Black* reporter, "I believe in quality education and our diplomas are at stake here. I didn't go here for four years just to have someone shit on my diploma." The students ended their demonstration with a march across the campus chanting,

"Hell yes, it's a mess!"

Georgia's Governor Joe Frank Harris also reacted noting that the trial was leaving unanswered questions which were creating negative reactions to UGA that he promised "will be answered." The misdeeds of UGA's administration were under an intense spotlight. The defendants were losing the public relations battle in dramatic fashion. Georgia's political establishment was alarmed. There were going to be consequences regardless of the outcome of the trial.

We wondered out loud among ourselves about how UGA's besieged administrators might react in the public arena to daily headlines about academic corruption, mistreatment of athletes, favoritism for the children of wealthy or politically connected families, and the cynical motives that were being exposed in the trial. Surely their public relations machines were gearing up to play Trotter's and Ervin's upcoming defense presentation to the hilt. It never happened!

# CHAPTER TWENTY-EIGHT
# THE DADDY WITNESSES

## Isaac Levy

Almand opened his case with a peculiar move designed to rebut Jan's testimony about ML, the student that she prosecuted through the student judiciary for making a profane telephone call to her home. Rather than calling ML to testify, Almand called his father, Isaac Levy, who had no direct knowledge of any relevant evidence. His testimony included a rendition of his efforts to have Davison vacate the student judiciary's verdict of guilty. He also gave hearsay testimony about ML's denial of making the profane phone call that Jan had testified about.

Levy was a graduate of UGA's School of Law practicing in Jacksonville, Florida. He was also a member of UGA's President's Club - a membership that he purchased for a $25,000 life insurance policy payable to the UGA foundation.

ML was initially denied admission to UGA by the Developmental Studies Admissions Committee. Levy reacted by contacting and then meeting with Ralph Beaird who introduced him to Ervin. Sure enough, after that meeting, Ervin recommended an "administrative admission" which Trotter approved.

ML became one of Ervin's racquetball partners soon after

his arrival at UGA. His father also arrived at UGA in a sense. He volunteered to participate in Ervin's Developmental Studies Parental Involvement Program (PIP) which gave him personal access to Ervin - a dubious privilege which some faculty members opposed as another pathway to the influence peddling that was destroying the integrity of their program. Isaac Levy was a member of both of the non-athlete favored classes of citizens under Davison's regime: the wealthy and the politically influential.

Jan was ML's English teacher. His first quarter performance was dismal, not only in English, but across the board in all of his Developmental Studies classes. She had received an abusive and profane phone call from ML which led her to file charges that were ultimately sustained in a student judiciary hearing in which ML was found to be guilty.

Levy was incensed. His son was not only charged, he was also convicted and sentenced to a one quarter suspension of his student I.D. and 10 days of "work discipline" at a local nature center. Refusing to accept that judgment, Levy decided to go straight to Davison to insist that he vacate it. Levy made numerous trips to Athens and phone calls to Davison's office, and then met with him personally.

Levy's testimony neither proved or disproved anything about the validity of charges against ML or the integrity of the student judiciary. His understanding of the facts was based on what his son told him coupled with his contempt for Jan who demanded consequences for ML's misconduct.

During Levy's cross-examination, he admitted that he

donated money directly to Ervin on two occasions, and then contacted him about the charges against his son. Levy said that Ervin promised him that he would investigate and suggested that he contact others at the University. Levy followed that advice. During one of his six trips to Athens, he got into a heated argument about ML's case with personnel in the academic affairs office. Later he met with Davison in the president's office. Levy told Davison that he "would do whatever action was necessary to bring this matter to a head." After that meeting, Levy received a letter from Davison reporting that he had reduced ML's punishment to an oral reprimand and had ordered the records of the student judicial decision to be purged from UGA records. As it turned out, Davison was even more generous to ML. No oral reprimand was ever imposed, and Davison ordered his Executive Assistant Jim Kenney to return ML's student I.D. to him immediately.

Levy acknowledged that ML's grades improved from the Fall Quarter's two "Fs" and a "D" to two "Bs" and a "C" after he was disciplined. He also admitted that ML used profanity when he told him about the charges Jan had filed against him.

Levy's testimony was naturally biased in favor of his son, but he made several serious mistakes that likely diminished his credibility with the jury.

First, he claimed that the law student that represented ML at the student judiciary hearing, whose name he couldn't remember, told him that Kemp had talked to the judges prior to the hearing - an uncorroborated hearsay statement by an unnamed law student. Almand never called the law student, the student judiciary judges, or any other witness to support Levy's assertions. Surely the jury must have wondered why no one with direct personal knowledge of such alleged gross misconduct by Jan and the student judiciary was available to testify. Almand and his team were experienced enough to understand that hearsay evidence was not persuasive, and they undoubtedly had the resources to locate ML's law student representative and the student judges - all of whom would have had personal knowledge of a breach of judicial ethics in the form of unauthorized communications with an interested party - if that was indeed the case.

Second, Levy, a wealthy experienced attorney, threatened to sue Davison via a "whatever is necessary" comment, thus demonstrating that he would cause trouble if he didn't get his way.

Third, Levy accused Jan under oath of being a racist in front of a majority black jury when he testified that "he (ML) felt that she resented that a black man was the coordinator of the program and she was subordinate to him." That outlandish accusation was lobbed before a jury who had heard Ronnie Stewart, a black football player who actually graduated from UGA, tell them, "There is not a finer person. Everything I know I learned from her." The jury had also already heard testimony in Jan's favor from Larry Blount, Fred Johnson, and Denise Ritter each of whom were also African American.

Unfortunately, this was not the defendant's only attempt to race bait - it was just the first of several outlandish plays using the race card that emerged throughout the rest of the defense case. Ervin's "she's a racist" strategy wasn't yet fully developed, but there was more to come - from Ervin himself.

We believed that Levy's appearance as the defendants' lead-off witness had actually shown the jury the picture we wanted the jurors to see: a wealthy influential person, a person whose son was admitted after being rejected by the Admissions Committee, a person who successfully demanded a meeting with UGA's president, a president who then intervened to decrease the punishment imposed by the student judiciary. Surely the jurors understood that regular people - people like them - would never have the leverage that the economically and politically elite possessed.

Although Davison capitulated to Levy to some extent, he refused to overrule the student judiciary's finding that ML had in fact made a profane phone call to Jan's home. He reviewed the student judiciary's case against ML and concluded that Jan's accusations against him had been proved.

Almand's lead off witness possessed no relevant evidence supporting any of Ervin's reasons for firing Jan as listed in his memo, all of which were limited to two categories: Jan's "failure" to engage in sufficient research and professional activities and her "disruptive" behavior for protesting the wholesale breach of UGA's academic integrity by the people responsible for protecting it. Levy's testimony proved nothing that mattered with one exception - he proved that the children of wealthy and influential citizens enjoyed immunity from the consequences of their misconduct. Every honest observer of Levy's testimony saw what we saw: Almand's lead off witness bombed.

Pat and I were somewhat astonished. Thanks to the credibility that our witnesses had brought to the case, we knew that Jan held a healthy lead when we rested, but we were both experienced trial lawyers who knew that trials are rarely so one-sided. We kept reminding each other that the defense would have good days too once Almand took control of the presentation of witnesses. So far, their first day wasn't one of them. Almand knew that he needed to open his case with a strong witness, like Levy, but his testimony ended up supporting Jan.

### Sheldon Leveston

Sheldon Leveston was Almand's second "daddy-witness." He was the father of a student who Jan identified by initials during her testimony. She had testified that the student made a statement to her to the effect that, "I'll tell you one thing. After my daddy bought my way into the University he didn't give that crook Leroy Ervin another dime." Of course, the father couldn't say whether that statement was true or not since he wasn't present when his son and Jan had that conversation. There was no reason Almand couldn't have called Leveston's son to the stand instead of his father who traveled from his home in Connecticut to testify that the statement attributed to his son couldn't be accurate because he never called him "daddy." We were so underwhelmed by this testimony we decided to just let the jury conclude the inescapable: Jan testified under oath that the statement was made. The only other witness to the conversation, the student himself, was inexplicably absent.

# CHAPTER TWENTY-NINE
# UGA POLICE PERSONNEL

Two UGA law enforcement employees - a former UGA police detective, Tim Stapleton, and UGA's Chief of Police, Asa Boynton, each took the stand to testify about the police investigation of Jan's charge against ML. They testified that they didn't believe there was sufficient evidence to bring criminal charges against ML and thought it should be handled in the student judiciary. Jan agreed. In fact, former Detective Stapleton, their witness, testified that Jan wanted to process the case through the student judiciary and that he found her to be "truthful and straightforward."

Asa Boynton was the police chief when the incident involving ML occurred, but he had been promoted to the position of Director of Public Safety by the time of his testimony. He testified that he was contacted by Ervin, whom he described as a personal friend. Ervin asked Boynton to speak to ML's father which he agreed to do.

Boynton also testified that he had conferred with Detective Stapleton, advised him that the evidence gathered was insufficient to file a criminal charge, and recommended referral of the case to the student judiciary. We didn't challenge the testimony of Stapleton or Boynton since Jan agreed with Boynton's assessment of the weight of the evidence as insufficient for purposes of a criminal prosecution.

Apparently, Almand's purpose for calling these witnesses was to contradict Jan's deposition testimony that Detective Stapleton told her that Ervin had asked Boynton to drop the case against ML. Stapleton denied making that statement, but he admitted during his cross-examination that there could be some confusion because there was a second police detective who actually opened the case and conducted the initial interviews. At a minimum, Detective Stapleton's cross-examination established that whatever was said to Jan by one or the other police detectives involved in the case wasn't clear.

Almand failed to deliver a single punch in his effort to demonize Jan's handling of ML's misbehavior, but that was only the beginning of a very bad day for the defense.

# CHAPTER THIRTY
# STRAIGHT FROM THE PRESIDENT'S OFFICE

Almand's next witness left little doubt that Davison had panicked. No trial lawyer with Almand's experience would ever put that witness on the stand in the absence of pressure from Davison. The witness was Sue McCaffrey. She was married to Jim Kenney, Davison's Executive Assistant. As such, he was at the epicenter of Davison's inner circle. Kenney was dubbed the "Undertaker" by some lower level administrators for two reasons: he was Davison's designee to deliver career death notices to disfavored employees, and his physical appearance fit the nickname - a short man with a stern facial expression who was always wore a black suit.

Kenney kept a low profile, but people who had dealt with him understood that he was Davison's enforcer. When he arrived at the door of any Davison adversary, three conclusions were inescapable: he was bringing a message directly from Davison, it was very bad news, and it was final.

McCaffrey was hired in 1971 to teach Library Orientation which was an elective course available to all UGA undergraduates including Developmental Studies students. *Macon Telegraph and News* reporter Randall Savage identified the Library Orientation course in his Pulitzer Prize winning articles on academics and athletics at UGA as a "mick" - the lingo that identified easy courses. McCaffrey was promoted in 1981 to the position of Assistant Director of Developmental Studies. Placing her in that position provided Davison with a confidential link through her husband to the internal affairs of Developmental Studies.

Carolyn Smith was McCaffrey's former graduate assistant in a 1981 Library Orientation course. Neither was scheduled to testify in the trial, but McCaffrey recruited Smith to corroborate her testimony and both showed up as defense witnesses. So, how was it that these newly discovered witnesses came to Almand's attention?

McCaffrey's story began with a discussion about the Kemp case with her husband after she "remembered" that she suspected that Jan had ghostwritten a student athlete's paper for a course she taught six years earlier during the Winter Quarter of 1980. Her "proof" was a term paper in her class that was turned in by one of Jan's students, and a subsequent meeting with Jan and Carolyn Smith.

Jan spent many hours working with the student to improve his writing skills, and her efforts paid off. So, she was puzzled when she learned that the student was failing McCaffrey's elective course. The student was making great progress in her class, so Jan asked for the meeting with McCaffrey who told her that the student was habitually absent, and his work product was poor. McCaffrey told the jury that Jan must have written the paper because it was "perfect." She thought Jan was aggressive during the meeting.

After discussing her recollection of that meeting with

her husband, McCaffrey contacted Almand to recount her story in case he wanted to use her and her former graduate assistant as witnesses. Her subsequent interview with Almand was the first time that she disclosed Jan's alleged misconduct to anyone other than her husband who undoubtedly passed her story on to Davison.

Pat was sitting next to me as we listened to McCaffrey's testimony. I glanced at him to check his reaction. He was staring at her, jaw dropped and eyes wide open. Then he passed me a note, "Let me take this one on cross!!!" I nodded my okay. This was a cross examiner's dream scenario. Pat certainly deserved the opportunity to rip McCaffrey's testimony to shreds, and that was exactly what he did.

We got a lucky break to segue into a devastating cross-examination that Almand himself set up. McCaffrey voiced her opinion that the student could not have written a "graduate level" paper given his failure in virtually every component of the Library Orientation course requirements except the term paper. Almand capped that testimony with a question that he may have regretted asking when he heard McCaffrey's answer:

Q. What grade did the student finally receive for the course?

A. Well, he took the final examination and flunked the final exam, but when I averaged out the homework assignments and the paper, he made a "D". He passed the course.

I could hardly believe what I thought I had just heard. A college instructor, who claimed to have a reason to believe that a student paper was ghostwritten by a UGA faculty member, included the "perfect" score on the supposedly plagiarized work product to arrive at a passing grade for the dishonest student. There couldn't have been a better opportunity to destroy the credibility of a witness.

Pat began his cross-examination by having McCaffrey admit that her husband, Jim Kenney, held his job at the pleasure of Davison. He had her repeat that she was certain that the student had not written the paper, and then asked, "What did you do about it?" McCaffrey answered, "Nothing." Pat was on a roll:

Q. So you could have gotten in touch with [the student], but you just didn't want to?

A. No.

Q. Did you talk to anybody else about it?

A. I talked to my graduate assistant about it.

Q. But you were so darn sure this wasn't his work?

A. I was at that time, and I still am.

. . . . .

Q. Besides your graduate assistant, when was the first time you ever talked to anybody about this?

A. I don't know. I don't remember talking to anybody else about it.

. . . . .

Q. Did Mr. Almand call you or did you call him?

A. I got in touch with him.

Q. Well, what prompted you to do that?

A. I felt like I needed to.

Q. To what?

A. Get in touch with him about this.

Q. After all these years?

A. Uh-huh.

Q. So you called Mr. Almand and told him that you suspected that six years ago Dr. Kemp may have ghostwritten a paper for some student?

A. Yes.

Q. But you didn't feel any need to talk to the student back in 1980? You didn't feel any need to talk to your department head?

A. No.

Q. Didn't feel any need to go to the student judiciary?

A. No. You can't prove something like that and in my department, you didn't discuss these matters with your department head."

Pat asked McCaffrey about her relationship with Ervin whom she claimed that she "only knew professionally." She acknowledged that she had written a letter of recommendation supporting his promotion and tenure.

To close his cross-examination, Pat dropped the question that the jury must have been waiting for:

Q. And this paper that we have talked about, do you, have it?

A. No. I gave back all papers and I don't remember whether I gave this student's paper back if he showed up or not. At the final exam, it was my practice to give back papers.

Q. You didn't make a copy or anything like that?

A. No.

Q. You thought it had been plagiarized but you didn't even make a copy of it.

A. No.

Brief redirect and recross-examinations reaffirmed that McCaffrey had done nothing for six years to disclose what she believed to be plagiarism. McCaffrey didn't even "remember" the alleged plagiarism until Jan blew the whistle on the systemic academic dishonesty of high level university officials.

Almand apparently didn't notice how implausible McCaffrey's story was when he called his next witness. "The defense calls Carolyn Smith, Your Honor."

Smith told the jury that she attended the meeting with Jan that McCaffrey had described and agreed in almost identical detail with her testimony. That was no surprise to us however because Almand interviewed McCaffrey and Smith together only a few days before they appeared as defense witnesses. Trial attorneys typically interview witnesses separately when they intend to testify about the same events to avoid any suggestion of witness collaboration in the preparation of their testimony. Almand's joint interview of McCaffrey and Smith was a gift to Jan because it raised an inference that their testimonies were coached to avoid inconsistencies.

Smith did have one surprise that McCaffrey had not mentioned. She testified that one of her students, RS, had also turned in a "perfect paper" that was prepared on paper carrying a UGA watermark. She elaborated—"the best paper I had gotten from students and that included freshmen through seniors at UGA and students from all the different schools within the university." She went on to state her opinion which was that Jan wrote the paper because she had brought up the student's name during the meeting with McCaffrey.

Pat then posed the obvious question, "What professional act did you take if you thought that you had a plagiarized paper in your possession?" Smith's answer was more than puzzling:

"I will be perfectly honest with you. I felt like it was a fault of my grading system that would allow this to happen, and I did not take any professional action on him." She went on to explain that the "professional act" that she did take was to change her grading system to divide the final paper into several smaller papers, and she thought that would discourage students from using plagiarized papers. Then Smith dug the hole a little deeper.

Q. But you didn't do anything about RS or FL?

A. No.

Q. You didn't contact your superiors?

A. No.

Q. You didn't contact the student judiciary?

A. No.

Q. You didn't even contact the students, did you?

A. No.

Q. Didn't even discuss it with him?

A. I didn't discuss it with my student because I felt like it was basically my fault for allowing him to do it.

Q. Did you ever bring any of these suspicions to Dr. Ervin's attention?

A. No. I did not.

Q. When was the next time you discussed either RS' or FL's paper with anyone?

A. I basically forgot it.

Q. Until when?

A. Until recently.

Q. Until how recently?

A. Until I was asked about it concerning this testimony.

Q. Ms. Kenney contacted you?

A. Yes. She did . . . The first time I heard any of this discussed was when I was contacted after this trial had started.

Q. By Sue McCaffrey?

A. Yes.

Q. What did she say to you?

A. She asked me if I would come to Athens and talk to someone about this.

Pat asked another obvious question, "Where is the paper for the jury to see?" Smith said she gave it back to the student, but that she had kept a copy that she threw away in 1982. According to Smith, McCaffrey never discussed taking any kind of action despite their belief that Jan had plagiarized the term paper for a student athlete.

McCaffrey and Smith never shared their respective plagiarized papers with one another, but since they had a joint interview with Almand, each obviously knew the content of the other's testimony despite being sequestered witnesses during the trial. Smith also admitted having two other conversations with McCaffrey about testifying but, "not in great detail."

The conduct of McCaffrey and Smith was not only self-destructive, the absurdity of their stories enhanced Jan's credibility. If Davison or Kenney actually knew of any other credible faculty member to blow the whistle on Jan, they wouldn't have dispatched those two to handle that job. Both testified that they had received term papers from students whom Jan was tutoring which were so "perfect" that they concluded that she had ghostwritten them. So, what did they do to remedy such a serious breach of basic academic standards? Surely no faculty member who ghost-writes students' papers should escape an investigation followed by severe discipline - probably termination of their contract for academic dishonesty. But there was not a peep out of these two until the trial was underway and was looking very dismal for Davison and his enforcer, Jim Kenney.

Neither McCaffrey nor Smith kept copies of the alleged ghostwritten papers; neither made any report to Jan's superiors; neither reported to their own department head; neither questioned the two students and neither confronted Jan. Neither did anything to expose their supposed discovery of a student paper that they believed Jan plagiarized. But then when Davison, the captain of Georgia's "flagship" university, realized that his ship was sinking, his Executive Assistant's wife suddenly remembered that Jan Kemp was an unpunished ghostwriter whom she was willing to point a finger at while under oath in a federal courtroom after remaining silent for years.

We didn't understand how Almand decided to use McCaffrey and her former graduate assistant to swear to such weak evidence. Obviously, Davison or one of his trusted advisors made that call and Almand fell in line. Davison and his allies made many mistakes behind the scenes, but this was a big one - eclipsed only by Davison's decision to testify as Almand's final witness several weeks later.

When McCaffrey and Smith finished, there was no doubt that they had inflicted substantial harm on the defendants' case. At best, they convicted themselves of academic negligence - plagiarism is not tolerated on American university campuses. I recalled what Davison's agents had done to David Dallmeyer: he falsely accused him of plagiarism which was grounds for termination of a faculty member's tenure. But in the Kemp case his Executive Assistant's wife goes to a Federal Court to swear that she failed to report plagiarism by Jan Kemp, but she isn't even mildly disciplined. Had any professor outside Davison's orbit ignored another faculty member's plagiarism of a student's paper, Jim Kenney would show up at that professor's office with bad news.

## CHAPTER THIRTY-ONE
## MARK HOGREBE

Almand's co-counsel, Randy Aderhold, conducted the direct examination of the next witness, Mark Hogrebe. Hogrebe reported directly to Ervin who hired him in 1979 as a research graduate assistant. In 1981, Ervin promoted him to the position of Developmental Studies Assistant Director for Research which he described in his testimony as a job to "stimulate research . . . teaching strategies . . . you know, as a stimulus to help do my own research and also to help others to do research." The reality however was that Hogrebe's actual job description, disclosed during his cross-examination, was to co-author research articles that Ervin was using for his own promotion and tenure resume. Virginia Trotter ultimately approved Ervin's research as sufficient to award him tenure.

I cross-examined Hogrebe to determine his relationship with Ervin - particularly any collaboration on research projects that were published with Ervin as a co-author. Hogrebe told the jury that they didn't publish articles while he was a graduate assistant for the first two years, but did "paper presentations" under both of their names. When asked who did the majority of the work on those projects, he said "mutual consideration," but then admitted that all of Ervin's contributions were "conceptual," and that, "Well, yeah, conceptual discussion. You know, as far as actually running the data and doing a lot of the actual write up, I did that." He agreed that he had never seen Ervin go to the library and that he, not Ervin, did all of the data analysis and all of the statistical calculations.

After becoming a full-time employee, Hogrebe published seven articles, six of which were co-authored with Ervin. All were listed in Ervin's promotion and tenure dossier that was forwarded to Trotter for approval.

Hogrebe was called to testify by the defense to attack Jan as a disruptive faculty member who opposed mandatory research functions for faculty members because Developmental Studies was strictly a "teaching component" program.

Hogrebe testified that Jan openly expressed her opinion that funding for a research coordinator, the position Hogrebe assumed in 1981, was a waste of money which should be allocated to new teaching assistant positions. Jan's opinion was not unique. A number of faculty members agreed with her. More importantly, Hogrebe failed to mention until his cross-examination that Jan had been appointed by Ervin to chair the committee charged with developing tenure and promotion guidelines. As such she had every right, if not obligation, to state her view of the relative weight of excellence in teaching and excellence in research when assessing Developmental Studies faculty members for promotion and tenure.

Jan didn't think Ervin particularly cared about tenure protection for the faculty, but that he was motivated by the desire to achieve national recognition for the program.

In fact, according to Hogrebe, Ervin wanted to institute a research component because "he felt that if he was going to make this into a nationally known type of a program it would also need a research function as we're part of a research institution." Jan and others correctly concluded that establishing research obligations for Developmental Studies was of minimal benefit to the program's mission which focused exclusively on teaching basic skills to marginal students. Moreover, Hogrebe acknowledged on cross-examination that the consensus of the members of the Promotion and Tenure Guidelines Committee was consistent with Jan's opinion. When asked on cross-examination if he, as a committee member, suggested ideas and concepts about developing research guidelines, Hogrebe replied "possibly but minimally – the group felt strongly that teaching was the main purpose and, you know – I – you know those initial guidelines did not really include anything about research that I recall."

On direct examination, Hogrebe had laid out his perception of issues that supported Ervin's decisions to demote and then non-renew Jan. He began with the allegation that Jan had demeaned Ervin's research by ridiculing him for installing research computers near his office so he could "play with the terminals." On cross-examination, I asked Hogrebe if he himself had similarly ridiculed computers by virtue of a plaque on his office door reading, "To Err is Human. To Really Foul Things Up Requires a Computer." He agreed that it was kind of funny, and that people who work with computers are as lighthearted about workplace humor as people in other endeavors. What he didn't remember was that Jan had given him the plaque, but he did agree that he considered it a joke regardless of who gave it to him. So, when fully vetted about her "ridicule" of computers, it became obvious that the joking by Jan about computers did not become a personality flaw until Ervin desperately needed it to become one.

Hogrebe also testified that Jan was "disruptive" and "combative" in committee meetings. However, he added that "interaction and some disagreement" occurred in any type of faculty meeting. I asked him to elaborate about disagreements by others involving "disruptive and combative" behavior, specifically by Ervin:

Q. Let me ask you about the coordinator meeting when you said you thought Jan was carrying arguments to a non-productive point.

A. Yeah.

Q. You told Ms. Pearson [the attorney who took Hogrebe's deposition] that Mr. Ervin did the exact same thing in those meetings, didn't you, it was a two-way street?

A. Yes. I mean, obviously when you get off on a tangent - yeah.

Q. So, the same criticism that you would level at Jan, you would level at Leroy Ervin also?

A. I would say they were initiated by Jan, and you know they were carried out by both parties.

Q. In an inappropriate fashion?

A. In my mind.

Q. Leroy Ervin, too?

A. Yes, to the extent they engaged in them.

Hogrebe also testified that faculty meetings remained "lively" after Jan left. Aderhold obviously elicited that answer to show that the faculty's free speech rights hadn't been chilled by Jan's termination. Later, on cross-examination, Hogrebe acknowledged that Jan was the only faculty member who threatened to go to the press with her complaints about the misuse of Developmental Studies.

Aderhold ended the direct examination by asking Hogrebe about Ervin's "reputation for truth and veracity." He said it was "good." Aderhold turned Hogrebe over to me for cross-examination.

The last answer was a good one for me to begin his cross-examination. Proof of reputation, good or bad, is a peculiarity in the law of evidence. It actually requires the witness to give hearsay evidence of what others said about the subject's character - not what the witness knows first-hand. That oddity creates the right to ask the sources of the "reputation" that the witness swears exists. Since the jury had already heard a number of faculty members describe Ervin's bad reputation as an untrustworthy person, I asked Hogrebe if he had made any effort to determine his colleagues' opinions about Ervin's reputation. His response revealed that he had asked no one about Ervin's reputation, so there was no basis for his opinion that it was "good."

Q. Did you ever ask Hyta Mederer about his reputation?

A. No, I had very little interaction with Hyta.

Q. Did you ever ask Ruth Sabol about his reputation for truth and veracity?

A. No.

Q. What about Annice Ritter, did you ask her?

A. No.

Q. Fred Johnson?

A. No.

Q. Who did you ask?

A. Nobody.

Hogrebe then agreed that he understood the difference between his personal opinion of someone and that person's "reputation." Pressed further to name people he talked to who voiced any information about Ervin's truthfulness and veracity, Hogrebe first answered, "the community at large." Pressed further for names, he finally said, "Ted Miller, an administrator in the College of Education." When asked when he had that conversation he responded, "Specifically about his reputation?"

Q. Well, now you did testify that you knew his reputation and that it was good, so I'm asking you about the basis of that now. You mentioned Ted Miller as a person you spoke to about his truthfulness, is that correct?

A. I - Okay, I did not specifically ask him about his opinion of Leroy's reputation.

Q. In fact nobody had ever told you that they thought Leroy was a truthful person, have they?

A. Those specific words?

Q. Right.

A. No.

Obviously, no one on the defendants' legal team had prepared Hogrebe for cross-examination on his testimony that Ervin had a good reputation for truthfulness. Like most experienced litigators, we had specifically instructed our "bad character" witnesses to ask others about their opinion of Ervin's character to prepare them for the expected cross-examination regarding the sources of their opinions.

We turned to Ervin's timeline for initiating the promotion and tenure guidelines for Developmental Studies which Hogrebe stated occurred in the Spring of 1982, thereby fixing the Regents' "up or out" seven-year deadline for Jan in 1989 or 1990. He added "I was not aware of much research going on at all in the division." These answers cast doubt on the defense's argument that Jan was fired by Ervin for failure to make sufficient progress in research. She was not the only faculty member who argued against a research component to the tenure requirements in Developmental Studies, but Ervin selected her alone to discharge for not making sufficient progress in research during the first year of what would be a seven-year time frame for acquiring tenure. Hogrebe acknowledged that, "when Ervin appointed Jan Kemp to chair the Committee on Promotion and Tenure Guidelines, he knew that she felt it was a teaching component and research should be deemphasized."

Q. Were you on the committee drawing the promotion and tenure guidelines?

A. Yes.

Q. Who developed them?

A. The committee.

Q. Did it have any emphasis on the fact that you were a teaching component?

A. Yes.

Q. And that was the consensus of the committee?

A. Yes.

Q. And that it would be foolish to emphasize research over teaching in Developmental Studies?

A. Yes.

Q. And you agreed with that?

A. Yes.

I turned the discussion to Ervin's contention that Jan failed to do sufficient research to satisfy the tenure and promotion standards. We introduced a memo into evidence from Hogrebe to the faculty notifying them of a scheduled

March 10, 1982 session by him entitled, "How to begin thinking about a research project?" That memo was dated approximately five months before Ervin non-renewed Jan's employment contract. At that point in time Jan had at least five years to satisfy the "up or out" limit of 7 years as an assistant professor which rank she attained in 1980. Moreover, Ruth Sabol, and defense witnesses Hogrebe - and later Bluie Diehl - agreed that Jan was working on a textbook which was a research project. Given those facts, it was more than obvious that Ervin was holding Jan alone to standards of time-consuming research activity within five months of notice to the faculty "to begin thinking about research."

# CHAPTER THIRTY-TWO
# MAY SMITH

Almand recalled May Smith for additional cross-examination as a ""hostile" witness to dispute her earlier testimony during her direct examination. The testimony of a "hostile" witness is considered an extension of their initial cross-examination.

Almand began by asking Smith to elaborate on the Developmental Studies faculty's 1976, 1977 and 1978 decisions expanding the program from one to four quarters subject to its Admissions Committee rule limiting students to a maximum of two quarters to earn at least a "D" in each course. He reminded her of her earlier testimony that the expansion of the program was only intended to accommodate athletes despite the fact that a number of non-athletes also needed additional quarters to exit into the normal curriculum.

Q. Is it your testimony that that is the reason the program was expanded from one to four quarters was to accommodate the athletes. Is that your testimony?

Smith's response was probably disappointing to Almand:

A. My experience with it is that the policies were made by violating previous policies. They were rarely made until a violation occurred and then the violation usually, as far as my memory leads me to believe, involved an incident over an athlete.

Almand then asked Smith if she agreed with his observation that there were a number of non-athletes who used up to four quarters to exit the program.

Smith responded:

A. There were students who did not meet exiting criteria every quarter and the decision would have to be made whether to exclude these students. If there were athletes on the list they got preferential treatment. We would call meetings and discuss just the athletes.

Almand quickly shifted the discussion to Smith's previous testimony regarding AA, a football player. His grades for three quarters were insufficient under the Admissions Committee's grading rules for him to remain in the program for a fourth quarter. Since he was an athlete, a faculty meeting was called to consider whether to grant him a fourth quarter which would be the Fall Quarter of 1978 - football season. In her earlier testimony, Smith had recalled a comment made by another faculty member during that meeting that AA had made a good play in a Georgia-Georgia Tech game. The faculty granted AA's petition to remain in the program for a fourth quarter. The problem with that testimony was the fact that the Georgia-Georgia Tech game wasn't played until the following football season several months after the faculty meeting.

After the press reported Smith's testimony, AA was interviewed for his response. In addition to his reaction to Smith's testimony, AA told reporters that he had "exited"

Developmental Studies after the preceding Spring Quarter. That testimony contrasted with the faculty's decision to grant him a Fourth Quarter in the program - not an exit into the normal curriculum. On the other hand, it corroborated the testimony of other witnesses who described a pattern of granting additional quarters and exits to student athletes who had failed to satisfy Admission Committee standards.

Smith explained that she may have been confused in her recollection in her original testimony. She said that AA had made a good play in a previous game, but she "remembered it as the Georgia-Georgia Tech football game because this was the one I associate with this student."

Almand continued to challenge Smith's honesty by asking, "In fact, at the time that play was made, the student was not even in Developmental Studies, was he?" That was true, but Smith finished the thought: "He was given another quarter, but he might have chosen not to take it. He probably, and I am just saying probably, highly probably, was given an administrative exit at the end of his third quarter." That testimony was likely correct given the pattern of administrative exits granted for athletes by Ervin and Trotter without faculty consent. It corroborated Smith's belief that AA was afforded preferential treatment.

Then Smith turned the tables on Almand by reminding him of his successful objection to her original testimony about AA's big play, since it was hearsay and the jury was instructed by the judge to ignore it.

Smith had also previously testified about another student athlete, GW, who received a grade change in a regular curriculum Introduction to Sociology course from an "F" to a "C", despite the fact that he attended only two lectures before he stopped going to class, never took a single test, and never turned in mandatory course work. She told the jury that Steve Ender, a Developmental Studies counselor and tutor, convinced GW's professor to change his final grade to a "C" from an "F." Ender denied Smith's allegation.

Almand cross-examined Smith on the details of the preferential treatment of GW. He produced GW's UGA records that showed that GW's final Sociology grade of "F" was changed to a withdrawal grade designated as a "W." Smith contended that the final grade had to have been changed after she examined GW's records that showed the final grade as a "C." None of this mattered to us or, as it turned out, to the jury. The change of the grade to a "W" was preferential treatment for GW because it removed the "F" from his records which would have lowered his overall grade point average (GPA). Normally, the final grade of a student who stopped attending class, stopped taking tests and failed to do mandatory course work would be a "WF", which would lower his grade point average.

Our redirect examination of Smith revealed additional evidence that showed the jury that while GW may have been a great athlete, he never actively pursued a college degree while attending UGA. Pat introduced GW's complete records for Smith to review for the jury as evidence of the methods used by the Athletic Association to shelter athletes who didn't have the ability to earn a college degree.

Those records portrayed a college "mick" course curriculum designed to maintain GW's eligibility to play football, which in turn generated millions of dollars in revenue that funded the salaries of coaches and Athletic Association management personnel that dwarfed faculty salaries.

In his first quarter in regular curriculum classes (Fall 75), GW received an "F" in History, a "Satisfaction" in P.E., and a "D" in Speech for a GPA of .5 which put him on scholastic probation. He raised his GPA to .96 in his second quarter. In his third quarter (Spring 76) he made "Bs" in First Aid, Personal Communications, and Health Problems. He also took two P.E. courses. The three "Bs" raised his GPA to 1.45. He was still on academic probation. GW returned to Developmental Studies (Summer 76). He took three courses that did not factor into his GPA which remained at a 1.45 GPA. The following quarter (Fall 76), GW took two P.E. courses which left his GPA at 1.45. His academic standing at that point in time mandated his dismissal from the University. Nevertheless, GW was readmitted to Developmental Studies (Winter 77) where he took an English course that did not factor into his GPA. He was also allowed to take the regular curriculum Sociology course that resulted in a grade of "F", which was then changed to a "C." After Smith confronted the professor whom she believed changed GW's grade from an "F" to a "C," his final grade was changed to a "W." The following quarter (Spring of 77), GW took special studies courses in English, Math and Psychology resulting in a GPA of 1.51. During the following quarter (Summer of 77) he took Beginning Workshop and Psychology scoring a "C" in each course, which raised his GPA to 1.6. GW remained on academic probation for the next two quarters (Fall of 77 and Winter of 78) during which he raised his GPA to a 2.01. That GPA cleared him from academic probation. During those two quarters, GW took courses in Industrial Safety, Safety, Nutritional Ecology, and two P.E. courses. By the end of the Fall Quarter of 1979, GW's GPA fell to 1.71. He was placed on academic probation again, and he was dismissed after one more quarter (Fall 79). Nevertheless, he was allowed to re-enroll for the Winter Quarter of 1980 but dismissed later. He never received the college degree that was implicitly promised in exchange for his athletic prowess.

# CHAPTER THIRTY-THREE
# DEFENSE FACULTY AND STAFF WITNESSES

Almand turned his presentation to an attempt to discredit the faculty members who testified in the presentation of Jan's case. Three witnesses testified—one by deposition.

## Steve Ender

The defense used Steve Ender's deposition to enter his trial testimony. He was a staff member involved in counseling and tutorial services for Developmental Studies students. Ender left UGA in 1979. His forty-two transcript pages of testimony amounted to almost nothing. He gave confusing testimony regarding the maximum number of quarters allowed for students to exit Developmental Studies after it had been conclusively established that athletes were first given an unauthorized fifth quarter, and then a sixth and so on up to eleven quarters. Ender stated his rationale for approving such abuse: "Higher Education is not geared to time limits. The system we set up is not conducive to a developmental student. All people can learn, but all people take various amounts of time to learn." The jury had already heard the testimony, not from staffers like Ender, but from the faculty in the trenches who unanimously agreed that the extra quarters and administrative exits afforded athletes was a scam. The victims were the student athletes who were not "better off" after their inevitable failure to graduate.

Surely, the jury had not forgotten that reality as clearly described by Ruth Sabol during her testimony - "It's a tragedy. They do not understand that the university doesn't expect them to graduate. It's a tragedy."

## William "Bluie" Diehl

William Diehl was a former Reading Coordinator who was called by the defense to criticize Jan's work on a textbook as acceptable research for purposes of acquiring tenure. We were able to undermine Diehl's testimony with a letter that he wrote to Kathryn Blake, the Chair of the Developmental Studies Promotions and Tenure Guidelines Committee on May 29, 1981. That letter stated, "Consequently, faculty members in Special Studies are engaged in a number of research and service activities. These activities tend to be limited because of constraints imposed by our instructional demands. Therefore, while we will continue to engage in some research and scholarly activity, we feel that the mission of our division precludes the attainment of a high level of performance in areas other than instruction."

Diehl also corroborated Jan's testimony that she was working on a textbook to satisfy any research requirements that might be encompassed by the new promotion and tenure guidelines under consideration by the committee charged with drafting those guidelines. On direct examination by Almand, Diehl challenged Jan's research production as "more exercise material and less instructional material than a textbook," but he flatly contradicted that assertion on cross-examination when he admitted that he had not reviewed her work product except in a cursory fashion while sitting on the witness stand during his direct examination. Upon closer review of Jan's work product while being cross-examined, Diehl finally admitted that the accordion folder containing her research was a "textbook in progress."

### Becky Galvin

Almand's next witness was Becky Galvin, yet another family member of a high level UGA official appointed by Davison. She was the daughter of Perk Robins, UGA Vice President for Research and Development. Galvin was the coordinator of UGA's tutorial programs. Her husband, Mark Galvin, was employed as a UGA School of Law recruiter. His boss was Ralph Beaird.

Galvin testified on direct examination that she had never said anything negative about Jan Kemp until her husband told her a prior witness had testified that Kemp said Galvin got her UGA job only because she was Perk Robins' daughter. She decided that Jan "would say anything" and that she no longer believed her and was offended by the press painting Jan as "sweet, innocent and lily white."

Galvin testified that she found Jan intimidating, aggressive and very self-assured. Then she added that she wasn't intimidated by Jan "because I've grown up a lot in the last four years."

One example of Jan's alleged misbehavior according to

Galvin occurred at a wedding bridal shower. She claimed that Jan gave her two gifts - a shower gift and a gag gift. The gag gift was a condom wrapped like a piece of candy. Galvin said that other people whose names she couldn't remember were present and she was very embarrassed. No witness corroborated that testimony, and Jan denied Galvin's condom story during our rebuttal after the defense rested. Then in the surrebuttal by the defense, Almand called a Developmental Studies secretary to corroborate Galvin's testimony, but that didn't happen. Instead the witness testified that Galvin herself brought a condom to the secretarial pool and showed it to a number of clerical workers and faculty members.

Galvin also admitted that she discussed trial testimony from other witnesses with her husband, who sat in on the trial for two days prior to her testimony. I thought that was a violation of the "Rule of Sequestration" which is intended to prohibit witnesses from learning of the testimony of other witnesses. Since Galvin knew she was going to be a witness and admitted discussing the trial testimony with her husband, I made a motion, outside the presence of the jury, to hold her in contempt for discussing trial testimony of other witnesses with her husband.

Judge Ward denied my motion because the Rule of Sequestration doesn't apply to courtroom spectators, but he admonished, "The audience is technically not within my jurisdiction but they certainly ought to understand the instructions about testimony." Even though he denied the motion, Judge Ward criticized the defense by offering his assessment of Galvin's testimony: "I can't understand why they called her in the first place, but I'm not trying their case."

I realized once again how wise and measured Judge Ward was in handling a touchy situation. He didn't want to hold Galvin in contempt if he could avoid it. He probably thought she was being used. So, he announced a ruling that didn't really address the motion for contempt because he said the rule of sequestration didn't apply to "the audience." He skillfully ignored ruling on the issue raised by our motion, which was directed toward the witness's conduct - not the audience's - while simultaneously hinting that Galvin had nothing to say that helped the jury decide the issues being tried.

Galvin was the final witness for that day. We were pleased with the weakness of the defense presentations to date. None of their witnesses had damaged Jan's case.

# CHAPTER THIRTY-FOUR
# DAN AND KATE KIRBY

Dan Kirby was a Professor of Education who placed his graduate students in Developmental Studies as interns. He was married to a Developmental Studies non-tenure track instructor, Kate Kirby. She testified the same day shortly after his testimony.

Kirby testified that he was "frustrated" over philosophical differences between the teaching in Developmental Studies and the theories that his graduate students were learning in the College of Education. He admitted he had interacted professionally with Jan over several years, and they both knew that they had different teaching philosophies - hers was more traditional than his since she taught marginal undergraduate students while he taught graduate students seeking Master's and Doctoral degrees.

Once again, Almand didn't call the students who had direct knowledge of their work with Jan. Instead the defense relied on Kirby. He testified that his students who interned under Jan complained about her methods, but there was no record of any such discontent. Also, despite his "frustration" with her teaching philosophy, he admitted that he continued placing his students in Developmental Studies internships under Jan "over a period of years."

On cross-examination, Kirby acknowledged that Jan had been his graduate student, that he had served on committees with her, and that he always found her conduct to be appropriate. He also acknowledged that his wife was a non-tenure track '"dischargeable at will" instructor in Developmental Studies, and Leroy Ervin was her boss.

Kirby made a number of other admissions that damaged the defendants' case. He acknowledged that his graduate students never taught English in classes that had the revenue-producing athletes enrolled. They only taught students who were admitted through the normal faculty-controlled admissions process. Kirby also admitted that he had no knowledge concerning the effectiveness of Jan's methods to motivate the athletes. He didn't even know that revenue-producing athletes were being admitted under relaxed standards, and he didn't think revenue-producing athletes received preferential treatment.

Kirby also contradicted Ervin's insistence that Jan didn't have enough time to generate the "research" required to acquire tenure when he fired her in the Summer of 1982. He agreed that under UGA tenure and promotion policies, Jan would not have been eligible to go up for early promotion until 1985 and would then have had two additional years to acquire tenure. The jury had already heard testimony about the de-emphasis on research in the Developmental Studies promotion and tenure guidelines that were implemented in 1982. We had no doubt that the jury would find that Jan could have easily satisfied those guidelines if, as Kirby testified, she had a full five years from the Fall of 1982 until the Fall of 1987 to do so.

To close out his testimony, Kirby acknowledged that he

was angry when he learned of the exit of the nine revenue-producing athletes despite their failure to make passing grades in Developmental Studies courses within the four quarter time limits. He said he understood the faculty's anger, and believed Jan and other faculty members had an absolute right to speak out about it. With that endorsement of the heart and soul of our case, Kirby left the witness stand seemingly as "our witness." The jurors must have wondered why Kirby was called as a "defense" witness.

Kate Kirby was Dan Kirby's wife, and a non-tenure track reading instructor. Her testimony was of little value. Basically, she had a philosophical disagreement with Jan's stern grading policy and strict adherence to the standards of excellence that she believed were unrealistic in most of the cases involving revenue-producing athletes. She believed Jan was an "elitist," who maintained an "intolerance of students using language in less than sophisticated, mature ways." To her credit, she admitted that Jan was a good teacher whose success rate in the normal curriculum was quite high.

When Kate Kirby left the stand, we shrugged our shoulders. How did that help the defense? When were we going to endure one of the inevitable "bad days" that all honest trial attorneys expect - particularly in a lengthy multi-witness trial?

## CHAPTER THIRTY-FIVE
## SHERRIE NIST

Sherrie Nist was another insider who served at Ervin's discretion as the Acting Associate Director of Developmental Studies. Nist's fiancé was seeking a faculty position at UGA. She acknowledged that Ervin offered to help him by making a few calls to find out more about the search being conducted and to determine the identity of the favored candidate.

Almand called Nist to testify to her view of the research obligations imposed on all tenure track UGA personnel, but she disregarded Developmental Studies' mission and the teaching-oriented promotion and tenure rules developed by the program's internal Promotion and Tenure Committee. Instead, she described the standard tenure and promotion guidelines applicable to faculty members in UGA's thirteen Schools and Colleges. Nist's expansive view of the scope of research obligations by those in teaching-intensive positions was simply that—a meaningless opinion by a low-level administrator that was not shared by the faculty as whole, and was specifically repudiated by the committee that drafted the tenure-promotion guidelines for Developmental Studies.

When Almand turned to questions about her view of Developmental Studies' mission, Ms. Nist's testimony reached the absurd. He asked her if she knew the student athlete, SP. She answered that she did because she interviewed him when he entered Developmental Studies. She remembered that he told her, "I can't read; I can't write; I don't belong in college." Nist claimed that "his first goal was to be able to read the Martin Luther King 'I Have a Dream' speech for his grandmother." Smiling at the jury, Nist added that SP succeeded in that endeavor and also "read his first book."

The introduction of an MLK theme into the proceedings several days after the first MLK national holiday was obviously directed to the four African-Americans on the six-person jury. What the defense didn't appreciate however was the fact that those jurors were also sworn to find the truth. Moreover, those jurors had heard African American witnesses like Fred Johnson, Larry Blount, and Ronnie Stewart all attest to Jan's exemplary work with minority students. They recognized racial pandering and understood that race was not an issue in the case - it was a smokescreen. But the urge was too powerful for the defense to resist as we later learned when Ervin took the stand.

Soon after Nist's "I Have a Dream" testimony was broadcast on the radio, something happened back in Athens that confirmed our view of the minority jurors' likely reaction. My wife, Carole, was teaching in an Athens public middle school with a significant African-American population. That evening, she told me that she was interrupted mid-day while teaching by a tap on the classroom door. When she walked to the door, Carole saw one of her African American colleagues beckoning her, so she quickly stepped into the hall. “Carole, you’re not going to believe what I just heard on the radio. A witness for Ervin and Trotter just testified that a black student wanted to learn to read so he could read Martin Luther King’s ‘I Have a Dream’ speech to his grandmother. . . Just how stupid do they think we are?”

After hearing about that reaction, I knew for sure that race baiting was a big mistake. Just how stupid did the defendants think the jury was?

So, at that point, two white defense witnesses had introduced race in front of a majority African American jury, but the black athletes never made any such claim. In fact, throughout the trial, no minority witness, except Ervin, accused Jan of racism - a false and unfair charge to make against an exemplary teacher who was admired for her dedication to helping undereducated minority students succeed in acquiring the promised college degrees.

# CHAPTER THIRTY-SIX
# STUDENT ATHLETES CALLED AS DEFENSE WITNESSES

## Antonio Render

Antonio Render was a scholarship athlete who exited Developmental Studies after four quarters because he satisfied the exit standards. He was in his fifth year at UGA when he testified and was two quarters away from graduation. He was a football player who suffered a career-ending injury during his sophomore year.

Jan had testified that Render was one of the students who she thought was solicited by Ervin to slander her. She acknowledged that her beliefs about his role were based on what she had heard from others. Randy Aderhold called Render to the witness stand to testify for the defense that Ervin never asked him for a letter criticizing Jan. That was it. Nothing Render said contradicted Jan's testimony describing what she was told by others.

Although Render's testimony didn't prove anything helpful to the defense, it did rebut the argument that Jan's strict adherence to a stern educational agenda for her scholarship athletes was unreasonable and harmful. Curiously, Aderhold asked Render about his experience as a student in Jan's class, and Render delivered—for Jan, that is! He answered, "I would say she was a good teacher." Aderhold followed up: "How would you characterize her teaching techniques?" We couldn't have scripted Render's response any better. "I wouldn't say she was a hard teacher, but she made you work. She didn't make it easy for you. If you made a grade I think you had to earn it."

Pat leaned over toward me and whispered, "We need to send Hale and Randy a fruit basket!"

I cross-examined Render—it was a pleasure. His was a Developmental Studies student athlete success story. He was intelligent, polite, articulate, thoughtful and straightforward. He represented the best of what the faculty labored to achieve.

Q. You are two quarters away from graduation?

A. Yes, sir.

Q. You did say they (other athletes) were afraid of her grading?

A. I said that they said she was a tough teacher, meaning whether it was grading, attitude or whatever.

Q. She was a tough teacher?

A. Yes, sir.

Q. And you are glad she was a tough teacher?

A. Yes, sir.

Q. And it helped you, didn't it?

A. Yes, sir.

Q. You need that help, that sort of discipline?

A. Yes, sir, discipline.

Q. That English 101 is kind of a rough course, isn't it?

A. It was tough.

Q. That's the one that sort of makes or breaks folks over there, doesn't it?

A. Yeah, it does.

Q. You better be ready for it when you go in - and you were ready?

A. Yes, sir.

Q. Thanks in large measure to Jan Kemp?

A. Yes, sir.

Kenny Sims

Aderhold rose to announce his next witness. "Your Honor, the defense calls Kenny Sims."

The jury had already heard about Sims. Hyta Mederer, the Developmental Studies English Coordinator, had testified earlier that Sims, a talented football player, was in a one student class that she was assigned to teach during the Spring Quarter of 1983 after he had failed to exit the program, despite multiple extensions granted by Ervin and Trotter. There was a lot more to his story—all of which was about to be told.

The defendants' main purpose for calling Sims was

to introduce his March 29, 1982 letter, addressed "To Whomever It May Concern", seeking readmission immediately after he was dismissed from Developmental Studies. The three-paragraph letter read in its entirety:

"Dr. Kemp has told the class that it was so hot in the classroom that she feels like taking off her clothes."

"Dr. Kemp stopped the class and started telling about this man who mistook her for a prostitute and he offered her some money so she took off running."

"Dr. Kemp said she had been on birth control so long that her skin had spots on it. She told me this while I was in conference with her."

There was no specific addressee, no stated purpose, nor any suggestion of harm to Sims in the letter. In fact, Sims testified on cross-examination that he wasn't embarrassed by Jan's alleged statements, and that his only complaint was the waste of classroom instruction time that he needed to exit the program—a claim not mentioned in the letter. After introducing the letter, Aderhold asked Sims to read it but then changed his mind and asked him to read along as Aderhold read the letter. Normally, a witness reads a letter that he or she has written. The "read along" method left the distinct impression that Aderhold was concerned about Sims' reading skills. If so, that concern was shared by our faculty witnesses—all of whom saw Sims as a victim. They deplored the decision to put him under oath thereby identifying him by name in a high-profile case. Of particular concern to those faculty members, they also knew that Sims had admitted to two of their colleagues that Ervin pressured him to sign the letter that his secretary had prepared.

When Aderhold finished reading the letter, he asked Sims to verify its accuracy:

Q. Did I read it correctly?

A. Well, the last - the last one, it was like it wasn't directly to me, it was someone else.

Q. The last paragraph?

A. It was someone else.

Q. Was that not correct?

A. She did not tell me that.

The letter wasn't mentioned again by the defense.

Aderhold's next series of questions hardly cured that shaky start. He established that Sims had received an "F" in his first quarter English class at UGA in the Fall of 1981, and that Jan had been his teacher. Aderhold then skipped over the rest of Sims' academic record in the program by asking the follow-up question:

Q: But in any event, you took every one of the Developmental Studies English courses?

A. Yes, sir.

Then, avoiding any question about Sims' grades in the program, Aderhold jumped from his first quarter at UGA to his academic status at the time of his testimony over five years later.

Q. I believe that you have said that you are now out of Developmental Studies and you are regularly enrolled in the University.

A. Yes, sir.

Q. And you are working toward a degree?

A. Yes, sir.

Q. Okay, and would you tell us what that degree is?

A. Business Management.

Q. All right. Do you know how much longer it is going to take you to earn that degree in terms of time?

A. Two quarters.

Q. Okay. Is that your expectation at this point?

A. Yes, sir. Depending on my past and everything.

That final qualification was significant because it showed that Sims didn't understand his academic status at the time of his testimony.

Sims entered the normal collegiate curriculum in the Fall Quarter of 1983 via Trotter's "administrative exit" from Developmental Studies at the end of the Spring Quarter of 1983. He testified on January 30, 1986, one month into his seventh academic quarter in the normal college curriculum. He was five quarters short of the twelve needed to graduate. To be only two quarters short as Sims testified meant that he would have needed to take more than a full load every quarter with no failing grades while laboring under considerable time demands imposed by the football coaches. Nevertheless, he thought he would graduate after only nine quarters - three quarters short of the normal twelve needed to graduate. Sadly, Sims probably actually thought that he was about to graduate which was clearly not the case. I wondered why he was in the dark about his academic status, and more ominously whether he had been intentionally misled by those whose only interest in keeping him at UGA was to exploit his athletic prowess.

Aderhold then turned to the circumstances surrounding the preparation of the "To Whomever It May Concern" letter. Sims' explanation raised more questions than answers.

Q: Did you have occasion to write a letter stating complaints against Jan Kemp?

A. Well, I – - I had a letter complaining to get back in school, you know, saying why I deserved an extra quarter first.

Q. Okay.

A. But in the process, I had some complaints on my own because, you know, I think that during the English class I wasn't getting taught English, rather wasting time. At times it wasn't all English, you know.

Aderhold realized that Sims' first answer was about a different letter he wrote in response to the letter of dismissal he received after his second quarter in the program - not the "To Whomever It May Concern" letter that had been introduced into evidence. Both letters were dated March 29, 1982. Sims' letter requesting readmission was never introduced into evidence. Aderhold continued:

Q: I understand that you had to write a letter saying why you should be readmitted, but specifically I will let you look at a copy of a letter. (handing him the "To Whom It May Concern" letter).

Sims identified the letter. He initially stated that he "told" the content of the letter to Ervin's secretary for her to type, but later stated that he wrote it out for her to type. He then elaborated on how both letters were prepared:

Q. Go ahead.

A. He said the main thing I should do was to go ahead and put it on paper, and that's what I done. I wrote it on paper and I gave it to the secretary, and so what I had to do at first was write two letters. I had to write a letter to get reinstated in school because I had got kicked out. You know, for failing Dr. Kemp's class, and then I had complained about her, you know on my side, so I guess they had to bargain the two letters together to see which one, you know, how it states and see would they let me back in school.

Sims was obviously confused. He wasn't dismissed for failing the class Jan taught in the Fall Quarter of 1981. He was dismissed under the program's rules that required students who failed an initial core course to achieve at least a "D" in their second attempt. If Sims had made a "D" instead of the "F" in his Winter quarter of 1982 English class taught by Art Stanley, he wouldn't have been dismissed but would have been afforded two additional quarters to achieve the mandatory "C" grade needed to exit the English component of Developmental Studies.

It was obvious that Ervin never intended to use the "To Whom It May Concern" letter to support any academic decision regarding Sims. When he testified later in the trial, Ervin said that he told Sims that he would not use that letter unless other students in Jan's class corroborated his accusations. Neither Ervin or Sims ever made any attempt to seek that corroboration from his classmates which begged the question: Why was it prepared? The obvious motive was Ervin's desire to create a paper trail to attack Jan, and that is exactly what happened when Aderhold tendered the letter as an exhibit in the Jan Kemp trial.

Pat conducted Sims' cross-examination. He had a full understanding of his Developmental Studies records which pierced any suggestion that Sims was qualified to successfully complete the curriculum required to obtain a college degree. Pat laid it out by showing Sims his records, which led to his dismissal. Those records documented his successful appeal from his dismissal followed by two D's that he earned in third and fourth quarter English classes taught by Dr. Timmons in the Spring and Fall Quarters of 1982. Ervin then granted Sims a single student fifth quarter class in the Winter of 1983 with Dr. Mederer in which he earned yet another D followed by a sixth quarter English class "audit" in the Spring Quarter of 1983. Sims was granted an administrative exit from Developmental Studies via a stroke of Trotter's pen in June of 1983 despite his uninterrupted string of failures in the program.

Pat also pinned Sims down on the circumstances when he wrote the "To Whom It May Concern" letter.

Q. How long did this conversation (with Ervin) last about?

A. Well, 20 or 25 minutes.

Q. And during that 20 or 25 minutes you never told him what the complaints were?

A. No. He just told me to put it on paper.

Then Sims described how Ervin's secretary prepared the letter and Ervin told him to sign it. Pat asked him to state the timing of that event.

Q. Do you know about how long it was before you came over with your parents, how long it was between the time you wrote the letter and the time you came over with your parents?

A. When I wrote the letter, I came in that Monday [March 29, 1983] with my parents. That Wednesday I came back being reinstated in school.

So, Sims' testimony established that his parents met with Ervin on the same date that that he signed the letter, and Ervin reinstated him two days later.

Sims also harmed his own credibility as a witness when Pat asked him to identify the student who told him that Jan talked about her birth control skin spots in a student-teacher conference. Initially, Sims admitted that he recalled the student's name but "would rather not say" who he was. Pressed further to reveal the name, Sims contradicted his first answer and said, "It was in 1981 and I don't know what guy said it." Pressed further, he said, "I said I don't know what guy said it."

Although we welcomed the opportunity to expose the real story behind Sims' letter, we were disappointed that the defendants decided to put his name and face on public display to bolster their character attack strategy. The overriding feelings of our faculty witnesses were empathy for Sims and anger with Ervin for exploiting him, but they were determined to ensure that the truth was told even though their testimony would challenge Sims' truthfulness. The decision to put Sims on the witness stand was also a tactical disaster for the defense in the courtroom and in the court of public opinion.

When Sims left the witness stand, the undisputed evidence proved that the letter criticizing Jan was a *quid pro quo* for a promise of additional time to exit from Developmental Studies. The defense had bolstered our case. Sims' testimony pointed towards reasons other than fairness to him for the existence of the letter, and the jury was yet to hear additional admissions he made to the two faculty members about his reasons for signing that letter. There was no doubt that Sims was being afforded unjustified and harmful preferential treatment by Ervin with Trotter's approval while he was being groomed to be a hostile witness against Jan. The defendants' decision to involve Sims backfired badly. His story was another element of the Defense's character assassination strategy, but instead it ended up damaging Ervin's character. Sadly, it also exposed an innocent young man to intense legal scrutiny—a naive student who had made admissions to two faculty members whom he trusted that contradicted his trial testimony regarding Ervin's motive for soliciting the letter. Calling him to testify was a colossal mistake.

## CHAPTER THIRTY-SEVEN
## LEROY ERVIN

Leroy Ervin carried the ball for the defense starting on January 30th, a Thursday afternoon, and ending the following Tuesday morning. He presented himself as a very charming man - handsome, well-educated, and articulate. But beneath his public persona his behavior caused wholesale violations of UGA's academic integrity, usually at the behest of UGA's highest administrators and athletic leaders.

Ervin faced an abundance of adverse evidence pointing in his direction. His credibility was already damaged by the undisputed "bad reputation" evidence given by a number of faculty members. His conduct, as described by many witnesses, was downright unacceptable. He had a lot of explaining to do.

Ervin's first afternoon on the witness stand signaled his method of responding to most of the questions asked during his three days of testifying. He was verbose, self-serving, and intentionally vague at times when he knew if he answered certain questions correctly, his testimony would support Jan's case. Almand used most of the first afternoon having Ervin describe his education, employment history, and the Developmental Studies program at UGA. Then Ervin wrapped himself in the model of a sensitive and understanding collegiate administrator who labored under unrealistic Regents' policies. That testimony was intentionally understated since he was not authorized to ignore the Regents' rules, but it was apparent that he elevated his personal judgment over theirs in many instances. In fact, he expounded throughout that testimony on his ideas and actions to mitigate the stringent rules for revenue-producing athletes through extra quarters in the program, one student classes, and administrative exits.

As he testified, Ervin inadvertently demonstrated how many of the revenue-producing athletes were grossly unprepared for college. He told the jury that "even the lowest of the low, they move, they make progress. What we've been able to demonstrate is that you can move a kid one grade level per quarter, but if a kid comes in reading at a sixth-grade level you move him in four quarters and you only have him at a $10^{th}$ grade level." Later he elaborated when asked by Almand, "Can you expect more or can you not from the man that starts out ahead than the man that starts out behind?" Ervin responded, "The point is that the person who comes in at the fifth-grade level may move five grade levels, but if they have not reached the level needed to exit and another kid comes in at the eleventh grade and moves, you know, one grade level, the person then can exit, so you put that person at a disadvantage."

Ervin elaborated extensively on the differences between his leniently flexible philosophy for teaching scholarship athletes and Jan's insistence that they be judged by traditional standards applied to the other students in the program. What Ervin missed was that Jan wasn't the only person who disagreed with the practice of acquiring young men's athletic skills in exchange for a college education knowing they would never achieve that goal.

Ervin's strategy components emerged during the second day of his testimony: 1) he faced heartbreaking dilemmas resulting from the admissions of unqualified revenue-producing athletes, 2) his actions were good faith efforts to ease the brutal effects of the "revolving door" for those athletes, 3) his departure from Regents and UGA academic rules was based on his "philosophy" learned through his self-proclaimed "superlative" graduate level education, 4) he decided to terminate Jan's employment because of her alleged failure to conduct the research activity supposedly needed to advance toward tenure, and 5) he claimed Jan was disruptive.

Ervin's storyline had him caught in a vise between the strict application of academic rules and what he claimed were his ethical and moral obligations to the student athletes. He agreed that a special classification for revenue-producing athletes created a group of students who were unprepared to succeed academically, but he blamed Regents and UGA policy makers who allowed special admissions of those athletes. He argued that his motives were always pure. Given the burden imposed on him by the special admissions system, he said he just wanted to do whatever he could to stop or slow down the "revolving door" that many student athletes were forced to endure. He contended that his philosophy was based on his extensive experience and his research. He saw his role as the savior of the innocent victims of a corrupt system—an empathetic leader seeking remedies for those victims.

Near the end of the next morning, Almand asked Ervin to explain the presence of his signature on a grade change form for Veronica Walker in Barbara Carson's English class. Ervin blamed his Assistant Director, Sue McCaffrey. Ervin had given her the authority to sign his name on work related documents. The Davison to Kenney to McCaffrey silent telegraph line that Jan had described became visible. The jury saw the real possibility of Davison's invisible hand manipulating others into doing his dirty work to avoid having his fingerprints left at the scene of the crime

To close out the morning session, Almand fired a cheap shot at Larry Blount, Jan's representative at her grievance hearing. He asked Ervin to explain how Blount, an attorney and law professor, supposedly chose the wrong procedure needed to obtain a substantive grievance hearing for Jan. Ervin obliged. He donned his pseudo lawyer persona to vaguely challenge Blount's understanding of UGA's employee grievance process without specifying the correct process that he supposedly overlooked. Almand obviously understood that he couldn't use a real lawyer to offer accurate descriptions of multiple grievance forums which didn't exist.

Direct examination by Almand continued throughout the afternoon beginning with another lecture by Ervin on how his special education philosophy differed from Jan's. Ervin pictured himself as someone with the courage to adapt rules to accommodate unprepared student athletes.

He described Jan's strict adherence to academic standards as insensitive and unrealistic. On the other hand, he did tell the jury that he shared the faculty's disgust over the use of false promises of college educations to academically unqualified athletes solely for their economic value to UGA's Athletic Association. He had no wiggle room to avoid that conclusion however since the jury had already heard his characterization of the athletes as "raw material" on the Timmons tape.

Later in the day Almand turned the discussion to the exit of the nine athletes whom he characterized as the "best" example of Ervin's humane philosophy that he believed should prevail over the application of normal academic standards. Ervin claimed that the nine revenue-producing athletes were exited from Developmental Studies without achieving the mandatory minimum grades because they were among the "poorest of the poor": student athletes in their fourth and final Developmental Studies quarter struggling to achieve the mandatory "C" during the football season—an explanation that ignored their failing grades over four quarters, three of which were not during football season. Ervin not only ignored Regents' policies, he closed his eyes to the inevitable failures those unprepared young men would encounter in the regular curriculum - a reality that both he and Trotter had acknowledged on the Timmons tape.

The defense presented no evidence that any of the nine athletes graduated from UGA after exiting Developmental Studies without the faculty's consent. The only evidence of academic success by the program's revenue-producing athletes were the stories of our witness, Ronnie Stewart, and their witness, Antonio Render. Both played football, but they also worked diligently to exit Developmental Studies within four quarters as required and ultimately succeeded in earning their degrees. Both credited Jan's adherence to strict academic standards as critical to their success. We were confident that the jury understood that the defense strategy had nothing to do with the promise of a college education and everything to do with the millions of dollars these athletes generated for the benefit of the Athletic Association.

It appeared that Judge Ward found the reasons for the exit of the nine as preposterous as we did. After exhausting Ervin's weak excuses for that blatant abuse of academic standards, Almand remarked, "I want to switch to another subject matter, Dr. Ervin." Judge Ward expressed his opinion of that announcement: "You can as far as I'm concerned."

Almand moved on to what we considered the weakest of Ervin's defenses - an attempt to prove that Developmental Studies was a promotional unit meaning, among other obligations, that the faculty was required to supplement their teaching responsibilities with academic research. The purpose of Ervin's testimony was to create a framework for his claim that he fired Jan for failure to progress toward tenure, but his explanation was vague and confusing. He based it exclusively on his interpretation of the promotion and tenure rules without accurate documentary or testimonial corroboration. Ervin's opinion necessarily included two assumptions of fact regarding the Developmental Studies faculty that were demonstrably false: 1) that they were subject to the research requirements of the normal tenure track rules despite the fact that it was not a promotional unit, and 2) that they were also subject to the tenure track rule mandating the nonrenewal of their contracts if they failed to acquire tenure within seven years of their initial date of employment.

Although Almand had introduced the *Red Book*, the official compilation of UGA's promotion and tenure rules, into evidence earlier in the trial, he carefully avoided referring to it during Ervin's testimony. That omission was understandable. The *Red Book* specified the time limits on employment for tenure track and non-tenure track faculty members at seven and ten years respectively. Ervin simply ignored the ten-year time limit then applicable to non-tenure track faculty members and claimed that Jan was subject to the seven years "up or out" policy. He concluded that Jan could not possibly satisfy promotion and tenure standards based on his erroneous assumption that she had not even begun a research agenda. That claim however had already been impeached by his own witness, William Diehl, who acknowledged that Jan, unlike most of the program's faculty, was making research progress by writing a textbook.

Given the existence of the *Red Book* rules, it was understandable why no UGA official, including his co-defendant, Vice President for Academic Affairs Virginia

Trotter, corroborated Ervin's interpretation of those rules as imposing research responsibilities on Developmental Studies faculty members. Almand failed to call a single witness to dispute the testimonies of the flood of faculty members who swore under oath that they were all told that they were not tenure track employees, that they were employed in a teaching unit only, and that they were not obligated to produce research to retain their jobs. In effect, Ervin's contrary testimony implied that numerous faculty members with impeccable integrity had all committed perjury in a federal trial.

Almand briefly switched topics to a subject that actually underscored the pettiness of the reasons Ervin claimed for Jan's dismissal. Under his questioning, Ervin overstated his reasons for Jan's demotion and firing to include her noncompliance with his directive to establish a more elementary level '096' English class that was even more basic than the existing Developmental Studies' curriculum. The English faculty opposed lowering the academic standards in place which they felt satisfied the minimal requisites for any hope of success by their students in the normal collegiate curriculum. That reason for Ervin's crusade against Jan was also an afterthought. There was no hint of it in his "reasons" memo that we had flushed out when we called him for cross-examination as our first witness.

Ignoring Judge Ward's comment about the extent of his focus on the exit of the nine, Almand returned to that topic. Under further questioning, Ervin acknowledged that a faculty protest erupted when the Admissions

Committee members noticed that some of the students appeared in the January 1, 1982 Sugar Bowl after being dismissed at the end of the preceding Fall Quarter under the Regents' four quarters limit rule. The issues that grew out of that discovery exploded during an ad hoc meeting a little more than two weeks later via a Kemp led unanimous vote condemning administrative interference with faculty prerogatives. Despite the timing of Ervin's removal of Jan as the English Coordinator on February 3, 1982, he denied that Jan's protest of the exit of the nine was a factor in his personnel decisions regarding her. He blew off the faculty protest on the grounds that the athletes involved would have been eligible to participate in the Sugar Bowl even though they had been dismissed from UGA because under NCAA rules failing athletes remained eligible until the following academic quarter begins, and in the cases of the nine, the Winter Quarter of 1982 began on January 2, 1982, the day following the Sugar Bowl. That observation missed the point. The faculty wasn't objecting to the athletes' eligibility to play in the Sugar Bowl. They were objecting to the audacity of UGA's leaders who ignored their academic judgments of those students' inability to succeed in college level courses.

Almand then tried to flip the conversation to allegations of preferential treatment of athletes by Jan and the faculty witnesses who had testified for her. For example, Fred Johnson had recommended a fifth quarter for Veronica Walker who satisfied exit standards, but whose academic progress suggested a need for an additional quarter, or at the minimum, for tutoring. Almand also introduced a letter written by Ruth Sabol recommending the exit of a student who had not earned the mandatory "C", and a June 1, 1979 letter from Jan seeking an exit for a student athlete who earned a "C" in his third quarter but was eight points short on the Basic Skills Exam. Jan doubted that the student would ultimately graduate but hoped for the best because he was diligent in his studies. Ervin incorrectly testified that the student was UGA's top running back when Jan sought that exit.

The problem with Ervin pointing his finger at Johnson, Sabol and Kemp was that they were faculty members charged with the academic supervision of the program's students based on their day-to-day interaction with them in the classrooms. On the contrary, the administrative grants of extra quarters and arbitrary exits were not premised on academic assessments of the students' potential for success, but instead on their potential to produce revenue for the Athletic Association.

Almand occasionally interrupted Ervin's narratives with questions that changed the cadence of the direct examination to "quick denial and move on" tactics. Ervin denied having any knowledge of Sue McCaffrey's change of Veronica Walker's English grade, that he ever asked Jan to lobby Barbara Carson to change grades, and that he ever told Velma Scott that, referring to Jan, he was going, "to get another pregnant woman out of his life, that she was a good teacher but was crazy as hell, and that he would get rid of her before letting her run the program."

Around mid-afternoon, Almand directed Ervin to

address the Sims' "To Whom It May Concern" letter. Ervin's answer was well-prepared and delivered in a concise practiced manner, but the content of his testimony cast more of a cloud than a clarification. He said that two students, one of whom was Sims, approached him after they received dismissal letters. Ervin testified that, "They had already written letters to their counselors. What happened was that when the students started articulating some of the things that had gone on in Jan's class, I immediately said, 'Put this in writing and I will take it up with Dr. Trotter.'" Curiously, Ervin then told Sims that without corroboration from other students, his letter would just "lie here," but it didn't just lie there. Ervin shamelessly used it in a federal courthouse not for the benefit of Sims, the student supposedly harmed by Jan's misconduct, but for himself as a part of his character assassination trial strategy.

After meeting with the students, Ervin met with Trotter, but he said didn't mention Sims' letter. Nevertheless, Trotter granted the extra quarters because, "there may have been extenuating circumstances that might have contributed to their grades and so forth."

Almand turned the narrative to the ML incident. ML was the student whom Jan prosecuted through the student judiciary. Ervin urged Jan to back off. He suggested an informal resolution between her and ML, but she stood her ground and successfully prosecuted the case against ML.

That's when ML's father, Isaac Levy, intervened. Levy had testified that he ratcheted up the pressure on Davison after ML's conviction by the student judiciary - that he threatened to do whatever was necessary to have it reversed. Ervin admitted that pressure to appease Levy came directly from the President's office. Ervin said that he got a call from Albert Jones, an executive assistant to Davison, who directed him to contact Jan's major professor at UGA in the English Department where she earned her doctoral degree to determine if Jan was a linguistics expert. Obviously, Davison had bought into Levy's false accusation that Jan claimed to be a linguistics expert before the student judiciary to explain how she recognized ML's voice during his profane telephone rant. Clearly, the Davison administration had once again kowtowed to the demands of a wealthy alumnus. How could the jury not be pondering the implausibility of ordinary citizens, including themselves, ever having that kind of access and influence?

At that point, Judge Ward adjourned. We all breathed a deep sigh of relief at the end of Ervin's daylong testimony - it was Friday - two days to rest and hopefully try to forget about the trial for a day or so. As it turned out, that was impossible. The trial was the only thing anyone that we happened to see that weekend wanted to discuss - local and national newspapers headlined it, and it seemed like everyone in Athens knew one or more of the players or witnesses. The defendants and their allies were on the ropes, and we still had some punches to deliver. Back on campus, Davison was in for a very bad weekend. The defendants and Davison were reeling back on their heels - Jan was winning the war on both fronts.

## Ervin's Return to the Witness Stand

Almand must have been upset over Ervin's previous testimony regarding whether or not Development Studies was a promotional unit because he began the following Monday morning's testimony using a copy of a memorandum that Ervin wrote to Trotter dated August 19, 1981. We intended to introduce that memo, but curiously, Almand preempted us. We understood. He used it before we had the chance to confront Ervin with it to create the impression that the defense wasn't trying to hide problematic evidence.

Ervin characterized the memorandum as a communication seeking "clarification about the promotion process." Almand followed up with a leading question to which we had absolutely no objection: "All right. Now, at the time this memo was written, August 19, 1981, the Division of Developmental Studies was not a 'promotion unit.' Is that right?" Ervin hedged in his answer: "Well, it was not clear." Then inexplicably, Almand directed Ervin to read from a different sentence in the memo: "If the division is not established as a separate promotion unit, faculty members will be placed in an untenable situation which will in all likelihood preclude promotion." Almand followed up by having Ervin point out language in his own memo characterizing the purpose of Developmental Studies to be "instruction and teaching." Pat gave me a quizzical look that said, "Is he trying our case or Ervin's?" Why would Almand open his last day of Ervin's direct examination by pointing out the virtual impossibility of any Developmental Studies faculty member being promoted and tenured thereby undermining his primary reason for firing Jan?

Ervin was on the defensive because of questions by his own attorney. He tried to explain how Developmental Studies faculty members could have been promoted before May of 1982 when the division adopted promotion and tenure guidelines. Curiously, he pointed to his own unsuccessful attempt to earn a promotion as an example of the availability of that method. Ironically, Ervin had waited to seek tenure again until the adoption of Developmental Studies guidelines. He made sure however that Jan wouldn't follow his example. He fired her three months later.

Moreover, while Ervin insisted that the Developmental Studies faculty had always been required to produce research, there were solid reasons why the jury shouldn't believe him. No witness corroborated him; there were no such expectations noted in any of the hundreds of documents admitted into evidence; no credible witness attempted to impeach the testimony of numerous faculty members who swore that they were all told that they were not obligated to engage in research activities; and a number of witnesses had testified that they would not believe Ervin even if he were under oath.

Additionally, Almand introduced a July 20, 1979 memo from Ervin to the teaching staff that listed "research" as the last item he believed should be included in the new promotion and tenure guidelines. Ervin acknowledged that the quantity of research to be required was not specified and the committee that was formulating the program's new promotion and tenure guidelines noted that the nature of the Developmental Studies' mission, "precludes the attainment of a high level of performance in areas other than instruction."

Almand then turned to his final line of questioning designed to suggest that Ervin's motives for removing Jan from the faculty were pure because he made that decision knowing that Jan would likely sue him for doing so. The implication was that Ervin was willing to be sued proving that he didn't fear the judicial scrutiny or the public disclosure of his conduct in the "Jan Kemp Affair." To support that assertion Almand offered a February 5, 1982 memorandum that Ervin wrote to Dean Ralph Beaird. Pat interjected to tell the judge, "It is not in evidence. We tried to put it in and they objected." Almand responded, "I will offer it at this time." Pat replied: "We won't object." Almand handed it to Ervin and asked him if he remembered the memo. Ervin acknowledged that he did write it to Beaird. Almand asked him to read it to the jury. He read, "Dr. Kemp's lawyer has advised her to charge a grievance against the University of Georgia. I am advised also that their grievance could lead to court action."

Almand had objected to the memo being introduced earlier in the trial because it disclosed the hidden hand of Davison controlling a grievance process by an untenured Developmental Studies assistant professor through his legal counsel, Ralph Beaird, and Beaird delivered. Although Beaird was not a panel member, he attended the grievance hearing. As Davison's counsel, he most likely created the ruse that rendered the hearing meaningless by limiting the scope of it to the question of whether or not the officials who caused Jan's demotion proceeded in a "procedurally correct manner." That decision eliminated any consideration of the merits of Jan's appeal. If any doubt remained about the highest UGA officials' involvement in the "Jan Kemp Affair," Beaird's appearance first as an observer at Jan's grievance hearing and later his presence at the trial in Atlanta resolved such doubt.

Then at the very end of Ervin's direct examination, Almand's questions disclosed his theory that the memo proved Ervin's character and the courage to face down a rebellious faculty member despite an impending judicial review of his conduct. Given the bad character evidence from numerous witnesses, it seemed to us that it was unlikely that the jury would buy into the hero role that he and Almand were trying to portray.

Almand completed his direct examination of Ervin and turned him over to Pat for cross-examination.

### Ervin's Cross-Examination

Pat began with an attack on Ervin's understanding of the "up or out" tenure rules as applied to Jan. He not only impeached Ervin's opinion of those rules, he also made Ervin's evasiveness obvious by asking questions that Ervin didn't want to answer. Pat handed Ervin UGA's *Red Book* which spelled out the "up or out rules" for faculty who were initially hired as instructors, and asked Ervin to read the relevant provisions.

Q. Let me show you what has been marked as defendants' Exhibit 35 and ask you to read the first sentence that begins on page 36.

A. "Non-tenured faculty are employed on a year to year basis. They may be terminated with timely notice by the appropriate procedures."

What Ervin read was not the first sentence on page 36. He simply perused page 36 to find a sentence that seemed to him to authorize the termination of Jan's employment for any reason without regard to her constitutional rights. Pat walked to the witness stand and pointed to the sentence in the *Red Book* that he had asked Ervin to read.

Q. I believe the first sentence begins right there.

A. I thought you said the last sentence.

Q. The first sentence.

A. "The maximum time that may be served in any combination of full-time instructional, appointment lecturer, instructor or professional rank without the award of tenure shall be ten years . . .."

Jan was promoted from being an instructor to an assistant professor in 1980 after earning her doctorate degree, so at that point she had six years remaining to become tenured and promoted to associate professor. After being confronted with the *Red Book*, Ervin admitted that six additional years were available to Jan in 1980 to acquire tenure but only if she was making progress in research in which he claimed she wasn't. That claim however was facially ridiculous given the emphasis on teaching over research in the tenure guidelines and the testimony from a defense witness, William Diehl, that Jan was in the process of writing a textbook that was considered appropriate research for Developmental Studies' faculty members.

Pat switched to the grade changes for Veronica Walker and another track athlete by English Associate Professor Barbara Carson that were processed through Sue McCaffrey in Developmental Studies despite the fact that both students had exited the program. Ervin admitted that his signature with his assistant's initials were present on the grade change forms. His explanation was that a perusal of the records demonstrated that the mistake was made on the assumption that the students had not fully exited the program. Later Ervin admitted that he had no explanation for the existence of that grade change form since Developmental Studies personnel had absolutely no authority to change grades in any standard curriculum course even if the students had remained in the program taking courses other than English. Pat pressed on and was scoring so effectively that Almand rose from his chair and stood in front of the defendants' table. It was obvious that he was trying to position himself where his presence would distract the flow of Pat's cross-examination from his position at the podium. Judge Ward temporarily abandoned his gentle manner of disciplining misbehavior by lawyers. He interrupted the cross-examination to sternly rebuke Almand. "Sit down, Mr. Almand."

Pat then had Ervin - a UGA Assistant Vice President

- describe his relationship with ML and his father, Isaac Levy. Ervin testified that he met Mr. Levy, who was accompanied by Ralph Beaird, for coffee at the Holiday Inn where, "We covered a number of topics. One of those was his son coming to the University of Georgia - he told me what he thought his grade point average was or something of that nature, but he was interested in getting his son into the University."

Pat pressed him further, but Ervin hedged to the point of aggravating the judge while Pat was asking about Ervin's role in ML's admission.

Q. Now, you admitted him into Developmental Studies, is that correct?

A. You mean I personally admitted him?

Q. Well, the Admissions Committee turned him down. Is that true?

A. Oh, all right.

The Court: "He is asking you did they turn him down?"

Q. Did they?

A. I really don't recall whether they did or not. They may have. I'm not sure.

Q. You don't recall having to take some action to get him admitted outside the Admissions Committee?

Ervin didn't respond, so Pat warned him of the consequences if he continued his silence:

Q. We can do this the long way if you want to.

A. No, we can do it the short way.

Q. The short way is for you to tell us he was admitted outside the Admissions Committee?

The Court: Come on. Answer the question. If you don't know the answer tell him you don't know it.

The Witness: That could very well be the case.

Pat forced Ervin to admit that he played racquetball with ML and had invited him to his home along with some other students. He also elicited admissions from Ervin about the pressure from Davison's office—the call from Davison's assistant, Albert Jones, regarding the false claim that Jan told the student judiciary that she was a linguistics expert. Although Ervin agreed that ML's and his father's voices were "pretty distinctive," he admitted that he followed up on Jones' complaint. He contacted Jan's major professor for her graduate studies to get his opinion on whether or not she was a "linguistics expert." He also admitted discussing the ML situation with Trotter and with Davison's Executive Assistant and Sue McCaffrey's husband, Jim Kenney.

Ervin's ugliest testimony emerged when Pat asked him if he agreed with ML's statement to his father that Jan was a racial bigot. We never thought Ervin would lower himself to playing the race card. He knew better. There had never been any hint of racial prejudice on Jan's part by anyone prior to the trial. But Ervin forged ahead with his eyes fixed on the race of the majority of the jurors. Pat asked:

Q. Finally, we heard Mr. Levy say his son told him that the basis of Dr. Kemp's problem was she was bigoted and she couldn't stand to be subservient to a black man. Did you find that to be true of Dr. Kemp, Dr. Ervin?

A. I have heard that, yes.

Q. You have heard that?

A. Yes.

Q. Well, let me ask you first, my question to you, did you find that to be true as a black man?

A. I think that – yes. I find certain situations existing, certain situations, yes.

When pressed for evidence to support that accusation, Ervin was unable to point to any concrete incident other than Jan's defiance in the face of the academic charade being forced upon the faculty. Ervin continued to waffle on questions seeking a basis for his opinion that Jan was a bigot,

Q. Can you think of any other example of Dr. Kemp's racial bigotry or conduct . . . ?"

A. You know it's very difficult many times to put your finger –

Judge Ward interrupted the cross-examination again to chastise Ervin for not answering the questions.

The Court: "Wait a minute. He said many other things. Can you ?"

Mr. Almand: He was explaining his answer and he has a right to explain his answer.

The Court: He hasn't given one yet.

Pat reframed the question: "Can you put your finger on any other examples of racial bigotry by Dr. Kemp, or conduct that you perceived to be racially bigoted?"

Ervin then gave his best answer which was no answer at all: "No, but it's very difficult to put your finger on something elusive. Many times, you can feel it, you know it is there, but it's very subtle and at a level that you cannot come right out and say one, two, three, this is it. But I've been in this world long enough to understand and have been confronted with those issues long enough to recognize them even in their most sophisticated form."

It seemed to us that Ervin's willingness to play the race card would backfire, and it did. The jurors' post-trial comments to the press uniformly praised Jan for her courage and devotion to her profession and to her students. Two-thirds of the jury were African Americans who were undoubtedly able to recognize subtle signs of racism as well as bogus claims of racism. Their verdict eventually proclaimed their conclusion—Jan was no racist, and Ervin's claim to the contrary was a fabrication.

In general, Ervin's responses were evasive and nonresponsive to the questions, but Pat was able to nail him on his responsibility for the decision to exit the nine athletes who failed to satisfy Developmental Studies criteria. He began by asking Ervin to review the records of the athletes. Ervin shamelessly allocated all of the blame to his co-defendant and boss, Vice President for Academic Affairs Trotter. Pat followed up with questions about the female student with better grades and basic skills exam scores.

Q. Now, why didn't you recommend to Dr. Trotter that she exit Developmental Studies?

A. Because this student's name did not come to my attention to refer to Dr. Trotter.

Pat probed further. He handed Ervin a list of the nine athletes and asked if he made any positive recommendations for any of the students listed. Ervin responded that he had made a recommendation to Trotter to exit one of the students, but insisted that it had nothing to do with the student's athletic status. Pat was laying a trap.

Q. Did you recommend any others?

A. I think I recommended one other.

Q. Wait - you think - you said you only recommended one?

A. There are two in there I recall recommending.

Q. You recall not recommending the other seven?

A. I did not give a recommendation on the other seven.

After Ervin elaborated in some detail on his reasons for recommendations for only two of the nine, Pat sprang the trap. He asked Ervin if he recalled his testimony in the initial hearing in the case before Judge Ward in 1983, to which he responded, "No, I don't recall." So, Pat handed him a transcript of that hearing and directed him to pages 120-121 to refresh his memory. Ervin read his testimony carefully, looked up and said, "According to my testimony at that time it said that I had not." Over strenuous objection by Almand, Judge Ward ordered Ervin to read the questions and his answers in the 1983 hearing. It must have been painful because this is what he had said and was now obligated to read to the members of the jury who would soon be deciding if he should be believed. He read:

Q. Well, who decided to exit those nine?

A. My superior.

Q. Who was that?

A. Dr. Trotter.

Q. Did you have anything to do with that decision? Did you make a recommendation?

A. No, I did not make a recommendation. Are you asking me did I make a recommendation to exit them?

Q. Yes.

A. No, I did not.

Pat pointed out to Ervin that his 1983 testimony predated his trial testimony by two and a half years, and asked Ervin to explain why his memory failed him then when he was under oath in a federal court hearing.

Q. Why didn't you tell us about that back in 1983?

A. Well, I mean, evidently what I consider an honest error there . . . a human error.

So, Ervin, whom numerous witnesses had sworn they would not believe under oath, asked the jury to believe that his testimony in 1983 was human error rather than an attempt to shift responsibility for his misconduct to someone else - in this case to his boss, Virginia Trotter.

Pat kept up the pressure. He made Ervin admit participating in episodes involving another ruse being used to maintain football eligibility for the scholarship athletes whom he habitually sheltered in Developmental Studies through as many football seasons as possible. For instance, Ervin had procured permission from the Regents to grant fifth quarters in Development Studies for five football players on UGA's 1980 SEC championship team. Ervin said he couldn't "recall" having any knowledge of the athletic status of those students - an implausible claim at best - an intentional lie under oath at worst. In any event, a 1980 letter from the Chancellor's office granting the request for an extra quarter for those athletes revealed what was apparent to the Developmental Studies faculty and should have been to everyone else. That letter had a handwritten note attached: "Good luck in New Orleans."

The exit of the nine occurred the following football season, Herschel Walker's Heisman Trophy year, and UGA's second invitation to play in the upcoming Sugar Bowl. Ervin admitted that those nine students were afforded preferential treatment because they were athletes.

Pat used the next segment of the cross-examination to pin Ervin down on the sequence of events surrounding the faculty uproar over the exit of nine. It was a tortuous endeavor given Ervin's continuing evasions as a substitute for straightforward testimony. The public got a good clue of how transparently unpersuasive Ervin was when a news reporter noted in his column the following day that some jurors, the court clerk, and Virginia Trotter nodded off during his testimony. Pat persevered however and further damaged Ervin's credibility.

The faculty ad hoc committee and Ervin met on January 18, 1982. The committee members unanimously condemned the exit of the nine despite their failure to satisfy Developmental Studies' exit rules. The minutes of that meeting recorded the committee's approval of Jan's proposal that the faculty formally protest the administration's brazen breach of Regents' and UGA's rules. The minutes of that meeting note that: "Jan proposed that we send a letter to the administration reflecting our concerns. It was decided that she would draft a letter and present it to the committee at next week's meeting. This letter would he shown to the faculty at the staff meeting next Tuesday."

The committee met again on the following Monday, January 25th. The minutes of that meeting summarized the faculty's deliberations and conclusions: "Jan distributed copies of the draft letter regarding fourth quarter students who did not exit but were allowed to transfer. A discussion about the minutes ensued. A suggestion was made to not only send a copy of the letter to Dr. Trotter but also to send copies to Coach Dooley and Coach Durham. The rough copy was gone through by the committee paragraph by paragraph and changes in wordings were made."

Jan agreed to have the edited copy of the letter typed and distributed to the committee for approval and distribution on Wednesday, January 27th at 3:00 P.M. The committee met on that date to approve the substance of the letter, but they asked Jan to make a few minor edits. She made those edits and had the final version ready on February 1st.

Ervin admitted that he was not present at the January 27th meeting, but he testified that "the committee couldn't reach a consensus." No one corroborated that claim. Nevertheless, Ervin collected all copies of the edited draft based on his false rationale "that the committee had decided that they were not sending the letter because they could not agree with Jan's wording and I suggested a meeting with Dr. Trotter." Ervin must have panicked. He arranged a meeting for the committee members with Trotter scheduled for February 2nd, one day after the committee received Jan's final draft.

Pat pressed Ervin for the source of his claim that Jan's edited copy of the letter was rejected. No one on the committee corroborated that claim. Ervin claimed that William Diehl told him. Diehl testified before and after Ervin's testimony. In fact, Diehl was the defense's final witness, but Almand never asked him to corroborate Ervin's claims. That omission by Almand clearly undermined Ervin's claim of discontent among the committee members with the final draft of the letter to Trotter, Dooley and Durham.

No experienced lawyer like Almand would have failed to ask Diehl if he told Ervin that the committee members rejected the letter if that was true. The most logical conclusion flowing from that omission was that Almand didn't believe Ervin because he knew that Diehl would deny making any such statement.

Pat then made Ervin acknowledge that he arranged the meeting of the committee members with Trotter for February 2 – a meeting that Jan was unable to attend because she had a doctor's appointment. Ervin demoted her the following day, February 3, 1982. That ominous decision triggered the onset of the "Jan Kemp Affair."

Judge Ward recessed until the following day.

### Day Two of Ervin's Cross-Examination

Ervin consumed a large chunk of his second day under cross-examination by Pat with evasions through exhaustive explanations of his understanding of the various rules and policies regulating Developmental Studies. He also questioned the authenticity of documents produced by UGA personnel during pre-trial discovery. He obviously had a reason to question and confuse the meaning of those documents - to minimize the effect of his written evaluations of Jan that portrayed a rising academic star during her first two years (1978-79) and (1979-80) in contrast to his contentions that she degenerated into an incompetent academic shortly after the exit of the nine. Ervin's first year evaluation gave Jan a score of

8.2 out of 10 which Ervin conceded was "a pretty good evaluation." Her star continued rising the second year to a 9 and Ervin added a comment acknowledging that, "She does an excellent job with any assignment undertaken. Dr. Kemp is a tremendous asset to the Special Studies Division. I'm convinced that within two to three years Dr. Kemp will develop a nationally recognized model for the Developmental English program."

Jan's star power fell precipitously according to Ervin's 1980-81 evaluation that he failed to have Jan review and sign as required by University policy. That evidence was a textbook example of personnel "file packing" - a common but foolish practice often used by employment case civil rights defendants.

Pat switched topics to begin asking Ervin about Velma Scott, the Developmental Studies' student who was a "close personal friend" of his. Although Judge Ward had suppressed the telephone records in our possession proving a more personal relationship between Ervin and Scott, he allowed her to testify that she was indeed a "close personal friend" of Ervin's. That gave Pat the right to ask Ervin if that was true to which Ervin answered, "No." We saw that answer as a golden opportunity to get the suppression ruling vacated so we could impeach Ervin's testimony through the phone records. We argued that a ruling limiting the introduction of evidence could not be used as an opportunity to commit perjury. Judge Ward seriously considered our request but decided to stick with his original order because he believed establishing a mixed-race administrator-student romantic relationship would be so prejudicial that it outweighed the "probative value" of the telephone records.

Judge Ward did allow us to make a record of the content of the phone calls outside the hearing of the jury. Our showing, which became part of the public record after the trial, documented 18 telephone calls between Scott at her home in a rural South Georgia town and Ervin during a two-month period in the Summer of 1981. Some of the calls were over an hour in length and were placed just before or after midnight. Ervin's attorneys had an opportunity to contest these details of our offer to produce the phone records but they never did - they just wanted to stop talking about them. Ervin's true relationship with Velma Scott was never revealed to the jury, but it was documented in the court transcripts that became another chapter in the history of the "Jan Kemp Affair."

Next Pat forced Ervin to impeach Sims' testimony claiming that he would graduate after two more quarters. He handed Ervin a copy of Sims' academic transcripts. Ervin agreed that 190 academic hours were required to graduate with a bachelor's degree from UGA. After reviewing the academic records, Ervin admitted that Sims needed ninety more hours to graduate. Since students could only earn 15-18 hours per quarter, Sims was at least five quarters away from graduating when he testified that he believed he would graduate in two quarters, "depending on my past and everything." This evidence laid bare the complete lack of empathy by Ervin and Trotter for the young men that they considered to be the "raw material" that they had exploited through the false promises of college educations in exchange for their athletic talents.

Neither Ervin nor Trotter ever demonstrated the slightest sense of concern over what they were doing to these young men. They staunchly defended their actions by consistently taking the position that the athletes were better off for having been at UGA. They had no reservations and no recognition of the painful reality so well stated during testimony by Ruth Sabol. Surely the jury recalled her powerful description: "They're damaged, being used in a system and told that they are going to get a college degree, and hoping, hoping so much from the bottom of their hearts that they will get a degree. It's a tragedy."

Pat then introduced a letter that Trotter wrote to Ervin granting Sims an "administrative exit" after he failed to make the grade needed to exit in his fifth quarter. The letter was addressed to Ervin and copied to Vince Dooley and Dick Copas, the Athletic Association's liaison to Developmental Studies. Curiously, the letter had a notation stamped on the first page, "Attorney-Client privilege," despite the fact that neither the writer nor the recipients were attorneys. That letter was dated March 23, 1982, six days before the date on Sims' March 29, 1982, letter accusing Jan of using class time improperly.

The purpose of the misuse of the attorney client notation was obvious: Attorney-client communications are privileged so they don't have to be produced in discovery or under Georgia's open records laws. Anyone who attaches that label falsely to a non-privileged communication intends to keep it secret. We had a copy of it because somehow someone in Almand's office included a copy in a "discovery dump."

After the trial, I also found additional letters in UGA's Hargrett Library of Rare Documents and Historical Records from Almand to Davison, who was not his client, but which were marked as attorney-client communications. It appeared that the attorney-client privilege was being misused as a matter of course.

Pat pressed on. He confronted Ervin regarding a student referred to as RC. The Developmental Studies Admissions Committee denied RC's application, but he was a member of a politically influential family. Pat handed Ervin a letter to him from Morris Phelps, a former Georgia football player and then Director of Admissions at UGA. The letter read in part: "RC is from a family with a tradition of University of Georgia and State of Georgia support. His grandfather, two aunts and an uncle are alumni. He also has an unusual background of family service to the state. His grandfather and his father served in the Georgia legislature." Tellingly, the letter also said, "He has been highly recommended by Fred Davison." RC was admitted.

At that point, Pat was ready to release Ervin from his intensive interrogation, but he wanted to end his testimony with a devastating admission by Ervin. He forced Ervin to acknowledge that it was his voice on the Timmons' tape stating that "we could count the number of black scholarship athletes who made it on one hand." Ervin admitted making that remark because he had no choice since it appeared on the tape recording, but he refused to accept any responsibility for the shameful conduct of UGA administrators, including himself, by adding, "I probably said that statement and it was probably an exaggeration."

Ervin was the defense's final substantive witness, but Almand wasn't finished. It was time for the dog and pony show: testimony by Vince Dooley and Fred Davison, neither of whom claimed to have any relevant information that might assist the jurors in the performance of their duty to resolve the issues in the case.

# CHAPTER THIRTY-EIGHT
# DOOLEY ON THE OFFENSE - DAVISON ON THE DEFENSE

Over the weekend, Vince Dooley emerged as UGA's public relations spokesman, Fred Davison took a snub from the University of North Carolina, and the *Athens Banner Herald* published a stinging public indictment of UGA's leadership in an editorial in its February 2, 1986 Sunday edition.

Dooley held a news conference on Friday, January 31. He made no bones about his negative opinion of Almand. He condemned his opening statement to the jury about teaching some student athletes enough to prepare them to become postal workers instead of garbage men. Dooley's candor about Almand's language must have stung. Dooley told the press he was subpoenaed to testify in the Kemp trial - not by Kemp's lawyers, but by Almand. Subpoenas are rarely used to compel the appearance of friendly witnesses - particularly witnesses whose interests in the outcome of the case are identical to those of the parties calling them to testify. Why would Dooley need a subpoena? One would assume that he'd be raring to go since the image of the program that he ran was being savaged in the press.

Dooley's statements to the press launched UGA's Athletic Association's counter-offensive. He blamed the NCAA for developing standards that compelled UGA to admit academically unprepared student athletes. That explanation didn't wash. He didn't get it. He didn't understand that the Kemp trial was about the wholesale breaches of academic integrity at UGA. That reality seemed to escape him - to him it was all about protecting the football program. UGA's mission, the provision of college educations to its students, didn't factor in, and in some cases, it got in the way.

Dooley, head football coach and Almand critic, also suggested that he intended to improve the truth-seeking process being conducted by a federal judge when he took the stand. He told an AP reporter he had to appear as a witness because: "There's been so much misunderstanding, so many half-truths, not the whole truth, that's being portrayed in the trial." Dooley never identified what "half-truths" he perceived were being foisted upon the court and the public. He simply ignored the sworn testimony by a number of faculty witnesses who detailed the academic scandal that ignited the "Jan Kemp Affair."

Dooley waited far too long to launch his public relations blitz, and then he chose the wrong forum. His courtroom performance the following week was a gift to Jan and her supporters - he made his pitch on direct examination. He must have assumed that he could engineer the cross-examination as easily as he handled his carefully scripted questions from Almand in his direct examination, but that didn't happen. I supposed he didn't realize that his revered status as UGA's football coach didn't afford any control over what we intended to ask. He wasn't as prepared as he purported to be during his news conference.

Davison had a very bad weekend. He began to really

feel the sting of the scandal that was capturing national attention - so did the Trustees of the University of North Carolina. Davison was an ambitious man who undoubtedly believed he could market his experience to heighten his profile. To that end, he offered himself as a candidate for the presidency of UNC. According to the *Athens Banner Herald*, Davison was considered to be a leading candidate, but the Friday before Davison's testimony, the UNC trustees announced that they had hired another applicant.

Davison took another hit in the *Athens Banner Herald* in its Sunday edition the same weekend. Editorial writer Rick Parham's column, "Random Thoughts on the Kemp Affair," targeted Davison and Almand. Parham wrote:

"The timing of the announcement that the University of North Carolina System has selected a new president - and it's not Fred Davison - is unfortunate for the head man at the University of Georgia. We must remember that Dr. Davison was one of a dozen or so persons seriously considered and there was never any assurance that he would get the job if he wanted it. We are all proud that he was in the running. But, of course with the Kemp situation, some might suspect that the UNC folks didn't want to bring in someone tainted by this affair.

Did I say tainted? Yes. Who else should be responsible? Of course, Drs. Trotter and Ervin are the top vote getters, but President Davison is right in the balloting. Of course, he did not personally oversee any of this - that's what vice presidents are for. But he gives the University its direction and he corrects the course when the ship goes astray. And so far, there have been no course corrections. Is the Captain at the helm?

But perhaps it's unfair to want answers now. I don't think so myself. Hale Almand says nobody can say anything until the trial's over. I don't think it will be 'over' until all the appeals, regardless of who wins, are decided. Yet the questions that cry out for answers are not really related to the testimony of why Kemp was fired. The University has flatly stated that it does change some grades for certain students (upgrading them for the wrong reasons); and it does admit some students but not others on the basis of who they knew or what they could do for the 'private' Athletic Association. What's wrong with addressing these concerns now?

Why haven't we heard from President Davison? When asked about the student demonstration last week, he could have responded with something like we're all concerned and will be looking into it or something reassuring. Instead we get a cold, "I wasn't there."

Parham's editorial also voiced a reaction to the defendants' case that we hoped mirrored the jury's sentiments. It included a "don't you wish" rumination that "UGA attorney Hale Almand would produce a few more witnesses besides those persons with a vested interest in the administration's defense, or those who have relatives in the administration?" Parham added, "A lot of what we've been treated to by the defense is just character assassination that has very little to do with why Jan Kemp was fired."

Davison was on the ropes. Jan was moving quickly toward her ultimate goals. The trial was going very well for her. She was winning battle after battle in the courtroom, but what was more important to her was the march toward victory in the war being waged in the public arena - a war that was overwhelming the enemy. Jan was close to decapitating UGA's corrupt leadership.

# CHAPTER THIRTY-NINE
# DOOLEY TESTIFIES

Vince Dooley arrived at the federal courthouse with all the fanfare of a pep rally prior to a championship game. He had no direct knowledge of the reasons that Ervin and Trotter claimed justified Jan's demotion and subsequent loss of her job. Almand knew that, but he obviously wanted to showcase Coach Dooley along with his covey of assistants and a throng of sports columnists, editorial writers, news and television reporters, and Dooley fans.

Dooley's mission became apparent when he took the stand with a script in hand - a cluster of papers that he continuously referred to while testifying. He had told news reporters that he was there to correct some of the "mistaken" testimony regarding the academic performance of scholarship athletes at UGA. He brought his public relations persona to the courtroom, along with his public relations team headed by Claude Felton, the Athletic Association's Director of Information. He referred to the papers in his hand repeatedly to offer misleading statistics about the academic performance of scholarship athletes at UGA from 1974 through 1984. He resisted our effort to see what he was reading from, but then had his staff hand out copies of those same documents at a press conference he held outside of the courtroom as soon as he left the witness stand.

Almand asked him how the NCAA 2.0 rule (a "C" average) affected recruitment at UGA. Once again, Dooley painted a picture of his philosophical reaction to a bad situation. He claimed that the new rule forced UGA to offer scholarships to student athletes who were "very poorly academically prepared." But, he claimed, "First of all, we don't take too many of them, and secondly, those that we do take, then we go the extra mile to help them help themselves in order to graduate." On and on he went claiming that he took extraordinary care when considering whether to recruit athletes with poor academic records. He would talk to their teachers and guidance counselors to determine if the prospect had "that motivation or extra drive." He then went into lengthy descriptions of two athletes with poor academic performance, one had the drive that the other lacked. He said his "heart went out to the one with the drive" whom Dooley retained on a scholarship even though he only played "three downs of football." Then he contrasted that student to several others who were great football players but poor students who failed out of school and lost their scholarships because they "just didn't make it." The jury must have been skeptical. They had already heard an abundance of evidence about the use of Developmental Studies Division's role as a safe harbor for a number of failing athletes in excess of the maximum four quarters – up to eleven quarters, the Kenny Sims saga, and the exit of the nine. They had also heard testimony about Dooley's and Dick Copas' lobbying Ervin, Trotter, and Davison to retain revenue-producing athletes who were demonstratively incapable of ever earning a bachelor's degree.

Almand switched topics. He led Dooley through a lengthy discussion of his opinion of UGA's prominent role in urging reform under Fred Davison's leadership. Dooley told the jury that Davison had urged the NCAA to reform its academic eligibility rules, all of which led to the 1968 adoption of Proposition 48 that imposed specific academic high school prerequisites. Then, in contrast to his self-portrayal as an "academics first" football coach, when asked for his opinion about the exit of the nine, Dooley endorsed Trotter's and Ervin's blatant disregard of the Regents' and UGA's academic rules.

Instead of insisting on academic integrity, Dooley lectured the jury on his version of the proper approach to dealing with the insurmountable barriers for students with "the low percentage chance of making it." He described the Dooley doctrine on that issue. "As long as they're making some progress and as long as they're trying, and I feel very strongly that way . . . that maybe, if you give them one more chance they might be able to go over that hump and they might be able to make it." Dooley's testimony, like Trotter's and Ervin's, didn't even pay lip service to the rules mandated by the Regents. The arrogance was palpable - we make the rules for athletes - let the Regents' rules control other students, but stay out of our business.

Dooley completely ignored the issues in the case. His appearance was obviously a public relations gambit and nothing more. But that was about to change when his cross-examination began.

I took Dooley on cross, and my very first question addressed one of the actual issues in the case: Jan's value and contributions to the student athletes who did "make it." Dooley's answers probably unnerved Almand. He praised her.

Q. Do you know Jan Kemp?

A. Yes, I do.

Q. And tell the jury how you know Jan?

A. I know Jan from Developmental Studies, and Jan was working with some of the athletes, and I would see Jan on occasion at night helping some students, and of course I knew about Jan secondhand a lot from some academic counselors, and from some of the athletes, including my son.

Q. Including your son?

A. Yes.

Q. What did your son think of her?

A. My son said she was a good teacher but she was tough, which I think was a compliment.

Q. That is what you want for your athletes, good tough teachers?

A. Yes, she got some compliments.

Q. And you say the athletes, you received comments from the athletes about Dr. Kemp also?

A. Yes, and I would have to rephrase that. I don't mean all the athletes, certainly Ronnie Stewart. There were some athletes that thought very highly of Jan.

Q. Would it be fair to say that her reputation among the athletes was as a hard but good teacher?

A. Well, I can't speak for all the athletes, but the ones that I know for sure, as I pointed out, like Ronnie, my son, and maybe a couple of others, that they did speak highly of her.

Q. All right, whatever you heard about her from athletes has been positive?

A. Yes, sir.

I asked Dooley to confirm Ronnie Stewart's testimony that he was only the 15th black scholarship athlete to ever graduate from UGA. Referring to his notes, Dooley acknowledged that Ronnie was the 15th black athlete to graduate, and the total number of scholarship athletes who graduated between 1974 and 1984 was 39, 16 or 17 of whom played revenue-producing sports. Three of the revenue-producing athletes were basketball players, so only 13 or 14 black football players graduated during that ten-year period. The remaining 23 or 24 black scholarship athletes were in non-revenue-producing sports such as track, swimming and gymnastics. Then, referring to his notes, Dooley proudly noted that one hundred per cent of the black female scholarship athletes had graduated. That answer was false and we knew it. At least one black female athlete, Veronica Walker had not graduated.

Q. All right. You say, now, a hundred percent of the black female athletes graduated?

A. During that period, yes.

Q. Between '74 and 84?'

A. Yes. There was a period of time when we didn't have the kind of women's program that we have now, so the numbers are smaller, naturally.

Q. What are the total numbers on that?

A. Oh, let's see. Eight.

Q. Let me show you these two names. (Herschel Walker and Veronica Walker) Did they graduate?

A. Not to my knowledge.

Q. Have they graduated?

A. They have not.

Q. All right. So, these students are not counted in these figures of a 100 percent graduation rate?

A. Oh, yes.

Q. So, she's graduated now you are saying?

A. They are - - They are counted in the percentages. They're not counted in the numbers. Was that your question?

Q. They haven't graduated, have they, from the University of Georgia?

A. No. Those two, no, they haven't, so they're not counted as the number of graduates but they were counted in the percentage of not graduating.

Q. They were counted in the number of black scholarship athletes that have not graduated?

A. That's - - yeah, I assume they were, but if you look at a hundred percent of female black athletes, that wouldn't be on - -.

Q. That doesn't quite add up, does it?

A. Now, let's see here.

Q. Did you prepare this thing you're looking at or did somebody else prepare it for you?

A. Obviously, I had someone else to prepare it, and I will certainly ask those that did the same questions that you are asking me now, and I hope I get a better answer from them than what you are getting from me.

Next, I attempted to lure Dooley into admitting the obvious: at UGA, particularly in Developmental Studies, revenue-producing athletes were not held to the academic standards that applied to other students. He zigged and zagged, Almand repeatedly interrupted with objections, and to some extent Judge Ward protected him from the aggressive cross-examination necessitated by his refusal to give straight answers to simple questions like should athletes in Developmental Studies be held to the same standards as others in that program. Dooley finally said "Yes", but he deferred to Dr. Trotter's prerogative when it came to the athletes. That was truly a disingenuous answer given the influence that he and the Athletic Association's academic advisors had with Davison and Trotter and any other administrator they needed to influence.

*The Atlanta Journal*'s Sports Editor, Furman Bisher, weighed in on Dooley's response in an editorial published on February 6, two days after his testimony. He focused on Dooley's witness stand demeanor and his concept of how to educate revenue-producing athletes. Bisher described his view from the audience: "This is not the kind of scene in which you expect to find Vince Dooley. He was the man in spectacles, sitting in a cage called the witness stand, seemingly strangely smaller than usual. Here on the 23d floor of the Richard B. Russell Building, he was in the supporting role of a legal show now playing its fifth week before a small gallery. Usually he is the star in arenas seating 80,000."

Bisher noted the finger pointing by Dooley and later by Davison blaming almost everyone but themselves for their admitted complicity in the numerous breaches of UGA's academic integrity: "That there has been preferential treatment for athletes goes unquestioned, especially those who can play games well enough to generate revenue for the athletic department whether qualified students or not. Dooley blamed the NCAA, the federal government and its guidelines." Bisher also referenced my question and Dooley's answer about his view of the preferential treatment of revenue-producing athletes:

Q. "You would not suggest that these athletes should be set aside from the academic standards of any other students at Georgia, would you?"

Then he introduced Dooley's answer characterizing it as "a stunning indictment of the state of college athletics in general, at Georgia in particular."

"If you raised academic standards to the normal student level, Georgia would not be able to compete on any level, and I'd be out of a job."

Bisher then informed his readers of Dooley's testimony that trivialized some very telling evidence about his recruitment of an illiterate athlete:

Q. "Is it true that you accepted an athlete who couldn't read a billboard?"

A. "We found out that he needed glasses."

Bishop ended his column with his reaction to that answer: "That's when I left."

We concluded Dooley's testimony late in the day, so Judge Ward recessed the trial. Dooley left the witness stand and walked directly to a nearby room in the courthouse where the Athletic Association had convened a news conference for him to elaborate on his appearance as a witness. When the horde of reporters filed into the room, his handlers handed out copies of the press release that Dooley repeatedly scanned during his testimony. I had seen many witnesses refer to notes while testifying, but this was the first public relations press release that I'd ever seen being used as notes by a trial witness. We weren't surprised. Anyone who took any notice of Dooley's career at UGA had to know that he was always on the script created by his public relations machine. What Dooley's handlers didn't get was that his routine "hype the Dawgs" public relations driven persona was not suited to communicate relevant information in concise factual statements to a federal jury in a United States Courtroom. The jury wanted to hear the truth - not a public relations pitch.

Neither Dooley's testimony nor his news conference accomplished his mission - to minimize the collateral damage that was inflicted upon the Athletic Association by a number of trial witnesses. He failed, as he acknowledged a few weeks later when the headlines from a press interview quoted him acknowledging that "We've been knocked to our knees."

An Associated Press writer, Scott Shepard, agreed with that assessment in an editorial two days after the verdict, but he went further and commented on Dooley's personal reaction in contrast to Davison's who belatedly banned the Athletic Association from making admissions decisions on academically unqualified student athletes. Davison announced just before the verdict that UGA would not take advantage of new NCAA rules that allowed the admission of academically weak athletes. Shepard noted that "Dooley, on the other hand, continued to complain about the 'inaccurate, incomplete and misleading' coverage of the trial by the media." As for the verdict, Dooley said, "I don't understand anything other than the involvement with us (the Athletic Association) and what's happened. As far as all other things, I don't have any understanding of it."

Shepard summed up Dooley's courtroom appearance:

"He punted."

# CHAPTER FORTY
# DAVISON IMPLODES

Fred Davison was scheduled to testify for the defense the following day, but that night he was a party to a conversation that probably sealed his fate with the Regents - a conversation that he never thought would see the light of day, but he was wrong.

What happened on the night of February 5, 1986 revealed the lengths to which Davison was willing to go to protect himself from any disclosure of his involvement in the academic scandals that led to the "Jan Kemp Affair." Davison was scheduled to testify under oath the next morning, February 6. Trotter, Dooley, Almand and Davison were staying at the same hotel. That night Trotter was summoned to Almand's room to meet with Davison to brainstorm potential questions that he should be prepared to answer.

Ray Cleere was a Regents' vice chancellor charged with investigating UGA's Developmental Studies program after the Kemp trial. His co-investigator was Elizabeth Neely, an associate vice chancellor. Their interview of Trotter during the investigation revealed a startling event that occurred in Almand's hotel room on the night before Davison's testimony.

Cleere: Okay. Ah, let's be a little more specific. During the trial, and at the time of the President's testimony, we had the impression that he was unaware of special exits for athletes, and so forth, and that all of this rested with your office . . . During the trial, did you discuss at any time with your lawyer, or with President Davison, the fact that you needed to substantiate his involvement in the process?

Trotter: Well, the night before he was to go on the stand, I did go to Hale Almand's room, and Vince Dooley and the lawyers and the President were there, and I had a list of questions, and so Hale said, "Well, Virginia, why don't you start with your questions?" And I said, "One thing I'd like to know is how we should deal with my discussions with the President about athletics, uh, on the stand." And the President said, "Well, you do understand that I knew nothing about any of this until after the fact."

Neely: Is that an accurate representation?

Trotter: That's exactly what he said.

Neely: But is that accurate in terms of substance?

Trotter: Well, no, because I have always discussed all of this with the President as it came about, because I really felt that I needed some guidance about what to do.

Cleere: So, when a major decision was made concerning an athlete and his status at the institution that involved your office, an exit or whatever, you discussed these things with the President in advance.

Trotter: And it wasn't … and I certainly didn't discuss them each individually, but I discussed each situation, like the exit of the nine, or the, you know, the fifth quarter, or … and, you know… I think that one of the hardest decisions was the students last summer on the BSE (Basic Skills Exam). Now, that I didn't discuss as much with the President because he was gone when that first came up. But, I did discuss it, he did know about it, and I did discuss it with his counsel.

Cleere: How did you react when the President indicated that, "of course, you know, I was unaware of these things until after they happened"?

Trotter: Well, I just said that if that's the case, why then, there isn't any further reason for us to discuss anything any further, and I left the room.

Cleere: What did your lawyer advise you on that; how did he advise you?

Trotter: Well, when he came back to my room after the President left, he said, "Virginia," he said, "I really do believe you, and I know that this was, you know difficult." He was sorry about it.

Neely: You're referring to Mr. Almand?

Trotter: Um-hum. I'm referring to Mr. Almand.

This segment of Trotter's interview by the Regents' investigators painted a picture of Davison's strategy to save his job - falsely deny, even under oath, that he had any knowledge of the widespread academic corruption being disclosed in the trial. Davison's dishonesty revealed his public relations strategy: Blame Virginia!

Ironically, we never intended to point the finger at

Davison regarding what we all knew was his complicity in the scandal for a simple reason: he wasn't a defendant in the courtroom. But Trotter's revelations to the Regents of Davison's role in the scandal and his intent to lie about it were very bad breaks for Davison in the broader war - the one being fought to dethrone him.

## CHAPTER FORTY-ONE
## FRED DAVISON'S TESTIMONY

Davison's testimony was pretty much in tandem with Dooley's, and, like Dooley, he followed up with a press conference as soon as he left the witness stand. They bolstered each other's worldview of competition for revenue-producing athletes—particularly the need to accept the NCAA's admittedly lax admissions rules to avoid what they both characterized as "unilateral disarmament." Davison's stance was apparently not well received by the Regents because he changed his tune shortly before the jury announced its verdict. He contradicted his own announced intent to defy any attempt to "unilaterally disarm" UGA's football program, and he announced that UGA would no longer take advantage of those relaxed NCAA admissions standards. Davison blinked while Dooley dug in.

Like Dooley, Davison offered no relevant testimony. Nothing either of them said assisted the jury in deciding the core issue in the case: Was Jan Kemp demoted and then fired for exercising her constitutionally protected First Amendment right of free speech? Their successive appearances as the final two witnesses for the defense, coupled with separate news conferences which echoed each other's narratives, were transparently designed to defend themselves in the court of public opinion - not to defend Trotter and Ervin. In fact, Davison explicitly blamed Trotter and Ervin as soon as he became the focus of public contempt after the trial and the publication of the Regent's Audit.

Davison not only failed to persuade the jury of anything helpful to Ervin's or Trotter's defense, he shot himself in the foot with testimony that did not sit well with the press, the public, and most importantly with Georgia's political leadership. During his trial testimony, I asked him if he agreed with Ervin's statement recorded on the Timmons tape admitting that there was no "sound academic reason" for many of the revenue-producing athletes to be UGA students. Davison's response was startling: "No, I think every student that comes to the University benefits by that. I can see absolutely no damage done by helping a student or teaching a student to read and write." Then, in his post-trial news conference, he blamed "accredited" high schools for graduating student athletes with a 2.0 average who couldn't read.

The President of the University of Georgia had affirmed under oath and in statements to the press that UGA conducted an elementary level reading program for illiterate students. That testimony invited nationwide ridicule of UGA and profoundly embarrassed those who held Davison's fate in their hands. The Regents and their political allies, including the Governor, were not amused.

When Davison left the witness stand, Almand announced, "The defense rests, Your Honor." We moved on to the Rebuttal stage of the trial. That process is a mini-trial limited to challenges to evidence of the opposing party admitted during the main trial. The trial wasn't over yet.

# CHAPTER FORTY-TWO
# PLAINTIFF'S REBUTTAL

## Jan Kemp's Rebuttal Testimony

We were in a long trial and assumed that the jury would like it to end as soon as possible. We agreed. On the other hand, we had to answer some of the critical testimony from defense witnesses. Jan and other credible witnesses were prepared to do so. If we didn't, Almand would argue to the jury that we had no answer to that testimony. Our strategy was to present a concise rebuttal at a steady pace. We had Jan and six other Developmental Studies faculty members available to help bring the trial to a conclusion.

We mapped out topics for Jan to address: the ghostwriting allegations by Sue McCaffrey; Ervin's claim of insubordination by Jan for canceling the basic 096 course; Dan Kirby's accusation that his graduate students who served internships under Jan complained about her methods; the conflict in the testimony of Barbara Carson involving student athletes in her regular curriculum English class; Kenny Sims' letter and testimony; Becky Galvin's testimony claiming Jan had given her a condom in a candy wrapper as a bridal shower gag gift; and Ervin's race baiting.

Jan reminded the jury that neither McCaffrey nor her assistant, Carolyn Smith, had accused her of plagiarizing student papers until they appeared as witnesses in the trial. She adamantly denied ever being involved in any ghostwriting of papers for two of her former students whom Ervin asked her to help in a Library Orientation class. Jan explained that she agreed to help the students but only to the extent of helping them understand the proper methods for writing term papers, reviewing their rough drafts, and pointing out grammatical errors. She testified that she strictly avoided making corrections on the student papers and did not critique the intellectual content of their work.

The next segment of the rebuttal addressed Ervin's claim that Jan was insubordinate because she abused her authority as the English coordinator to abandon the 096 English courses – a course that was more elementary than the normal Developmental Studies courses. Jan testified that she originally supported having a more basic course for students who opted to begin their study of college level English in the most elementary class available. However, since 096 was scheduled for the first Quarter in the program, the faculty had insufficient information to identify the incoming students who could benefit from it. Jan suggested dropping the course for that reason. Ervin refused, but he agreed to moving the course from Fall Quarter to Winter Quarter to give the faculty the opportunity to determine which students should be placed in that class. The faculty soon realized however that placing the slowest students together in one class was also problematic. Jan explained. "Dee-Dee Yaw taught that course. It was primarily composed of athletes who were not the delight to teach that the original mixed level 096 class had been."

Jan told the jury, "They wouldn't behave, they wouldn't do the work, and it was a dismal failure." So, with the consent of Ervin's assistant, Sue McCaffrey, who acted for him in his absence, the faculty decided to abolish 096 and distribute those students among them so no teacher would have more than three at a time. McCaffrey agreed and told Jan that she would advise Ervin of that decision. Jan also testified that she heard nothing more about the 096 class until Ervin accused her of insubordination for canceling it during his trial testimony.

We shifted to Dan Kirby's accusation that Mary Phillips, one of his English Education graduate students who served as a teaching assistant in Developmental Studies, had complained about Jan's teaching methods. Jan described the problems she had with Phillips and another of Kirby's graduate students - a male whose name she couldn't remember. She did recall something about him. "The only thing I remember about him was that he dismissed his class on Fridays and took his students to T.K. Harty's to drink beer, and I thought that was entirely inappropriate for a freshman student, and I spoke with him about that."

Then Jan described the more problematic issues regarding the other graduate student, Mary Phillips. She graded more leniently than the rest of the English faculty. Some of the undergraduate students who served as tutors in Developmental Students began complaining about their inability to work with her students. "The tutors came to me and said, 'We don't know how to work with her students. She can't recognize a comma splice. She comes and argues with us about whether they need a semicolon between two independent clauses,' so I talked to her about it and she said she didn't believe in marking all the errors. She believed in grading on content only."

Additionally, some of the student evaluations from that class blamed Jan for the graduate assistant's shortcomings. Jan testified, "When the student evaluations came in, eight or nine of those students had written on the evaluations, 'We don't think it's fair that Dr. Kemp, the Chairman or the Head of English faculty, didn't tell her that she had to teach grammar, and we're not going to exit and we're mad about it.'"

Jan acknowledged that those comments angered her. She testified that Phillips "came in and wanted to see her student evaluations. I checked in pencil all the ones that blamed me for their inability to exit. I asked her what was the story. She started crying immediately and said 'I didn't say that. I didn't tell them that.'" I asked her to "look me straight in the face and say to me how eight or nine students could independently write virtually the same comment and it is untrue." Phillips continued to deny making the comment, but Jan told her that she believed her students were being truthful. Moreover, Jan told the jury that Dan Kirby never mentioned any problems with his graduate assistants, and she only learned of those allegations in the first hearing in the case in April of 1983.

We turned the narrative to English professor Barbara Carson's denial that she authorized Jan to provide assistance to former Developmental Studies students in Carson's

English class. To rebut Carson's testimony, Jan had prepared a packet containing documents proving her version of the agreement with Carson. She flipped through the packet and described each document: 1) A list of students that she had agreed to help and a few dated notes of phone calls to and from Carson, 2) notes on individual students and how they were doing, 3) a note that simply said, "Call Barbara," and, 4) a "rather silly" note that Jan wrote to the students: "Dear Blank. I hope you are doing well this quarter. If you have any problems that relate to your performance in class this quarter [or any quarter] please get in touch with me. I'm available to help you with grammar or writing. If you are still splitting your infinitives, dangling your participles, or suffering worse maladies, please call me to help restore you to healthy uses."

Moving on, I asked Jan to address the contents of the letter that Ervin had solicited from Kenny Sims. She acknowledged that there was a classroom discussion that included a story about a prostitute which Sims mentioned in his letter. Jan explained that the story was taken from a textbook used in Developmental Studies. She acknowledged that she did make a comment about skin blotches on her face due to the use of birth control pills, but that comment was not made in class as Sims claimed in his letter. It was a private conversation with an older mature female student who asked Jan about it.

Then, changing subjects, I asked Jan if she had ever given Becky Robins a condom wrapped in a candy wrapper as a gag gift. She responded, "No, sir, I have never seen a condom disguised as a piece of candy."

There were two other issues that we needed to address: First, Ervin's charge that Jan was a racist, and, second, his claim that she was insubordinate and disruptive. Her answers were straightforward.

Q. You don't particularly like Leroy Ervin?

A. He is not my favorite person.

Q. Is that because he is a black person?

A. That has absolutely nothing to do with it.

I concluded by asking Jan if she had been "disruptive" as Ervin had testified. Her answer was delightfully candid: "I was disruptive, but it was high time for disruption with all of the corruption going on in Developmental Studies."

Almand's cross-examination followed. It revealed just how concerned he was about the outcome of the case. His demeanor was harsh to the point of nastiness. As a result, the cross-examination was a dismal failure from our viewpoint. Jan handled Almand's attacks flawlessly. His four hour cross-examination didn't land a punch. Her clear and concise answers were consistent with her rebuttal testimony. Almand's pattern of long-winded argumentative questions accomplished nothing, but it did reveal the paucity of firepower by the defense. He would have been better served by keeping his seat.

## Ruth Sabol's Rebuttal Testimony

Our next witness was Ruth Sabol, the faculty member whom Ervin assigned to take over as the Coordinator of the English component of the program after he demoted Jan. Despite repetitive "speaking" objections from Almand which the judge consistently overruled, Sabol established several critical facts concerning the faculty's research responsibilities. She was initially employed for the 1982-1983 academic year. She was told that the division of Developmental Studies was beginning to expect research from its faculty members under newly developed promotion and tenure guidelines that became effective after being approved by Trotter in June of 1982. Although there were guidelines, the method for implementing them were not complete.

Then, after heated objections from Almand, Judge Ward allowed Dr. Sabol to testify on her comparison of the book that Jan was writing to a book written by Sherrie Nist.

Q. Tell the jury whether or not the textbook Jan Kemp is preparing has any similarity to what Sherrie Nist claimed in this courtroom to be the kind of research that is expected over there.

A. Yes. Given that they are in two different fields, they are, in fact, quite identical. Sherrie took a previous text, revised it, changed some wording, used most of the previous text that Bluie Diehl and Annice Ritter had written, and revised it. It is a very fine textbook. It, in fact, presents major ideas in the field of the teaching of reading that have been in the discipline for years and years. It does not represent new knowledge. Jan's chapter that I have looked over essentially does the same thing. It takes ideas that have been in the field for several years, and it presents them in a cogent meaningful fashion so that a student could use them. The difference is that Jan Kemp's wording is her own throughout, but Sherrie Nist took much of Bluie Diehl's previous wording and used it, but essentially, they're the same, and I want to make sure that people understand that *Developing Textbook Thinking* by Nist and Diehl is a fine book as is the promise of the text that Dr. Kemp is in the process of producing.

With those few words, Sabol positioned a dagger in the heart of Ervin's assault on Jan's alleged failure to satisfy his imaginary version of faculty research responsibilities.

Almand tried to undermine Sabol's testimony on cross-examination in an aggressive to rude manner, but Sabol fought him blow for blow. At one point, he asked her, "Dr. Sabol, are you mad today?" She answered, "Beg your pardon?" Almand answered, "Are you angry today?" She put him in his place with her response, "No. I'm trying to respond with your same tone of voice."

## Fred Johnson's Rebuttal Testimony

We recalled Fred Johnson, one of Jan's African American colleagues, to rebut Ervin's suggestion that Jan was a racist. He testified that he had worked under Jan's supervision for approximately three years and had also served as the

English coordinator for a short stint after Ervin demoted Jan. Pat asked him if he had ever observed any racist behavior by Jan while she was either his superior or his subordinate. He responded, "None whatsoever." Pat followed up, "Even when she was working for you?" Johnson's answer was firm. "No, definitely not."

### Rebuttal of Kenny Sims' Testimony

We recalled two faculty members, Theresa Timmons and Hyta Mederer, to rebut Kenny Sims' testimony claiming that he failed Jan's class because of her classroom behavior, and that he voluntarily documented his complaint in his three-sentence letter dated March 29,1982. Timmons and Mederer were waiting in the witness room to testify that Sims sought counsel from each of them after Ervin promised him additional time to exit Developmental Studies if he wrote that letter.

Timmons taught Sims in the Spring and Fall Quarters of 1982. She testified that "I was walking to class, I believe it was the Fall Quarter. Sims walked up to me on his way to class and said that he was troubled. He wanted to talk, and I said shoot, and he said he had been to see Dr. Ervin who said if he wrote a letter about Dr. Kemp that he could have some more time."

Mederer also retook the witness stand to testify about a conversation that she had with Sims whom she taught in a single student class in the Winter Quarter of 1983. "He was absent from class one day because he had to meet with some lawyers and when he came back the next day he talked to me about that. He was concerned about having to meet with lawyers, and he explained to me that when he was dismissed from the program Dr. Ervin had told him that if he wrote this letter, then he would be readmitted to the University and he could play football as a Bulldog again."

Timmons and Mederer proved that Sims' letter was solicited by Ervin to slander Jan in a court of law. Sadly, the use of Sims as a witness by the defense caused his name to be included in the trial record, and publicized by the reporters covering the trial. It also caused a vulnerable young man to suffer the indignity of being impeached as a witness in a highly publicized case.

### Katie Blackburn's Rebuttal Testimony

Our next witness was Katie Blackburn, a former Developmental Studies Math instructor who resigned after one year because she "didn't want to work there." Her reason for leaving UGA was made crystal clear. Despite Almand's vociferous objections to her testimony, the court allowed her to testify that she left because Ervin had a dismal reputation for truthfulness. She swore that his reputation in the community was "terrible" and that she would not believe anything that he testified to if contradicted by any other witness.

Almand conducted her cross-examination, but he must have regretted that decision because he opened the door to an opportunity to heap more damaging evidence on top of the cascade of bad reputation evidence that the jury had already heard. He began with a series of questions designed to limit the scope of her knowledge of Ervin's reputation to the Developmental Studies faculty, which he contended was too small to represent a "community" for purposes of gauging Ervin's reputation. Blackburn clarified the scope of the "community" that she was referencing as the "University of Georgia" including "upper administrators."

Almand took the bait. He asked Blackburn to elaborate by naming people whom she was referring to, "outside of Developmental Studies." She provided seven names: Jim Wilson, Tom Koon, Ed Davis, Nathan Dean, Larry Hatfield, and Sigrid Wagner.

Almand sat down. He had just asked the questions that we wanted him to since we had told our witnesses to be prepared to identify whom they had talked to about Ervin's reputation. Pat followed up with the ultimate question, and he got a classic answer.

Q. Without going into what any individual said, did they specifically tell you, you can't believe that man under oath, or did you learn - did you form an opinion based on things they said?

A. They told me that I couldn't believe that man and also other things that they said verified and supported that.

Q. Is this basically the whole Mathematics Education Department at the University of Georgia?

A. Yes.

Q. And Mr. Almand didn't ask you about people in Developmental Studies at the University of Georgia?

A. No, but I would be glad to mention names there too.

Pat didn't follow up. He didn't have to. Almand wisely opted to decline any additional cross, so the Judge dismissed Blackburn and directed me to "call your next witness." After a five and one-half week trial, I called our final witness. "The plaintiff Calls Paula Yaw!"

### Paula Yaw Rebuttal Testimony

Paula Yaw earned her Master's and PhD degrees in English at UGA. She was hired by Ervin as an English instructor in Developmental Studies the Fall of 1980. I began her direct examination by asking her if Ervin ever mentioned anything to her about any expectations regarding research requirements for the Developmental Studies faculty. Her response was unequivocal: "No, he didn't. There was nothing mentioned about research. I took the job with the understanding that it was purely a teaching job. We taught a full load of courses, three courses a quarter, and we gave our time to the students rather than to our own research."

She then testified that Jan was an "excellent teacher - a dedicated teacher who never behaved unprofessionally in her relations with her colleagues or superiors."

Yaw was also present at the Parent Involvement Program when Isaac Levy talked about giving blazers to

Developmental Studies faculty members. She corroborated Jan's testimony that Levy wrote a check and handed it to Ervin in the presence of herself and other faculty members.

I asked her if she had heard any statements from Jan regarding the conversation she had with Ervin when he asked her to contact Barbara Carson in an effort to get grades changed for athletes. She answered, "I don't remember what time of the year it was. I don't remember what quarter it was, but I remember Jan's mentioning that to me, because she was very upset about it, that Dr. Ervin had asked her to call Barbara Carson and ask her to change the grades of some athletes whom she was teaching."

I then asked her for impeachment testimony regarding Ervin's claim that she had told him that she was quitting her job in part because of Jan Kemp. She answered, "No, I did not."

During Almand's ensuing cross-examination of Yaw, he attempted to dispute her denial of making that statement, but he failed miserably. She stood by her testimony despite Almand's attack based on alleged contradictory statements that he claimed she had made when he interviewed her in the Courthouse just prior to her testimony.

Yaw denied Almand's version of that conversation. We were actually pleased that Almand, in essence, "testified" through his questions that Dr. Yaw was not being truthful. She was no longer employed by UGA - she had no reason to testify falsely, and her calm and measured demeanor contrasted sharply with Almand's aggressive questioning premised upon his own impressions of their corridor conversation. We were convinced that the jury believed Yaw and not Almand, and amazed that Almand implicitly put his own credibility before the jury for their judgment. Who did he think the jury would believe - a disinterested witness testifying under oath or the lead defense lawyer? The verdict answered that question. The jury believed Yaw.

At the end of Yaw's testimony, I was more than ready to announce the words that we, the jury, the gallery, and the UGA community had been waiting to hear - "The plaintiff rests, Your Honor."

Almand advised the judge that his surrebuttal, the final phase of trial testimony, was limited to defense witnesses who contradicted the testimonies of the plaintiff's rebuttal witnesses, and that it would be brief. Judge Ward called the jury back and told them that the trial testimony would conclude the following day, a Friday. He also told them that they would hear closing arguments and the court's final instructions on Monday before beginning their deliberations.

# CHAPTER FORTY-THREE
# THE DEFENDANTS' SURREBUTTAL

## Carolyn Faust's Surrebuttal Testimony

Almand began the surrebuttal with an attack on Jan's denial that she had given Becky Robbins Galvin a gift-wrapped condom as a gag gift at her bridal shower, but he failed to present the testimony of anyone who was actually present at that shower. It was apparent that Galvin could not provide him with the identity of any of her friends or relatives to corroborate her accusations. Almand's only witness was Carolyn Faust, Ervin's secretary who didn't attend the shower.

Faust testified that Becky Galvin had come into the secretarial pool one day to complain about something that had happened to her. She said Galvin was upset, and showed the secretaries some red wrapping paper and what she thought was a balloon, but the other women there laughed and told her it was a condom. Faust testified that "Galvin said, 'Oh,' and I chuckled and I went back to doing my job." She also confirmed that the incident was insignificant to her. "I could not understand why she was upset about it." She assumed that it was because Galvin wasn't married.

On cross-examination, Faust said that Jan came in while they were looking at the condom, laughed and said they did it because Galvin was shy. I pressed her to identify "they." "Did she (Galvin) say anything about Jan Kemp?" Her answer disclosed the insignificance of her testimony.

She responded, "No, I don't remember her saying anything about Jan." Then she changed her testimony about Jan even being present. She testified that, "There were a lot of people in our office in and out and remembering back to the years I cannot remember who was in the office."

Q. "You can't remember Jan even being present, can you?"

A. "I probably couldn't, but I remember the incident happening."

She added that she remembered Jan mentioning the incident to her, but she couldn't say when. I asked her if that was the same day, and she said she couldn't remember. She testified, "It might have been - it might not have been."

### Mary Phillips' Surrebuttal Testimony

Almand's next witness was Mary Phillips. She was Jan's graduate teaching assistant who had been assigned to teach a class that concentrated on grammar because that was the subject of the students' exit test. Jan gave her the course syllabus that emphasized grammar. Phillips admitted seeing that syllabus, but said that she felt like she could do her own syllabus. She testified that didn't know that grammar was emphasized on the exit test until the last two weeks of the quarter when she "crammed it down their throat."

### Sue McCaffrey's and Carolyn Smith's Surrebuttal Testimonies

Sue McCaffrey and Carolyn Smith took the stand as Almand's next two witnesses. Once again, Almand had interviewed them together the preceding night. Neither had any information other than what they had testified to when they first appeared as witnesses to swear that Jan had plagiarized a paper for a student. Judge Ward remembered their testimony, so he severely limited what he allowed them to say. Nothing was added to bolster the defense.

### Nathan Dean's Surrebuttal Testimony

Almand called Nathan Dean who was the Acting Vice President for Research under the direct authority of Trotter and Davison. He was called to contradict Katie Blackburn's testimony that he was one of the people whom she knew held a poor opinion of Ervin's reputation for truthfulness. Dean hedged when asked twice whether or not he said anything to Blackburn about Ervin's reputation. His answers were, "I don't believe so" and "No, sir, I don't believe so." Almand was obviously dissatisfied with those equivocal responses, so he asked the same question for a third time, but he rephrased the question. "Do you have any reason to doubt his reputation for truth and veracity?" Dean said, "No, sir." Almand followed with a leading question: "You never told Ms. Blackburn anything of that nature." Dean responded, "No, sir." Almand quickly ended the dialogue with Dean. "I have no further questions." We noticed that his abrupt end of his questions omitted the critical question: can you identify anyone with whom you have discussed Ervin's reputation for truthfulness?

That omission gave us an open field that we could drive

a tank through. I couldn't help but wonder why Almand didn't prepare Dean better for his testimony by simply advising him of the rules governing reputation testimony. Had he known the rules, he could have simply contacted a few people whom he knew would vouch for Ervin's good reputation for truthfulness, but that obviously never happened. That gave me a great opportunity to undermine Dean's testimony on cross-examination.

Q. Do you know his reputation for truth and veracity?

A. Pardon?

Q. Do you know his reputation for truth and veracity?

A. I can't speak for his reputation with other people, but I have no reason to doubt his truth and veracity.

The judge interrupted to advise Dean. "It has to be communicative or areawide. Let me explain that to the witness." Then Dean fell into the trap we were setting.

Q. Do you know one or another, not what you think or what you have no reason to believe or disbelieve, but what his reputation is for truth and veracity?

A. I know what people that I know think of him.

Q. Let me get the names that you know of.

A. I'm not talking about individuals, but about the general reputation he has in the group of University members with whom I'm familiar.

Q. Give me their names.

A. We have a Monday morning meeting of the president,

all the vice presidents, the various other people to which Dr. Ervin - - in which Dr. Ervin is a participant.

Q. The deans and the vice-presidents?

A. Yes, sir.

Q. You never went over to Developmental Studies to ask anybody about the reputation.

A. No, sir.

Q. In fact, the deans and the vice presidents have never discussed his reputation?

A. No.

Q. So you do not know his reputation, do you?

A. No, sir. As I said, I can only tell you my judgment of him.

Dean's denial of Katie Blackburn's reference to him as someone who challenged Ervin's credibility was insignificant given the testimony of other unimpeached witnesses who did know of his poor reputation for truth and veracity.

## Sherrie Nist's Surrebuttal Testimony

Almand then recalled Sherrie Nist, Ervin's Acting Associate Director, to contradict Ruth Sabol's testimony that Jan's textbook was similar to the one that she and William Diehl had authored. Nist was hardly in a position to make that assessment since she admitted on cross-examination that she had never seen Jan's book. Specifically, I asked her if she ever sat down and compared her book and Jan's book to determine whether or not Dr. Sabol's testimony was correct. After attempting to avoid the question, Nist finally admitted, "No, I have not."

## William Diehl's Surrebuttal

Almand's final witness was William Diehl who also took the witness stand for the second time. Almand asked him to compare Jan's book to the one that he co-authored with Nist. Diehl concluded that the two books were not similar because Jan's was "a workbook" and his was an "instructional book." That evidence was next to meaningless – the jury had already seen Diehl testify about the nature of Jan's unfinished book based solely on a one-minute and ten-second perusal of it while sitting on the witness stand. Moreover, the Developmental Studies faculty was never expected to conduct any research until 1982 around the time that Jan was fired. In other words, all of Almand's rigmarole about the faculty's research obligations were immaterial. The jury had already heard that Diehl himself had minimized research for Developmental Studies faculty members in his own report to the chairman of the department's committee that formulated the promotion and tenure guidelines. Ervin was the single witness who contradicted Diehl and a number of other faculty members who testified that there were no research expectations until the faculty Promotions and Tenure Committee delivered its 1982 recommendations.

After Diehl's testimony, Almand's surrebuttal ended with his announcement that the "defense rests." The presentation of evidence was finally over. All that remained were the closing arguments, the court's charge to the jury summarizing the applicable legal principles, the jury's deliberations, and the return of the verdict.

Judge Ward addressed the jury. He told them that the evidence was closed, that the next stage of the trial would begin on Monday morning. He explained that he was excusing them on that Friday afternoon. They were to return Monday morning when the lawyers would deliver their closing arguments. After that, he would give them instructions on the legal principles that controlled the case before they began their deliberations. He wished the jury a restful weekend and discharged them.

After a recess, Judge Ward heard and denied the defendants' motions for directed verdicts in their favor. Then he convened the final hearing, the charge conference, to review both sides' specific requests to include certain principles of law in the instructions that he would give to the jury. When the final set of instructions was completed, the judge gave a copy to the attorneys to refer to in preparing their closing arguments.

## CHAPTER FORTY-FOUR
## THE "JAN KEMP AFFAIR" ERUPTS

The verdict was still pending, but the public relations battle was devastating UGA's leadership. Jan's top priority was already assured - there would be reform at UGA to stop the abuses revealed by the trial witnesses - there were too many eyes watching. I couldn't imagine a better platform for her to lobby the public to insist on the reform that she and other faculty members were demanding. The witnesses had delivered a damning indictment of UGA's leadership. The trial attracted nationwide attention that shamed the academic and political leaders of the State of Georgia. The defense of indefensible academic malpractice by UGA's top tier administrators drew virtually unanimous condemnation from UGA's faculty and students, the citizens of Georgia, and Georgia's political elite. The press was eviscerating the decision makers who had paved the way to the judicial disaster in the United States District Court before a federal jury sitting in Atlanta - Georgia's capital city.

*The Atlanta Journal Constitution* Editor, Jim Minter, summed up the public relations fallout in an editorial published on Sunday, February 9, 1986. He announced the public's verdict regardless of what the jury's verdict might be. Describing his mood as someone who approached the Jan Kemp trial with "a sick feeling in the pit of my stomach," Minter wrote, "The jury has not spoken, and yet the trial is over. The University of Georgia lost." Minter, who had been a sports writer for 20 years, understood that "collegiate athletes are not universally a hotbed of academic excellence." He continued, "I have not been shocked to learn that football practice at the University of Georgia is not a meeting of Phi Beta Kappa. It doesn't have to be. I have, however, been surprised to learn that we now have athletes who cannot read billboards. And I've been stunned by the University of Georgia's defense, by attempts to defend the indefensible, by Administration officials from Athens driving over to Atlanta each day and shooting the University in the foot. The University has committed the cardinal errors of a defendant on trial. It lost its temper, lost perspective, and just plain lost, terribly."

After reading Minter's editorial and reflecting on the preceding five weeks I knew that the Jan Kemp trial was almost over, but the "Jan Kemp Affair" was accelerating toward its conclusion - Fred Davison's resignation as UGA's President.

# CHAPTER FORTY-FIVE
# CLOSING ARGUMENTS

We returned to the Federal Courthouse Monday morning ready to end the Kemp case with a bang. We were confident that we had carried our burden to prove Jan's case and were anxious to review the damning evidence provided by our witnesses throughout the trial. The court allocated an hour and a half to each side for the final summations. The plaintiff is always entitled to opening and closing arguments because the burden of proof remains with the plaintiff throughout the trial. The defendants' closing argument is sandwiched between the plaintiff's two opportunities to address the jury.

Pat and I split our arguments. He was tasked with the opening which is designed to review the evidence by reminding the jury of the testimonies of the plaintiff's witnesses and the content of the documents in evidence. Almand would then review the evidence of the defense witnesses, and try to undermine our case. I was responsible for the closing argument which affords the plaintiff an opportunity to challenge the defendants' closing argument, attack the defense witnesses, and urge the jury to return a substantial verdict for Jan in order to send a message to the defendants and other collegiate football factories.

### Pat's Summation

Pat began our summation by outlining the major events

proved during the trial: Barbara Carson's change of grades for Veronica Walker and another female track athlete, Isaac Levy's successful lobbying of Fred Davison to negate the student judiciary's decision to sanction his son for making an obscene phone call to Jan, and the exit of the nine. He told the jury that the court would tell them in his instructions that Jan's criticism of those events was protected speech under the First Amendment, so the sole issue for the jury to decide was "causation"; specifically, the core question that the jury had to consider was whether Jan's exercise of her constitutional rights of free speech was the cause of her demotion and/or the nonrenewal of her employment contract.

Pat's outline of the overwhelming evidence supporting our answer to that question was superb. He talked about Jan's meritorious evaluations by Ervin preceding the Veronica Walker grade change incident, Ervin's subsequent negative evaluation planted in Jan's personnel file without notice to her, Ervin's "not yet" response when Larry Blount asked him if Jan's personnel file contained any evidence to support the adverse actions taken against her, and Ervin's statement to his "close personal friend" Velma Scott that he intended to get rid of two pregnant women in his life - Jan and his wife.

Then Pat asked the jury to focus on the timeline linking Jan's constitutionally protected speech to the series of punitive actions that Ervin took against her. He catalogued the meritorious content of Jan's evaluations prior to 1981, her superlative professional reputation among her colleagues, students and administrators - some of whom, including Vince Dooley, were defense witnesses. He reminded the jury that Ervin agreed with those sentiments until the Barbara Carson incident in the Spring of 1981 and Jan's refusal in October of that same year to abandon her successful prosecution of ML with the student judiciary.

Pat pointed out that Ervin didn't waste much time retaliating against Jan. He offered her English coordinator position to Theresa Timmons in November, but Timmons refused the offer. Ervin also removed Jan from the Promotions and Tenure Committee that was forming guidelines for the impending effort to have Developmental Studies become a promotional unit.

Pat reminded the jury that the faculty rebelled in January of 1982 when Trotter, with Davison's permission, agreed to exit the nine after being lobbied by an Athletic Association agent, Dick Copas. An ad hoc faculty committee met three times in January to consider a letter that they asked Jan to draft protesting the exit of the nine. Pat called the jury's attention to Trotter's and Ervin's presence at the committee's January 27 meeting that Jan wasn't able to attend. He asked the jury to look at Trotter's notes of that meeting. Despite Jan's absence, Trotter made extensive notes during or immediately after that meeting referencing Jan's activities in connection with the protest of the exit of the nine - a matter that had not been discussed at that meeting.

Pat recalled Ervin's actions following a January 29 meeting. He ordered Jan to schedule a meeting with him as soon as possible. She contacted his office and scheduled it for the following Monday, February 1. Ervin failed to appear at that time and again on Tuesday at another rescheduled time. The following day, February 3, he notified Jan that he was demoting her from her coordinator position. Jan appealed that decision and hired law professor Larry Blount to represent her. Pat outlined Blount's trial testimony - how, to no avail, he had notified Ervin that he represented Jan who preferred an internal resolution of the problems with the athletes and her demotion from her coordinator position.

Pat asked the jury to consider Ervin's reaction to Blount's appearance in the case. On February 5th, Ervin notified Blount's boss, Ralph Beaird, the Dean of the Law School and Davison's counsel, that Jan had retained Blount to represent her and that the situation might end up in litigation. On that same day, Ervin solicited former English graduate student program instructor Mary Phillips' memo that criticized Jan.

Beaird and Trotter then created a ruse to render Jan's scheduled March 10 formal grievance hearing meaningless. Trotter notified Jan that she was not entitled to a grievance hearing since there were no allegations of discrimination. Jan would only be allowed to pursue a challenge of the process that led to her demotion. The hearing panel then added insult to injury by claiming that Blount failed to utilize the "correct procedure" to challenge the merits of the decision to demote her when, in fact, there was no such procedure. Pat reminded the jury that one of Jan's grievance panel members, Vice President Eugene Younts, testified at the trial and was unable to identify any 'correct' procedure when asked to do so. Nevertheless, Jan insisted on stating her case before the grievance panel even though she understood that an unsuccessful outcome was preordained. Her truthful testimony about Ervin infuriated him. Pat described the undisputed testimony about Ervin's misconduct during that hearing. Ervin completely lost control of his temper. He broke a pencil and threw his glasses down on the table while excoriating Jan's constitutionally protected actions.

Eleven days later, Kenny Sims signed the letter falsely accusing Jan of making improper sexual remarks while teaching her Fall 1981 class. At that point, he had failed Jan's class and another professor's class with grades of F. That second F resulted in Sims' expulsion from the program under the Admissions Committee rule which only allowed two quarters for a student to earn at least a D in the core courses. Ervin ignored that rule and readmitted Sims by a letter dated March 29, the same date as Sims' letter. Then on June 2, after receiving a third F in English, Sims was dismissed for a second time, but Ervin readmitted him again despite the absence of any information justifying either readmission on any academic grounds.

Pat reminded the jury of Trotter's April 21, 1982 memo in which she underlined the phrase, "She's going public," a notation that proved her awareness of Jan's intent to exercise her First Amendment constitutional rights. On that same date, Ervin notified Jan that he was reducing her contract from twelve to nine months because she was no longer a coordinator despite the fact that several other faculty members who were not coordinators had 12-month contracts. Ervin's decision reduced Jan's annual income by approximately $4,000, a considerable amount in the early 80's.

Pat turned to an attack on Ervin's attempt to prove that Jan's research efforts were insufficient to allow her to be promoted and tenured within the seven-year time frame allowed for tenure track faculty. He reminded the jury that Developmental Studies wasn't approved as a promotional unit until June 26 of 1982, and significantly, that Ervin, who consistently argued that Jan didn't have enough "time in rank" to achieve promotion and tenure under the newly adopted standards for promotion, had no idea of how "time in rank" was calculated. That fact was proved by an August 5, 1982, letter from Ervin to Trotter seeking clarification on the "time in rank" limitations for Developmental Studies faculty members. That letter was dated four days after Ervin notified Jan that her contract was being non-renewed. He didn't notify her of the reasons for that decision, but he did retroactively record his seven reasons in the September 2, 1982 memo to his files that we forced him to reveal at the beginning of the trial.

Pat made sure that the jury understood that the decision makers at UGA, with the collaboration of the Regents, remained unrepentant. He reminded them that on December 9, 1980, the Regents approved fifth quarters for five football team players. The Regents' memo granting those extra quarters had a handwritten note attached to it stating, "Good luck in New Orleans!" referring to UGA's pending appearance in the upcoming January 1, 1981 Sugar

Bowl game against Notre Dame that it won to claim the 1980 National Championship. Then in the Fall of 1983, Theresa Timmons taped Ervin and Trotter acknowledging the validity of the faculty complaints as well as the virtual certainty that those athletes, as well as the athletes involved in the "exit of the nine," would never graduate.

Pat encouraged the jury to consider the character evidence - to weigh the testimony of numerous witnesses, including defense witnesses, who praised Jan's energy and talent along with the ten witnesses who swore that Ervin had a bad reputation for truthfulness, and that they would not believe him even if he was under oath.

Pat asked the jurors to be mindful of the unique opportunity that they had to make a difference by ruling for Jan and against the defendants - a difference that no one else was willing to deal with. He noted that Davison certainly was not willing to address the serious breaches of academic integrity clearly proved during the trial. In fact, Davison testified that he supported the defendants' disregard of stated academic standards because the athletes would be "better off" for remaining as students at UGA despite their inability to acquire a college degree. Pat also noted that the Athletic Association had no motive to ensure that the athletes complied with UGA's academic standards as illustrated by the lobbying of its agents of UGA's academic leaders to exempt the athletes from the rigors of normal academic standards. Their interests were unrelated to the academic success of those students. Their goal was winning football games - period.

Pat concluded his argument with a review of Jan's outstanding career as a UGA undergraduate and graduate student whose talents were recognized when she was awarded a UGA professorship. He reminded the jury of her superior service as a professor, and most importantly of her courage as proved by the professional risk she took by standing tall in protest of the blatant breaches of academic integrity by the defendants. Then he gave the jury an eloquent summation of the compelling reason that demanded a verdict for Jan. "But if you do the wrong thing, there won't be another Jan Kemp, and I doubt there will be another Jan Kemp anywhere around here, because if this woman can't win the lawsuit based on the facts presented to you - the clear and convincing evidence that has been presented to you, based on her record - if she can be fired and this jury says that is okay, you can be sure there will never be another Jan Kemp at the University of Georgia."

Before concluding his summation, Pat outlined the reasons for the jury to award not only compensatory damages to Jan for the loss of income, but to also award punitive damages to send a message by imposing a penalty on the defendants for their conduct:to "hurt them" to deter further misconduct and to send a message not only to the wrongdoers at UGA, but also to administrators at other football machine universities who undoubtedly accepted or even encouraged similar misconduct.

## Almand's Summation

Almand opened his summation by admitting the core of our case: athletes did receive preferential academic treatment at UGA, the exit of the nine did occur, extra quarters were afforded certain scholarship athletes in violation of the four quarters limitation, and failing scholarship athletes were administratively exited. He acknowledged that "certain actions" were taken against Jan after she resisted the events that gave rise to the faculty rebellion. He acknowledged that Ervin discharged Jan from her positions as the chair of the Promotion and Tenure Committee and as the Coordinator of the English Department and then nonrenewed her contract. He also acknowledged that Jan did speak out on "matters of public interest."

Given those admissions, Almand correctly noted that the jury could rule for Jan if they decided that her protected speech was a substantial or motivating reason for the actions taken against her. Almand effectively reduced the jury deliberations to a single issue: were Ervin's seven reasons noted in his September 2, 1983, memo a pretense or were they the actual and sole reasons for the actions that he and Trotter took against Jan?

Almand's summation didn't answer that question. Instead, he recalled the character assassination tactics that he used earlier in the trial. His opening salvo began, "If you find that she spoke out and she spoke out loudly, that is not sufficient. You must also go and find that we had no other reason to do what we did other than the fact that she spoke out, and I will remind you at this point of the number of witnesses whom we presented concerning Ms. Kemp and her personality and her actions - the things she did and the things she didn't do."

Almand characterized Jan's self-image as that of a "perfect teacher, a perfect person, a person without any human frailties, a person that never did anything wrong . . . she is assuming a role of one of the English knights of folklore, going on out to do battle against the evil magician." He argued that Jan was "cloaking herself in this mantle of outraged virtue, to divert your attention away from the real issues in this case which was her and her conduct." Almand reiterated his belief that Jan's conduct revealed that her motive wasn't a simple attempt to salvage academic integrity at UGA, but instead an effort to seek revenge against Ervin, an "individual who found her lacking in some respects and took action against her for this reason." He asked the jury to decide if Jan was speaking out on corruption or if she was seeking her own form of revenge which was to hurt these defendants and to obtain large sums of money.

Almand then suggested that Jan was not acting in good faith because she failed to report the misconduct of Trotter and Ervin to "her superiors and to the Regents" - an argument that seemed preposterous to us given the collaboration in that misconduct by the administrators to whom she would report, Virginia Trotter and Fred Davison. Almand's mention of her "failure" to report to the Regents was equally absurd since they had given Trotter permission to grant fifth quarters to failing scholarship athletes in the December of 1980 memo with the handwritten note wishing the football team "Good luck in New Orleans."

Almand finally shifted his focus to an actual issue in the case by addressing the favorable treatment afforded the children of individuals who contributed money to UGA or had political influence. He began with another rhetorical question: "How much in the way of generalized statements do we have, and how much in the way of specific evidence do we have for that?" Then he answered his own question by throwing Virginia Trotter under the bus. "There were some few students who came in at a low level. The Levy boy is one. Okay. He was admitted before his father's financial contribution, not after. And I don't have any excuse for Dr. Trotter admitting the daughter of her maid. What can I say? It happened."

Despite the complete absence of any evidence of preferential treatment for other students - those whose parents were not wealthy donors or influential citizens, Almand told the jury that every case of parental intervention was handled without regard to social status or economic standing. That argument was particularly disingenuous since the jury had heard the testimony of ML's father Isaac Levy - a wealthy Florida lawyer and a graduate of UGA's law school. He understood the process - a *quid pro quo.* He met for lunch with Ervin andRalph Beaird, the law school dean. Beaird contacted Davison, Levy's son was admitted, and Levy donated money to UGA.

The jurors were also aware of Isaac Levy's contacts with Davison, who then vacated a student judiciary's decision to impose sanctions on Levy's son for making the obscene phone call to Jan. They had also heard testimony about a grade change for Herschel Walker's sister on request by a UGA track coach. Almand's claim that UGA had actual policies in place to control influence peddling was disingenuous at best.

Judge Ward broke for lunch at that point. The afternoon session reconvened exactly one hour later. Almand began the afternoon with his rendition of the validity of the "educational philosophy" that led Ervin to construct his version of how educationally unprepared student athletes should be treated. He brazenly admitted that "Dr. Ervin and Dr. Trotter were faced with an impossible situation with a University policy, of which, as they and others have testified, they did not agree." He made that statement with the confidence that the jury would accept the proposition that high rank meant that University officials were exempt from compliance with official UGA and Regents policies if they disagreed with them. He emphasized that the defendants' proposition was reasonable and acceptable as a remedy to the "revolving door" syndrome that admissions of unqualified students created. Almand was seemingly blind to what he was saying. We couldn't believe that he was telling the jury that UGA and Regents policies could be ignored if they violated an administrator's educational philosophy. Surely, the jurors pondered that argument since Almand's proposition would render official Regents and UGA policies meaningless.

Almand turned his attention to the Athletic Association which was the subject of the public relations portion of the defense featuring Vince Dooley. He urged the jury to consider the value of the Athletic Association's financial contribution to UGA—its sponsorship of non-revenue-producing sports such as track, tennis and swimming. He also noted the Athletic Association's one million dollar annual contribution to UGA—a contribution that paled in significance compared to the excessive salaries paid to the coaching staff and the director of the Athletic Association.

Almand then launched an accusation of insubordination against Jan for dropping the lower than normal basic 096 class, even though that accusation wasn't mentioned in Ervin's ""seven reasons" memo. Moreover, no witness corroborated Ervin's testimony disputing Jan's claim that Sue McCaffrey Kenny, acting as Developmental Studies Director in Ervin's absence, authorized the decision to discontinue that class.

Almand continued in a vague sort of way to criticize Jan for failing to do sufficient research, but added nothing to the testimonies of numerous witnesses, including the defense witnesses, Mark Hogrebe and William Diehl. Hogrebe, the program's Director of Research who also served on the Promotion and Tenure Committee, had agreed with the other committee members that it would be "foolish to emphasize research in Developmental Studies." Diehl wrote a letter to the chair of that committee stating, "We feel that the mission of our Division precludes the attainment of a high level of performance in other areas than instruction."

Almand was approaching the time limit for his summation, so he turned to the evidence against Trotter and suggested that we had not made a case against her. "What has been the role of Dr. Trotter in this case? She's almost like the disappearing person. I've heard so little testimony about her role." Shortly after drawing that conclusion, Almand finished his summation.

Almand did what he had to do - discuss the case for an hour and a half by presenting what he considered to be the best arguments available for a litigator in the face of overwhelming evidence that favored the opposition.

### My Closing Summation

Pat had comprehensively summarized the evidence proving Jan's claims of retaliation for exercising her rights of free speech under the First Amendment. His presentation provided the jury with ample reasons to find that the defendants' violations of her constitutional rights justified an award for her lost wages and emotional distress. His summation had systematically outlined the facts the jury needed to reach that conclusion. What a relief I felt listening to his words. It was not only a textbook summation of the facts that overwhelmingly favored Jan's case, it allowed me to make my favorite kind of closing argument speaking from the heart and the gut to convince the jurors that they needed to go beyond a verdict for Jan's monetary damages.

I began by reminding the jury of Almand's admission that there was preferential treatment for scholarship athletes, but it wasn't for any academic purpose. In fact, it demeaned normal university-level academic standards. Most faculty members refused to accept that reality, and some of them created their own version of "preferential treatment." They used their personal time to provide preferential academic treatment to marginal athletes who they believed could attain undergraduate degrees if given a chance to make up for their substandard high school educations. No one could reasonably criticize that version of preferential treatment since it placed a huge burden on the faculty. They used their own time, sometimes virtually hundreds of hours, to tutor challenged students. Their problem with UGA's leadership was the preferential treatment of scholarship athletes via the stroke of a vice president's pen without regard to the educational impact of such actions. Faculty witnesses called to testify by both sides agreed that administrative exits from the program and/or the granting of extra quarters for failing athletes was gross misbehavior in contrast to accommodations made with faculty consent for a reason and in a reasonable manner.

I tried to summarize the faculty's mindset about the harm that UGA's and the Athletic Association's leader were visiting upon UGA's student athletes. I argued that, "Philosophically, they're telling these athletes that 'you don't have to accept the demands of a college curriculum - that you can forget about studying because you can come to the University of Georgia, and you won't have to study. Academic exceptions will be made for you. You're going to be given benefits to help you get a college degree, but exceptions to normal academic standards will be made for you so you can play football.' They're telling the other undereducated high school kids that they will not get similar preferential treatment because they're not athletes."

I argued that these signals sent by the administrators to

revenue-producing athletes were also signals to the faculty – they were being told that their academic judgments were irrelevant because it all boiled down to Trotter's judgment which had nothing to do with UGA's mission to educate its students. Focusing on why Trotter should pay punitive damages, I argued that, "She just made the decisions arbitrarily. Did Trotter tell you the information she used? No. Did she go to the faculty? No. Did she have the records in front of her? No. Did she have any recommendations in front of her from faculty members? No."

I turned to another obvious curiosity about how Ervin assessed the academic viability of scholarship athletes. He admitted that he talked to Vince Dooley about LC, a scholarship athlete. I asked the jury to scrutinize that testimony. "Ask yourselves, Ladies and Gentlemen, what in the world has Vince Dooley got to contribute about the academic treatment of LC? What does he know? Why was he involved in that process – the academic treatment of these kids? He's not on the faculty. He's not a teacher. Why is Leroy Ervin even talking to Vince Dooley about whether or not to make exceptions from the academic rules for athletes, and how did that conduct advance the athletes' academic progress toward obtaining a college degree?"

I also challenged Almand's claim that there was no preferential treatment for the children of influential and/ or wealthy people by reminding the jury of the Levy and Leveston cases as well as Trotter's administrative admission of her housekeeper's daughter. Those cases revealed Ervin's, Trotter's and Davison's disrespect of educational standards that were intrinsic to the very idea of a university education. I also reminded the jury of other administrative acts that provided preferential academic treatment by UGA's leaders for political reasons. I asked them to recall the admission of the student, RC, whose politically connected relatives were mentioned in his UGA files because his grandfather and his father were or had been members of the Georgia legislature. Perhaps the most revealing example of political preferential treatment of students was the case of SR. He was readmitted by Davison personally after failing out of Developmental Studies. I asked the jury to review his file where they would find a series of memos signed by Ervin and Trotter. One of those memos addressed to Ervin's assistant Sue McCaffrey Kenny contained the admission that "Trotter is going to see Davison about it." Handwritten notes in SR's file corroborated the truthfulness of that comment. One of those notes ordered SR's readmission. It read, "Remove this flag per the orders of President Davison."

Then I turned to the legal principles that governed the case. The charge conference we had with Judge Ward allowed both sides to review the jury instructions he had prepared, to give the parties an opportunity to submit requests for additional instructions, and to put any objections to those instructions on the official record. That process is very helpful because it enables the lawyers to blend the facts of the case with the instructions the jurors are about to hear. I told the jury that the first element of our burden of proof, to establish the constitutional protection of Jan's speech, had already been resolved – the judge would instruct them that Jan's speech regarding preferential treatment for scholarship athletes, her protest of Ervin's request that she ask another UGA teacher to change grades for female athletes, and her criticism of favorable treatment for the children of wealthy and influential people were protected by the First Amendment as a matter of law. On the other hand, we had the burden of proof to establish the second element, that Jan's protected speech was more likely than not a substantial or motivating factor for the actions taken against her by the defendants. If the jury decided that it was, the burden of proof shifted to the defendants to prove by a preponderance of the evidence that the actions taken against Jan would have been taken even if she had not engaged in constitutionally protected speech.

The intent of those instructions was to focus the jury's attention on determining the real reasons for the actions taken against Jan. So, I reiterated the evidence that the jury could consider to determine that the defendants' real motives were limited to her criticism of their misconduct. I reminded them of the timeline of Jan's annual evaluations, the sudden change of those evaluations from superlative on the ones that Jan signed to the unsigned derogatory one written by Ervin after she exercised her right to speak freely. I also argued that Almand's failure to produce any evaluations of the other coordinators for the jury to compare to Jan's evaluations was purposeful because they would highlight her value to the program.

Second, Ervin confessed in the most provocative language to his close personal friend, Velma Scott, that Jan was not going to run his business, and that he was going to get rid of her as "another pregnant lady in my life." Ervin denied making that statement, but Almand failed to produce independent evidence challenging Scott's testimony.

Third, Ervin never denied Jan's testimony describing his explosive conduct during her grievance hearing. He slammed his glasses on the desk, broke his pencil point and called Jan a liar, all without any reprimand by the three vice presidents who were present.

Fourth, Ervin was recorded on the Timmons tape saying that he was willing to speak truthfully about the situation with the athletes in a meeting with the faculty, but that he would not do so outside the meeting.

I asked the jury to listen carefully to the court's instructions on witness credibility. They would be told to consider the relationship of witnesses to the parties, and the interest of the witnesses themselves, if any. I reminded them of the "parade of vice presidents and their family members" who testified for the defendants. I suggested that they compare the demeanor of Jan's colleagues who corroborated her testimony to the demeanor of the defense witnesses, and to compare Jan's demeanor to Ervin's demeanor when he testified. Jan had been badgered by Almand, but she stood up to him, answered his questions concisely in a dignified manner, and conceded that she had made a couple of mistakes in some of her testimony taken in an earlier hearing and in her deposition because she was under considerable stress flowing from her discharge as a professor. Also, unlike Ervin, Jan apologized to the jury for the inaccuracy of any misstatements she had made.

I implored the jury to ask themselves if Ervin and Trotter

had testified clearly, candidly and concisely. "Did you get straight answers from Leroy Ervin? Did he ever give you answers that were actually responsive to the questions? What about Virginia Trotter's testimony?" I asked them to ponder why Trotter was left sitting at the defense table instead of being called as a witness in the presentation of the defendants' case in chief. "Why didn't Almand call Trotter back to the witness stand for comprehensive testimony during the presentation of the defense?" I reminded the jury that when we finished cross-examining Trotter during the presentation of our case, Almand asked the judge to instruct the jury that the defense was not allowed to question her extensively on direct examination until the presentation of their case. That request clearly implied that Almand intended to question Trotter later in the trial, but he never called her to testify and successfully objected to our request to recall her in the rebuttal phase of the trial.

Almand suggested in his closing argument that we hadn't proved the case against Trotter, so I argued that we had, but that even if we didn't, the jury could find that she had proved her own guilt. "What about the direct evidence on Virginia Trotter? Virginia Trotter was responsible for doing what led to the faculty protest. She is the one that exited the nine in an arbitrary manner. She is the one who admitted in a faculty meeting that, 'we are really talking through our hats if we think these kids are going to graduate.' She is the one that engaged in the wrongdoing. The faculty was protesting her misconduct."

I reviewed the evidence about the faculty meeting to protest the exit of the nine that Jan couldn't attend. Trotter's notes of that meeting were in evidence, and they contained almost nothing to do with the faculty's vigorous protest over that incident, but they were very critical of Jan who was not discussed during the meeting according to the faculty members in attendance.

I reminded the jury that Trotter claimed under oath that she had nothing to do with the decision to fire Jan. She said that she just approved Ervin's recommendation and sent it forward, but her assertion of being a purely disinterested observer was proven to be false. Her own notes recorded her conversation with Larry Blount. He called to notify her that he was going to represent Jan at her grievance hearing, and that Jan intended to use legal process if necessary. Blount's statement about a possible lawsuit were underlined in Trotter's notes of that conversation. When asked about that, Trotter swore that she compulsively underlined when making notes, but the numerous documentations in evidence of Trotter's various writings regarding the case contained no underlining other than the one documenting her conversation with Blount.

I turned to a brief discussion of the claim made by the defense that all faculty members, including the Developmental Studies faculty, were expected to engage in research. That claim was denied by every faculty member who testified, including defense witnesses, but the defense impugned the integrity of Theresa Timmons, Hyta Mederer, Fred Johnson, Ruth Sabol and others who swore to tell the truth and did so.

By way of contrast, I asked the jury to consider who the defense called as witnesses – witnesses who had no direct knowledge of what they were testifying about. With the exception of Kenny Sims, Almand didn't call any students who complained about one thing or another regarding Jan. Instead, he called their fathers who knew only what their sons had told them. Why didn't Almand call the students? He had no reservations about putting Sims on the stand to tell an improbable story about Jan - one Sims later admitted to Theresa Timmons and Hyta Mederer was bought and paid for by Ervin with a promise that Sims could remain as a UGA student in the face of the overwhelming consensus of the faculty that he was not going to make it academically.

As my remaining time neared ending, I returned to our request for punitive damages. "The purpose of punitive damages is to deter these people and others from similar conduct so you do have to send a signal beyond this courtroom. Ladies and Gentlemen, regardless of what Mr. Almand would like you to think, you are sending a proper message beyond this courtroom; you are not deterring administrators who act in good faith and have good reason to get rid of a subordinate. You are deterring people acting out in bad faith. If they are acting in good faith, they have nothing to fear. But if they act in bad faith, you are doggone right that they ought to be deterred." With a nod toward the defense table, I looked back to the jury: "Do it and you will answer to a jury and you will answer in a substantial way." As it turned out, that is exactly what happened when the jurors returned their verdict.

I closed with a plea to the jury to protect the University of Georgia, which the people of Georgia love. As jurors, their responsibility was to protect our University which compelled them to do the right thing – "to react as if it were your own child who needed protection." I reminded the jury that, "These people do not personify the University of Georgia, regardless of what they would like to think. They are not the University of Georgia. I suggest to you that people like Jan Kemp and her colleagues, the people of this state, and these jurors have a trust relationship with this university that requires us to return it to its former glory. That is what you need to do with your verdict, and it has to be a substantial verdict or they won't hear it. Money is all that they hear. That is what we are asking you to do."

## CHAPTER FORTY-SIX
## THE JURY'S VERDICT - "DEFINITELY"

Judge Ward's soft but confident voice solemnly charged the jurors to carefully review the evidence, apply his instructions in their deliberations, and try in good faith to reach a just verdict. The jurors were focused. They listened intently to his charge. No one in the courtroom doubted that each juror understood the importance of their obligations.

When he finished the charge, the judge directed the jurors to retire to the jury room. They left the courtroom accompanied by a bailiff who would insure the privacy of their deliberations. The wait began.

Jan, Pat and I stayed in the corridors, talked with news reporters, and cut up with the television cameramen. The defendants and their legal team cloistered themselves in a locked witness room. The trial was over for us, but the "Jan Kemp Affair" raged on for Davison, Trotter and Ervin, and it was about to get worse.

We remained pretty confident during the deliberations. The jurors had been exceptionally attentive throughout the trial. They all took copious notes, and they never asked the court a single substantive question during their two and a half days of deliberation. They deliberated that Monday afternoon and all of the following day. The only thing we heard from them was a request for assistance in locating Ervin's "sevenreasons" memo. They returned their verdict mid-morning on their third day of deliberations, February 12, 1986.

The verdict form was retrieved from the jury foreman by a courtroom marshal and handed to Judge Ward for his perusal to ensure that it was in proper form before passing it to the clerk for publication. The clerk then read it to an eerily quiet courtroom. "We the jury find as follows: For the plaintiff against both defendants for lost compensation in the amount of $79,680.95, for compensatory damages for mental distress in the amount of $200,000, and for reputation damages in the amount of $1. We find punitive damages against the defendant Virginia Trotter in the amount of $1,500,000, and against the defendant Leroy Ervin in the amount of $800,000." Judge Ward asked the jury foreperson, Melanie Mims, if she agreed that the verdict was in fact the verdict of all of the voting jurors. She answered, "Definitely!"

We knew that the news reporters would be anxious to interview Jan, but we needed a few minutes to decompress; so we retired to the witness room that was assigned to us. Of course, our excitement was palpable—hugs all around before we sat down to talk and do some deep breathing to calm down before meeting the ravenous cluster of reporters on the other side of the door. After about 15 minutes, we left so Jan could meet the press before we returned to the hotel where Pat had two suites reserved. He had anticipated the "happening" of a large party as the news leaked out to Jan's supporters and our families and friends.

Jan met the press attired in *red and black* clothes—UGA's

colors. She wore a large button that was given to her by UGA students who came to Atlanta to hear the verdict. It read, "Restore Academic Integrity at UGA." She thanked her family, the faculty members who supported her, and her attorneys. She told the press that the amount of damages in the verdict was "beyond my wildest dreams" and expressed her hope that it would lead to the substantial reform needed to address the academic dishonesty disclosed during the trial. That was more important to her than any amount of money that she might ultimately recover. Her interview lasted for about ten minutes before the reporters turned to several jurors who were waiting to be interviewed.

We watched intently as the jurors explained their decision to the news reporters in words that tracked our trial strategy. Juror Archie Collier told the reporters that "we wanted to make sure that it never happens again." Juror April Hamm said, "We wanted to stop it right here with this case." All of the jurors agreed that the deliberations focused on the core issue in the case. They wanted their verdict to affirm the constitutional right of faculty members to speak out against a university's practices without fear of reprisal.

The jury's foreperson, Melanie Mims, explained the one-dollar award to Jan for damage to her reputation. Her explanation was a great compliment to Jan. Ms. Mims said, "It was obvious from the testimony that Dr. Kemp was a good teacher." She noted that Jan's colleagues, including the ones who testified for the defense, acknowledged her teaching skills, so it seemed apparent to the jury that Jan's good reputation remained intact despite the actions taken against her by the defendants. In some respects, that compliment was the most satisfactory aspect of the verdict. Jan had not only scorched the defendants financially, her reputation as a great teacher was trumpeted by six citizens who sat through five weeks listening to a malicious attack against her character by UGA's top officials through their spokesman, Hale Almand, one of Georgia's most heralded trial attorneys. The jury's wholesale repudiation of that attempt at character assassination was golden.

Jurors Mims and Collier were also quoted in a February 15, 1986 *Atlanta Journal* article. Ms. Mims told news reporters that the jury "wanted to give it to them on the wrist where it hurts. You know how your mama used to whip you down, hit you with a switch." She went on to explain that the largest amount was assessed against Trotter because "she had the most power."

Mr. Collier elaborated on his earlier comments. He told the reporter that "the impression I got was that Dr. Trotter was very evasive." Collier went on to describe his overall impression of her testimony. "I viewed her as a person in a high position, not used to being asked those questions and called upon to answer for her actions." Commenting on the weight of her testimony, Collier said it was "confusing" and that "she was very hard to follow. Her thought patterns completely eluded me. So, in the end, I wasn't sure what she said and what she didn't say." He also criticized Almand's performance. When asked for his opinion of the lawyers, his comment on Almand was, "There were times when I felt that Almand was just inclined to make speeches."

# CHAPTER FORTY-SEVEN
# POST-TRIAL REACTIONS

## The Regents

Within hours of the verdict, the Board of Regents announced that it was delaying the traditional annual one-year reappointments of the University System's presidents pending the outcome of system-wide audits of all Developmental Studies programs. That announcement by H. Dean Propst, the Chancellor of the University of Georgia System, used ominous language in response to Davison's and Dooley's sworn testimonies that adherence to academic standards by scholarship athletes would constitute "unilateral disarmament." Propst condemned Davison's testimony claiming that UGA would not raise its standards as applied to athletes unless UGA's athletic opponents did the same, and that UGA's academically unqualified athletes had a "utilitarian value" to the University because of their revenue-producing potential. Propst concluded that the questions raised during the trial regarding athletic favoritism, "... must be directly addressed without equivocation because it is neither an effective excuse nor a sound justification to argue that certain things are done because everybody else does them."

For the first time during his 19-year tenure as UGA's president, Davison found himself in jeopardy of being forced to resign. He panicked. The following day Davison announced that UGA, unlike the other Southeastern Conference (SEC) universities, would not accept any athlete with a Scholastic Aptitude Test score lower than 700 and a high school grade-point average lower than 2.0. The timing of that concession spoke volumes—Davison knew what an audit of UGA would reveal. He was suddenly confronted with the reality that Jan Kemp had probably delivered a fatal blow to his presidency. He was guilty of complicity with the Athletic Association's trashing of UGA's academic reputation. The trial evidence was overwhelming, and Davison's active role in the Kemp disaster was about to be proved by the Regents Audit.

## The Political Establishment

The reaction to the verdict was instantaneous in the corridors of the State Capitol. *The Atlanta Journal Constitution* described it as "shock and disbelief." Governor Joe Frank Harris told the reporters that he was "amazed" and that "My first reaction would be, it's a little excessive, unbelievable really." Harris went on to criticize the Regents for not settling the case. "There's no doubt about it - it would have been an ideal situation to have been handled on campus by people in positions to handle it." He characterized it as a "personnel matter" that harmed the University's image because of the evidence heard during the trial. He described his feelings upon hearing the verdict as, "sadness . . . because we have gained so much in the last few years in education, there's been momentum from kindergarten through higher education. Something like this certainly overshadows it." Harris also issued a written statement promising that the State of Georgia would carry out "whatever action is required to restore the University's integrity." He also wrote a formal statement predicting that the audit ordered by the Regents would "help restore the public's faith and confidence in the University of Georgia and preserve the integrity of our system of higher education."

Tom Murphy, the legendary Speaker of the Georgia House of Representatives, reacted to the news of the verdict exclaiming, "Good God. All I can say is I hope the attorney general appeals." Murphy also adopted Harris' criticism of UGA's leadership. "There's no question in my mind that they shouldn't have taken some of those students into the Developmental Studies program. And there's no doubt in my mind that they should have weeded some of them out."

A number of state legislators from the Athens area, including Representatives Bob Argo, Hugh Logan, and Senator Paul Broun blasted the amount of the verdict. State Senator John Foster of nearby Cornelia, Georgia, the Chairman of the Senate's Education Committee, introduced a resolution to set up a joint House-Senate Committee to examine all of Georgia's Developmental Studies programs - a meaningless gesture since the Regents had already ordered a comprehensive statewide review of those programs immediately after the verdict.

## The Press

The national press reaction was uniformly critical of UGA's leadership. The New York Times published a comprehensive review of the trial on February 13, 1986, one day after the verdict. That article noted the Regents' disgust with Davison's trial testimony. *The Times* followed up the next day with a humiliating editorial opinion stating in part that, "the instructors were the weak link at Georgia, situated in the town of—as Socrates rolls over in his grave—Athens."

Other national publications followed up within several days. *Sports Illustrated* published trial testimony which showed that, "Since the color line was broken for athletes at the University of Georgia in 1969, approximately 200 blacks have worn Bulldog uniforms. And how many of them have graduated? Perhaps as few as 30."

The *Detroit Free Press* reported that "a lawyer for the University of Georgia has admitted in Federal Court that the University enrolls some athletes who are unable to read and write."

The *Baltimore Sun* wrote, "This particular can of worms has proven to be economy style … Ugly, untidy, shameful. It's enough to make you want to throw up your arms in disgust."

The *Miami Herald* noted the scope of the problems unveiled in the trial: "The rumors that swirl around many of the nation's big-time athletic programs—that academic standards are compromised to keep ball players eligible—are surfacing as harsh courtroom testimony against the football-mad University of Georgia."

The *Los Angeles Times* expanded the blame beyond Trotter and Ervin—"Trotter and Ervin may be co-defendants in the U.S. District Court of Northern Georgia, but the University of Georgia is on trial in the court of public opinion."

National syndicated columnist James Kilpatrick also weighed in with a column titled, "Reflecting on Kemp's Trial." Addressing the UGA administration's role in the endless keeping of some athletes on academic probation, Kilpatrick concluded, "Who is to blame? One place to start is with the University's gutless president, Fred C. Davison, who professed not to know what was going on. It was all news to him. Davison was named to his post by the State Board of Regents. Where were the Regents when the lights went out?"

Other newspapers and magazines also covered the Jan Kemp trial. Those publications included *The Washington Post*, *Chicago Tribune*, *Boston Globe*, *Orlando Sentinel*, *Newsweek*, and *People Magazine*.

Newspapers across Georgia published editorials criticizing Davison's mishandling of the Kemp case. The *Macon Telegraph and News* blamed Davison, Trotter and Dooley. "Are they the best physicians for a wounded University at this juncture in its life?" Characterizing the trial as a cancer corrupting a great University, the editorial concluded that, "Bringing it under control again has to begin with a hard look at the leadership at the University of Georgia."

*The Atlanta Constitution* concluded that the Developmental Studies program "clearly was more the victim of misuses than the cause of them." While recognizing that Georgia's "public school systems are often scandalously bad, such programs are essential if the University System is not to be the unwitting enforcer of a virtual caste system and what is worse, a caste system disproportionately based on race." Its editorial went on to note that the trial revealed instances of "disturbing indulgence of academic fudging by the campus administration, a certain lazy cynicism about the sometime fiction of the scholar-athlete." The editorial concluded that UGA and its Athletic Association "now needed to address the large concerns that were animated by the trial, to step beyond legalistic alibis and speak strongly to the school's academic mission."

*The Augusta Chronicle* quoted Jan Kemp's post-trial statement describing the verdict as "a victory for academic integrity." That editorial condemned UGA's leadership and complimented Jan. "Everyone who is sickened at the spectacle of the nation's institutions of higher learning treating athletes like prima donnas has to hope she's right because the recruiting of athletes then returning them to their homes without degrees is exploitation, not education. It should no longer be condoned."

## UGA's Campus

The Kemp verdict set off an open rebellion against Davison by students and faculty members. A group of students supporting Jan were present when the verdict was announced. They attended the post-trial press conferences and watched Jan's interview while wearing a gift they had given to her: a large button proclaiming, "Restore Academic Integrity at UGA." Earlier that day, another group of UGA students picketed the Regents meeting to demand Davison's discharge.

Meanwhile, back on the UGA Campus, a group of students organized "Students Against Campus Corruption" and began a protest designed to force Davison's resignation. They demonstrated outside Davison's office on at least two occasions carrying signs reading, "Fred Davison: World-Class Lie Master."

Davison initially reacted like Davison–he refused to accept responsibility for the scandal and drew a line in the sand rejecting calls for his resignation. He told the *Gwinnett County News* that he would not quit his job as UGA's president. He minimized the devastating effect of the trial on his career by proclaiming that "I've got a job to do, and I can't worry about the Kemp verdict." Davison then doubled down publicly. He proclaimed that the verdict was a miscarriage of justice that unfairly victimized UGA when there was nothing done that was wrong. He also resorted to the standard intimidation tactics previously used against student protestors—the presence of uniformed campus police officers taking photographs of the demonstrators.

Simultaneously, a number of faculty members demanded investigations and reform to remedy the corrupt academic practices disclosed during the trial. The faculty of the College of Arts and Sciences successfully petitioned its Dean to call a faculty meeting to discuss those issues. Approximately 350 of the 700 Arts and Sciences faculty members attended that meeting which resulted in decisions to call upon Davison to relieve Trotter and Ervin of their administrative duties pending the appeal of the Kemp verdict and to form a committee to investigate a full agenda of the Kemp trial issues. The faculty also voted to publish a letter criticizing the administration's handling of Developmental Studies, endorsing other UGA Schools and Colleges' similar actions, and expressing appreciation of Jan Kemp for disclosing breaches of academic integrity by UGA's leadership.

The faculty of the School of Journalism voted to create a committee to investigate the issues as did the University Council which convened a similar six-member committee composed of faculty, students and administrators.

Ten members of the Law School faculty signed an open letter to the UGA community requesting an immediate reassignment of Trotter and Ervin who were being allowed to retain their positions pending release of the Regent's Audit of Developmental Studies. The letter also criticized Davison for his inaction regarding Trotter and Ervin pending a Kemp trial report by Attorney General Mike Bowers. The letter stated, "Given the central role that the First Amendment plays in a democracy and in the life of a University, this is a serious matter. A judge and jury have found a constitutional violation. The ideal of academic freedom has been tarnished. We urge that pending appeal the defendants be reassigned from their administrative duties." The letter criticized Davison's refusal to take such actions by ceding his responsibility to control his top assistants to

Georgia's Attorney General. It read, "This decision must not be left to the attorney general of Georgia. To delegate the decision to him, as the president apparently intends to do, is an evasion of responsibility." The letter went on to criticize Georgia's private Athletic Association's role in setting policy in Developmental Studies. It stated, "The idea of a private entity setting policy in an area so closely identified with the University is a shameless charade."

The pressure on Davison was intense. He finally capitulated to an outraged faculty for the first time in his 19-year career as UGA's president. He recognized that the campus scandal precipitated by the Kemp verdict was a threat to his future which precluded him from continuing to allow the abuse of academic standards by UGA's administration and the Athletic Association without faculty oversight. He had to take action to remedy what he implicitly agreed was a shameless charade, so he announced that he was going to ask the Regents to transfer Developmental Studies from Academic Affairs to the College of Education where it would be subjected to academic oversight by the faculty rather than by the Vice President for Academic Affairs, who was subject to pressure by the Athletic Association. That decision was welcomed by the faculty, but it was too little and too late to salvage Davison's presidency.

# CHAPTER FORTY-EIGHT
# THE TAKE DOWN

UGA's Developmental Studies program was the first to be audited under Chancellor Propst's mandate. It began during the week of February 23, 1986. The preliminary findings of that audit were discussed by Vice Chancellor Ray Cleere during a two hour and forty-five minute session of the Regents at their March 12, 1986 meeting. At the conclusion of that meeting, Chancellor Propst advised the Regents that the UGA Audit would be completed by the following Friday. He also recommended that the Regents grant the traditional annual renewals of the contracts of all 30 of the system's other presidents while continuing to defer Davison's annual reappointment until the UGA audit was completed because, according to Board Chairman Arthur Gignilliat, there was "no indication of problems in the other institutions." The handwriting was on the wall. Davison's 19-year tenure as UGA's president was in its death throes, and the Regents made sure that he got the message.

Davison did get the message. He resigned the following day, March 13, 1986, exactly one month after the Kemp verdict. That day's weather featured a severe thunderstorm on UGA's campus. Davison read his angry letter of resignation at a meeting in his office with UGA's thirteen deans and six vice presidents. The letter characterized the decisions reached in the Regents' "star chamber proceeding" as a "personal and professional insult and a questioning of my integrity which I will not tolerate." Davison blamed his imaginary "political enemies," former Governor George Busbee, then Governor Joe Frank Harris and Tom Purdue, the Executive Secretary for both Busbee and Harris.

Legions of Davison critics joyfully reacted. His opponents, including students, faculty, and citizens celebrated his demise. An *Athens Banner Herald* editorial published the day of Davison's resignation captured the spirit of the local community's reaction. "We don't doubt that Dr. Davison has some legitimate complaints. His job is not easy. When you're the boss, everyone else thinks they can do your job better than you. But Dr. Davison's fall from grace could be characterized as more of a jump. His personal style is not that which endears itself to all persons. He has been characterized as obstinate, arrogant and vindictive by critics. His supporters would rephase the characterization as self confident, assured and unwilling to compromise his principles. Dr. Fred Davison has certainly had an impact at the University of Georgia. And perhaps it is fitting that his resignation this morning came in the midst of a thunderstorm."

Davison was still a tenured UGA veterinary faculty member. He remained there for two years before leaving to serve as the president and chief executive officer of the National Science Center Foundation in Augusta.

# CHAPTER FORTY-NINE
# UGA'S ATHLETIC ASSOCIATION PUNTS

## Vince Dooley

Immediately after the trial, Vince Dooley, UGA's Athletic Association Director and football coach, adopted a hostile reaction to the verdict and the ensuing investigation by the Regents, but he changed his tune in an interview by an Associated Press reporter published in the *Los Angeles Times* on March 23, 1986, ten days after Davison's resignation. During his testimony at the trial, Dooley swore that UGA could not raise academic standards for athletes without sacrificing its athletic competitiveness. Davison concurred during his trial testimony. Both characterized the prospect of higher academic standards as an act of "unilateral disarmament."

After allowing time for the devastating verdict to sink in, Dooley told *the Times*' reporter that he no longer believed his own trial testimony that the restoration of UGA's academic integrity would be unilateral disarmament. "As I look back on it … I would try to have done a better job of being more selective than what we were. Obviously, anybody that would say after what we've been through, that I would do the same thing all over, that would be foolish. I mean, it's like my people asking me would I run the same play again after it was unsuccessful. I'm not that dumb."

## The Athletic Association's Bosses

Prior to the verdict in the Jan Kemp trial, the private UGA Athletic Association refused to open its financial records for inspection by the public. Its leadership, controlled by Dooley as Athletic Association Director and Head Football Coach, resisted disclosure of the financial records claiming an exemption from Georgia's Open Records Act because it was not an agency of the State of Georgia. *The Macon Telegraph and News* had filed a lawsuit to compel disclosure of those records. The Athletic Association vigorously opposed the Macon newspaper's lawsuit, and convinced a Superior Court in Athens that its records were not subject to the Open Records Act. Despite that judicial victory, the Athletic Association punted shortly after the Kemp case verdict. It announced that it would open its financial records despite its status as a private corporation, but it continued asserting an exemption from the Open Records Act in the *Macon Telegraph and News* case, which was on appeal. In November of 1986, the Georgia Supreme Court reversed the trial court, and ruled that the Athletic Association was subject to the Open Records Act.

## CHAPTER FIFTY
## THE REGENTS' UGA AUDIT

The *Athens Banner Herald* headlined the results of the UGA audit in their April 4, 1986 edition, "Audit Finds 1,823 Violations." *The Atlanta Constitution's* headline proclaimed, "Audit: Breaks for Athletes Widespread."

The UGA audit identified five categories of violations of Regents' rules governing Developmental Studies: 1) admissions of revenue-producing athletes who did not satisfy admissions standards, 2) grants to athletes of more than four quarters in the program and, in some cases, enrollment in noncredit courses, 3) administrative exits by Ervin and Trotter for athletes who failed to satisfy exit standards within four quarters, 4) the substitution of an Athletic Association funded "laboratory" that enabled selected athletes to avoid the Developmental Studies regular requirements, and 5) a pattern of Athletic Association '"advisors" steering athletes to crip courses.

The findings of the Regents' audit were stunning. Given the sheer number of violations, it was unlikely that Davison, UGA and Athletic Association's President, was completely ignorant of the facts that led to the "Jan Kemp Affair." He must have had some awareness of the massive number of violations discovered by the auditors. If he didn't, his incompetency was more than enough reason for the Regents to end his presidency.

The Conclusions of the Audit were:

1) Neither Dr. Trotter nor Ervin denied their responsibility for decisions that resulted in preferential treatment for athletes and selected students in the areas of admissions, additional time in Developmental Studies, and administrative exiting.

2) The admissions of many academically deficient students via athletic and administrative influence were clear violations of equity in the application of admissions standards at the institution.

3) Allegedly, because of pressure from the Athletic Department, Dr. Ervin and Dr. Trotter made numerous exceptions to University and Regents policies by administratively exiting revenue producing athletes from the Developmental Studies program.

4) Apparently because of the large number of academically deficient athletes who were admitted to the University, the Athletic Department chose to directly fund the establishment of a Developmental Studies laboratory that was subsequently used as a route for an athlete to bypass the established academic standards of the approved Developmental Studies program.

5) After the auditors were told by representatives from the Athletic Department that the athletes were advised in the various departments of the University and then encouraged through counselors in the Athletic Department, it became clear that, in many cases, the advising process was abrogated and the Core Curriculum, in practice, ignored.

6) It was verified by reviewing transcript after transcript that the Athletic Department was instrumental in placing weak students in courses of study that were designed to maintain academic eligibility and not move students sequentially toward a college degree.

7) According to Dr. Ervin and Dr. Trotter, the President was made aware of requests for exceptions to policies governing the Developmental Studies Program.

## CHAPTER FIFTY-ONE
## POST-TRIAL SETTLEMENT

Georgia's Attorney General Mike Bowers took control of the post-trial defense of Ervin and Trotter. A very capable young Assistant Attorney General, Patrick McKea, was assigned to represent them. He filed a comprehensive motion for a new trial. Judge Ward entered his order resolving that motion on April 22, 1986. He denied the motion on all issues except one: the amount of the punitive damage provision of the judgment. He ruled that the punitive damages award totaling $2,300,000 was "excessive" as a matter of law and granted the defendants a "conditional" new trial. The "condition" was that Jan accept $400,000 as punitive damages, which Judge Ward found to be a reasonable amount based on the facts of the case. If she refused, a second jury trial would be convened to determine a reasonable amount of punitive damages, and the jury's finding in that limited trial would become the final judgment.

We assumed that the Attorney General would appeal Jan's judgment. Pat McKea confirmed that assumption during a conversation with me many years later. That was no surprise because I knew that the Attorney General consistently appealed every judicial defeat. For instance, in the Larry Williams case, the Attorney General unsuccessfully appealed the verdict to the U.S. Fifth Circuit Court of Appeals and then to the U.S. Supreme Court despite the fact that it was a case involving egregious police misconduct.

Judge Ward's reduction of the punitive damages put us in a tight spot. If we accepted the judge's order, Jan's punitive damages would be reduced from $2.3 million to $400,000. That amount plus the compensatory damages that he upheld, $279,681.95, equaled $679,681.95. The court still had to rule on Jan's post-trial attorney fees and litigation expenses motion. Jan was entitled to an award of those expenses by law in successful federal civil rights cases. We estimated that he would find a total award to reimburse those expenses at approximately $200,000 resulting in a final judgment of approximately $879,681.95.

We recognized that Judge Ward's reduction of the punitive damages would probably be upheld on appeal. The amount of that award was over eight and a half times the compensatory awards. The Order reducing the punitive damages was meticulous. It cited a number of cases in which appellate courts had affirmed reductions of excessive punitive damages. So, it seemed that our best option was to choose a retrial of the amount of the punitive damages award in hopes that we could boost the final numbers above Judge Ward's assessment but not high enough to risk a reversal on appeal. We also favored that approach because it would increase pressure on Georgia's leadership since a retrial would encourage continuing scrutiny of the scandal.

I found out several years later during a conversation with Pat McKea that Bowers was anxious to settle the case for a number of reasons including a strong desire to decrease the flow of negative publicity surrounding the verdict. The Governor and other officials had already criticized the failure to settle the case before the trial, so it made sense to assume that considerable pressure was being put on Bowers to avoid further litigation. McKea also told me that Bowers was under political pressure to end the case because we had filed judgment liens attached to the homes of both Trotter and Ervin. Those liens panicked Georgia's highest officials for fear that the state would lose critical employees who might be unwilling to assume the risk of a judicial seizure of their personal assets if successfully sued individually for illegal acts or omissions in their official capacities.

Bowers approached us in hopes of reaching a settlement. He offered $750,000. We declined that offer because we knew that the state had the authority to pay up to one million dollars. Its insurance company would be liable for the excess of any judgment over a million dollars, but it had bankrupted shortly before the Kemp verdict.

Soon after we refused Bower's initial offer, we got an invitation from him to meet personally to try to hammer out an agreement. The ensuing meeting was the strangest that I had ever attended. Bowers wanted to meet secretly to avoid publicity by the press regarding the settlement discussions. We agreed and met with him several days later at a hotel located inside the state-owned Stone Mountain Park near Atlanta. When Pat and I arrived, we were surprised to learn that the hotel appeared to be empty. There was only one car in the parking lot, and it was a State Patrol squad car. There was an eerie feeling about these circumstances—a police guarded meeting with Georgia's Attorney General to resolve a civil rights case in an empty hotel in a State Park with a Civil War theme.

Our meeting was brief. Both sides had strong incentives to resolve the case—Bowers needed to end it to placate the Governor and give UGA's new leadership space to begin restoring its battered reputation. We wanted to avoid the expense of additional post-trial proceedings—especially a retrial in the trial court followed by an inevitable appeal to follow that proceeding if the new jury's verdict pushed the total judgment above $1 million. As it turned out, that was the figure that we all agreed upon that day to satisfy Jan's compensatory and punitive damage judgment. We also insisted that she be reinstated to her faculty position, receive compensation for the income she lost by reason of the unconstitutional discharge from her faculty position at UGA, and be assigned supervisory personnel other than Ervin and Trotter. Bowers agreed.

The deal was immediately leaked to the press by an unknown informant. Its terms were published two days later. Several days later we met with Judge Ward to get his approval of the settlement agreement and to pick up a check in the amount of $1,079,681.95. The Jan Kemp case was over.

*Pleased with settlement: After emerging Monday afternoon from the judge's chambers with a check for $1.08 million on Tuesday May 6, 1986, Jan Kemp said during a press conference she looked forward to returning to her old job. She started back at UGA July 1, 1986. The check was made out to Dr. Jan Kemp and Hue Henry. (Steve Deal/Atlanta Journal-Constitution via AP)*

# EPILOGUE

To me, the power of this story is found in the courage of Jan Kemp and the UGA faculty, students, and employees who confronted its leaders for habitually violating their constitutional and other legal rights. The lesson they taught was invaluable—we can defeat wrongdoing by powerful people. It takes courage, but we can level the playing field lawfully by asking a judge and jury to decide who is right and who is wrong.

Jan Kemp's case is a model of how an individual can use lawful means to affect societal objectives. She consistently said that her main reason for filing the lawsuit was the need to eliminate the academic frauds being foisted upon the faculty and students. "Reform" was always Jan's response when asked about her motives. That wasn't something that a court could order, but her case unveiled enough evidence in the trial to create the public and political backlash needed to ensure an investigation of the academic fraud at UGA. Her victory spawned the internal Regents' audit that uncovered massive violations of rules and policies leading to Davison's resignation.

The "Jan Kemp Affair" triggered the restructuring of UGA's presidency from Davison's authoritarian model to a more inclusive style that respected faculty input and corralled the Athletic Association. After Davison's resignation, the Regents convinced the retired President of the University of Miami, Henry King Stanford, to serve for one year as the acting president of his home state's University while a national search was conducted to find a permanent replacement to restore UGA's damaged reputation. Jan's admirers were delighted to learn that Dr. Stanford was the perfect antithesis to the imperial presidency of Fred Davison when he traveled from his South Georgia home to Atlanta on a Trailways bus to formally accept the Regents' offer!

Stanford served honorably for a year while the Regents searched for a new president. He immediately restructured UGA's leadership. On his first day in office, Stanford telegraphed his intent to erase the damage to the University's reputation and its academic integrity. He appointed another UGA administrator, Louise McBee, to serve as interim Vice President for Academic Affairs. McBee was a refreshingly revered administrator whose impeccable integrity made her a perfect fit for the task of restoring academic credibility. She was also the only high-level administrator who candidly admitted that Jan Kemp's lawsuit contributed to the reform of UGA's Athletic Association and collegiate athletics nationally. McBee recalled the "Jan Kemp Affair" in an interview several years after the trial. She acknowledged the damage done to the scholarship athletes who had no chance of attaining a college degree and praised Jan's revelation of that reality. She told the interviewer, ". . . and so, it was Jan Kemp's thinking that it was not fair to the institution or the student to bring someone in who could not make the grade, and she kept saying that, and I think rightly so, and we probably didn't listen as well as we should have. She sued the University, and, as I said, it gave national exposure to a problem that was not just ours, and, believe me, in our cleaning up our shop, other institutions did the same."

Confidence in UGA's next generation of high-level administrators was permanently restored when the Regents hired Charles Knapp in 1987 to serve as its President. He was the perfect choice to impose discipline and academic integrity on UGA's Athletic Association. Knapp was Tulane University's executive vice president and academic overseer of its athletic programs. His authority over sports was instrumental in the highly publicized abolition of Tulane's men's basketball program in 1985 as the result of a point-shaving scandal. His arrival in Athens two years later sent the right signal to UGA's athletic programs. Academic favoritism for scholarship athletes would not be tolerated.

Knapp took the necessary steps. With the assistance of an ad hoc faculty committee, he imposed the necessary reforms. Developmental Studies was discontinued. An "Academic Assistance" program was substituted. It was available to all students, including athletes, who needed remedial preparation in reading, writing or math. That program also offered "elective institutional or degree-credit courses" to improve the academic performance of those students. It provided peer tutorial services and converted its Learning Lab into a Learning Center open to all UGA students.

In 2002, the Athletic Association opened its seven

million-dollar Rankin M. Smith Student-Athlete Academic Center. Its 31,000 square feet of space includes a 230-seat study hall, 20 tutoring rooms, 60 computer stations, a student lounge, an awards banquet hall, a writing lab, and a high-tech classroom that seats 55 students. It has an annual budget of $800,000, ten full-time staffers headed by an associate athletic director, three counselors, and more than 80 tutors comprised mainly of graduate students and volunteers from the community. According to a 2014 NCAA report, graduation rates for black football and basketball athletes have steadily increased. The biggest jump of 13% occurred in 2013-2014. UGA's current 53% graduation rate of black male athletes ranks third in the SEC.

No informed observers of collegiate athletics doubt that the Jan Kemp case stimulated the reforms that elevated the academic performance of UGA's minority athletes. Despite that reality, she has never been formally recognized by her alma mater for her courage in exposing these wrongs and in helping restore the University's academic integrity. Regrettably, UGA has had a history of initially ignoring its heroes who attacked racial injustice by its leaders. For instance, Horace Ward, the Jan Kemp case federal judge, was denied admission to UGA's law school in the 1950s because he was an African American. The University's leadership ultimately recognized that injustice and awarded Judge Ward an honorary doctorate of law degree at its 2014 graduation ceremony - sixty years after he would have earned a UGA law degree if he had not been rejected based solely on his ethnicity.

Hamilton Holmes and Charlayne Hunter were the first black students admitted to the University. They applied to UGA for the fall 1959 quarter but were denied admission. Their legal team included Constance Baker Motley of the NAACP's Legal Defense and Education Fund and Atlanta attorneys Donald Hollowell, Vernon Jordan and Horace Ward, by then a graduate of Northwestern University School of Law. They re-submitted their applications each new quarter but were consistently rejected for reasons supposedly related to space or application procedures. In September of 1960 their attorneys filed for an injunction to prohibit UGA from "refusing to consider their applications and those of other Negro residents of Georgia for admission to the University." Their request was refused, but a full trial on the matter was later held in Athens in December 1960. On January 6, 1961, United States District Court Judge William Bootle issued his ruling, stating that Holmes and Hunter "would have been admitted had it not been for their race and color."

Holmes and Hunter registered at the Academic Building on January 9, 1961. They were met with crowds shouting racial slurs and chanting, "Two, four, six, eight. We don't want to integrate!" On January 11 a riot broke out after a basketball game outside of Myers Hall, where Hunter lived. Bricks, rocks, and bottles were thrown; the mob dispersed only after Athens police, armed with tear gas, and Dean William Tate arrived. That night the University suspended Hunter and Holmes, citing safety reasons, and the State Patrol escorted the students back to Atlanta. Within a few days, they returned to campus following a new court order.

Forty years later, the University renamed its academic building the Holmes/Hunter Academic Building in honor of the two students who first integrated it.

The "Jan Kemp Affair" was similar to the Ward and Holmes-Hunter stories in one respect. Racism was a common feature of each of these cases, and also like the others, Jan's contribution to the University has been ignored by its leaders for over thirty years. Jan and her colleagues knew that many of the revenue-producing black athletes would never graduate with a college degree. With their support, she took action – an action that exposed the façade being imposed by UGA's leadership in collaboration with its Athletic Association coaches without regard to the harm to the young men who were being victimized. It is now time for UGA's leaders to openly recognize the exploitation of dozens of young black athletes and Jan's courageous disclosure of that reality. It is also time for the name "Jan Kemp" to be added to the group of UGA heroes who demanded racial equality and condemned racial exploitation. At a minimum, a plaque honoring Jan's memory and contribution to UGA's legacy should be erected on the North Campus Quadrangle near that iconic chapel bell that pealed out the news of her victory on March 13, 1986 – the date of Fred Davison's resignation.

College and university faculty members are the guardians of their institution's academic integrity. Unlike administrators and other employees, professors make judgments through grading that reflect the caliber of their institution's educational standards. Jan Kemp's story has and will continue to inspire faculties and administrators nationwide to insist on the highest levels of academic integrity including a duty to resist and, if necessary, to reveal misconduct that threatens the core missions of their institutions.

## ACKNOWLEDGEMENTS

After the Kemp trial, a number of people asked me when I was going to write the book. My attitude dictated my consistent response to that question. "Never. Been there, done that." Frankly, I saw the idea as terribly burdensome and completely unnecessary given the volume of newspapers, magazines, books, and mass media reports that covered what seemed like every aspect of the Jan Kemp Affair during the trial and for many years after the verdict. Then, several newspaper reporters called me for comments on Jan's passing in 2008, a year after Pat Nelson's death. One of those calls changed my mind. After I commented on Jan's death, the reporter asked me if I was going to write the book. I gave him my standard answer. But, his response planted the seed. He said, "Well, you have to. You're the last man standing. Mr. Nelson and Jan Kemp have died. You're the only person left who can write the inside story." That was true. No one else had access to the inside information needed to tell the whole story. I pondered the idea for quite a while, and the more I thought about that conversation, the more convinced I became that I actually had no choice. So, over a longer period of time than I had expected, I researched and wrote this book. That news reporter's comment was a critical moment leading to this project. So, while I cannot remember his name, I have to thank him for his words of wisdom that led to the writing and publication of this book.

My wife Carole was my first reader, editor and critic. She is a retired University of Georgia Josiah Meigs Distinguished Teaching Professor of Art Education – UGA's top teaching award. Everyone who knows us would agree that Carole is the family scholar. Her dedication to this project was essential. Our son, Jason, a Fairfax, Virginia fifth grade teacher, was also an instrumental participant in this project – he spent hours in UGA's library helping me assemble a comprehensive collection of the multitude of UGA internal documents and press coverage of the Jan Kemp trial.

Other old and new friends weighed in. Randall Savage, a 1972 UGA graduate and co-recipient of a 1985 Pulitzer Prize for a *Macon Telegraph and News* series of articles on athletics and academics at UGA and the Georgia Institute of Technology, provided invaluable assistance and support. He reported the Jan Kemp trial for the *Telegraph and News.* He not only read earlier drafts of this book and made spot on recommendations to improve it but also wrote the Foreward. His contributions were formidable and for that I'm deeply appreciative.

Pete McCommons, the editor of Athens' popular weekly *Flagpole* newspaper, encouraged me and introduced me to Mary O'Brient, a book editor who shared her talents to ensure that this book would appeal to the UGA 'nation' and others who are interested in athletics and academics at the college level.

Other friends acted as 'readers' of early drafts to catch the errors that I missed, and to encourage me to keep going. My thanks go to Paul Tilton, Amy Bramblett,

Al Templeton, Bruce Romanchak, and Professors R.G. Brown, Sylvia Hutchenson, and Bill Martin.

Last, but certainly not least, my thanks go to Debbie Seymour and Hope Hilton. Debbie is an Athens Superior Court reporter. She also worked for me for many years as a secretary, and before that, as a secretary at UGA's Art School. Debbie was the perfect person to proof read the book. Hope is my graphic book designer. She is talented, energetic and funny – a delightful person to have on my team. Debbie's and Hope's work was instrumental in bringing this book to fruition.

CPSIA information can be obtained
at www.ICGtesting.com
Printed in the USA
LVHW11*0016250918
591272LV00002B/17/P

9 780692 152614